PLURAL IDENTITIES – SINGULAR NARRATIVES

PLURAL IDENTITIES –
SINGULAR NARRATIVES

The Case of Northern Ireland

Máiréad Nic Craith

Berghahn Books
New York • Oxford

First published in 2002 by **Berghahn Books**

www.BerghahnBooks.com

© 2002 Máiréad Nic Craith

Library of Congress Cataloging-in-Publication Data
Nic Craith, Máiréad.
   Plural identities--singular narratives: the case of Northern Ire-
land/Máiréad Nic Craith.
      p. cm. --
   Includes bibliographical references and index.
   ISBN 1-57181-772-7 (acid free paper). -- ISBN 1-57181-314-4 (pbk. :
acid free paper)
   1. Northern Ireland--Ethnic relations.   2. Culture conflict--
Northern Ireland.   3. Group identity--Northern Ireland.   4. Ethnic
groups--Northern Ireland.   5. Northern Ireland--Civilization.   I. Title.
DA990.U46 N53 2001
305.8'009416--dc21   2001035609

British Library Cataloguing in Publication Data

A catalogue record for this book is available
from the British Library.

Printed in the United Kingdom on acid-free paper

ISBN 1-57181-772-7 (hardback)
ISBN 1-57181-314-4 (paperback)

Für Ulli
Ohne dich wäre alles nur halb so schön!

CONTENTS

Tables

Map

ACKNOWLEDGEMENTS

I am indebted to several colleagues for their thoughts on various parts of this book. In particular, I wish to thank Anthony Buckley, Gerard Delanty, Jürgen Elvert, Amy Hale, Seán Loughlin, and Philip Payton who commented on individual sections of the book. Harvey Cox read all the chapters at an early stage and Don Akenson read a later version of the manuscript. All these colleagues offered very many useful comments, criticisms, and insights.

I am grateful to the University of Liverpool for a grant towards research expenses. Marianne Elliott, Director of the Institute of Irish Studies at the University of Liverpool, ensured teaching relief to enable me complete this book. Helen Carlyle, Eleanor Crook, and Tracey Holsgrove provided research assistance. During my visiting research fellowship at the Institute for British-Irish Studies, University College, Dublin, I had many opportunities to discuss my work with John Coakley and Carmel Coyle. Marion Berghahn, Seán Kingston, and an anonymous reader at Berghahn Books provided some helpful comments during the process of publication.

Staff members in a variety of institutions and organisations such as the Department of Education, Northern Ireland, and the Representative Church Body Library, Dublin, responded promptly to my queries. Yvonne Murphy and Traolach Mac Giolla Bríde gave me access to various collections at the Linen Hall Library, Belfast, while Aodán MacPóilin and all the staff of the ULTACH Trust, Belfast, have always proved a great source of information since my initial speculations regarding language and culture in Northern Ireland. Walter Kirwin, Assistant Secretary in the Northern Ireland division, Department of an Taoiseach, offered insights on matters relating to the Forum for Peace and Reconciliation, Dublin. Padraigín Nic Alastair of the Central Community Relations Unit and John Kirk of the Queen's University, Belfast, were helpful in relation to the question of Ulster-Scots. Every effort has been made to trace original copyright holders and I wish to thank Appletree Press Ltd, Belfast and the Ulster Folk and Transport Museum, Holywood, Co. Down for permission to reproduce the tables in Chapters 1, and 3.

I cannot forget my parents, Tom and Máiréad, who introduced me to the joys of reading at a very early age, generously indulged my love of books, and supported my writing from my days as a student. I with to thank my siblings and friends for their support and patience while I was writing this book. Finally I want to thank Ullrich Kockel who ensured that this manuscript was completed rather than abandoned! Most of the ideas here have been shaped by our conversations while walking by the sea in Crosby. Without his encouragement this work would not have been written and it is dedicated to him with great love.

Máiréad Nic Craith

ABBREVIATIONS

BBC	British Broadcasting Corporation
CLAR	Committee on Irish Language Attitudes Research
CCRU	Central Community Relations Unit
CTG	Cultural Traditions Group
DENI	Department of Education in Northern Ireland
DUP	Democratic Unionists Party
EU	European Union
FC	Football Club
GAA	Gaelic Athletic Association
GFA	Good Friday Agreement
INLA	Irish National Liberation Army
IRA	Irish Republican Army
IRFU	Irish Rugby Football Union
MEP	Member of European Parliament
MSP	Member of Scottish Parliament
NICEM	Northern Ireland Council for Ethnic Minorities
NISAS	Northern Ireland Social Attitude Survey
OBE	Order of the British Empire
PUP	Progressive Unionist Party
RUC	Royal Ulster Constabulary
SF	Sinn Féin
SDLP	Social Democratic and Labour Party
UDA	Ulster Defence Association
UDP	Ulster Democratic Party
UUP	Ulster Unionist Party
UK	United Kingdom
USA	United States of America
UVF	Ulster Volunteer Force

INTRODUCTION

When the present is finished with the ornaments of the old and the 'original', the future often seems merely the projection of a lost past.
(Bausinger 1990: 127)

My central aim with this book is to explore the politics of cultural traditions in Northern Ireland. While I am interested in the historical evolution of the two major traditions, my primary focus is on the essentialisation of the dual paradigm in a contemporary context. Any review of this aspect of Northern Irish culture generates many questions. Why is the 'two traditions' paradigm so widely accepted? Are there really two traditions and if so, are they opposites, mirror images of one another, or simply unalike (Buckley 1988; Loftus 1994)? What generates tension between diverse traditions and how are their differences established and consolidated? Do they share any common historical or newly-evolving narratives?

Much of my book focuses on the interplay between cultural symbol, politics, and identity. In many societies cultural icons are constantly re-evaluated in terms of their prestige, and 'valuation contests' are ongoing (Harrison 1995). Throughout this work I explore the affirmation of historical and contemporary cultural and linguistic symbols by loyalists and republicans, nationalists and unionists. Interactions between differing groups often expresses itself in terms of rivalry for what Bourdieu (1990: 112-21) terms 'symbolic capital'. Sometimes this quest takes the form of 'symbolic competitions', where ethnic minorities symbolically assert the superiority of their symbols in relation to those of the majority (Schwimmer 1972). On occasions these contests can generate political theatre or political factionalism which I explore with regard to parades and sporting rituals in Northern Ireland.

My initial focus is on the reductionist nature of the two traditions paradigm. Having briefly reviewed the establishment of the Northern Irish State, I query the legitimisation of the two traditions model in the political agreements of the late twentieth century. I assess the inadequacy of this model by considering the sheer number of ethnicities in Northern Ireland and question the recognition of the multicultural dimension at government level. In divided societies minority groups often protest against government restrictions on the expression of multiple identities. Traditionalists, even in peaceful regions, frequently lament the erosion of local identities by modernisation, globalisation, and materialism.

This hegemonic trend is occasionally called the 'McDonald-isation' of modern culture – a term inspired by the predominance of similarly mass-produced fast food in almost every city in the world. But even McDonald's aims to adapt to regional cultures and modifies recipes to local requirements! A customer in Italy can choose *insalata caprese* in lieu of French fries. In Norway a client can eat a salmon burger instead of a Big Mac. McDonald's salad dressings in France differ in their levels of sugar and mustard (Pells 1998). Contemporary society is gradually coming to terms with its cultural diversity and is increasingly intent on policies of pluralism.

While the focus of my work is on the current consolidation of the two traditions paradigm in Northern Ireland, it is essential to recognise the significance of historical narratives for this model. Throughout my book I analyse the way in which the past has been and continues to be used as a symbolic resource in the arena of cultural politics. 'Since the past serves as such a powerful authority in culture, no society could afford letting it just be; it must add to it, subtract from it, mold it in its own image' (Ben-Amos 1984: 115). Williams (1961) described this process as selective traditions.

In the second chapter I explore the contemporary significance of particular historical trajectories. Whether it is possible for any historian to be totally objective and non-partisan is debatable (Hobsbawm 1997: Ch. 9), and here I review the competing histories of the two traditions. I pay attention to the process of selectivity that generates an impression of polarity. In this context I explore the role of memory and the part played by 'amnesia' in the consolidation of cultural memory.

In the third chapter I review the essentialisation of the two traditions in terms of the religious divide. Here I contend that certain attributes associated exclusively with one tradition or the other, are in fact shared by Protestants and Catholics alike. Although distinct religious beliefs should not in itself generate conflict, social and historical segregation has ensured that different religious denominations view one another with suspicion (Elliott 2000; Harris 1986; McKay 2000).

In the next three chapters I focus on cultural and linguistic symbols that are promoted as traditional and exclusive. Both Williams (1961) and Hymes (1975) regard the construction of tradition as a purposeful action. As in all cultures, different groups in Northern Ireland designate aspects of culture as belonging to specific traditions, thereby infusing them with particular meaning and authority. In chapters three, four and five I explore aspects of Celtic, Ulster-Scots and English cultural traditions and locate the origins of these traditions in distinct territories. While these sections attempt a separation of identities in order to acknowledge the different singularities in the Region, they quickly debunk the notion of exclusivity and establish that the concept of two or three traditions does not correspond to reality. Separate traditions have been artificially constructed, often in the light of political concerns. In fact, cultural traditions in Northern Ireland have always altered in the shifting contexts of British and Irish political history.

In these chapters I provide further examples of the use of similar symbols and traditions by different groups and explore the anomaly that boundary formation is sometimes reinforced by a perception of resemblance as much as recognition of difference (Blok 1998; Harrison 1999; Ignatieff 1999). In some instances groups may be in conflict because they perceive themselves not as possessing different identities, but as having incompatible claims to similar or equivalent identities. Parallel aspirations can generate greater conflict rather than harmony, and competing groups may go to great lengths in order to justify their claim to particular symbols or traditions. Often, as I observe in chapter four, icons, such as that of the Celt, resonate with opposing narratives to different groups. In this chapter I explore the racialisation of the Irish, particularly in the nineteenth-century, and the dichotomy between Anglo-Saxon and Celt, which was a historic precursor to the contemporary two traditions paradigm.

In the fifth chapter I draw attention to the commonality of symbols with reference to the figure of Cú Chulainn. In this instance, the symbolic conflict between competing traditions takes the form of what Harrison (1995) calls 'proprietary contests'. While republicans and loyalists agree on the prestige of the character of Cú Chulainn, the ownership of this symbol is disputed. Conflicts concerning claims to symbols provide evidence of their value and significance as cultural property (Harrison 1992). Such cases are common worldwide and are exemplified in the dispute between Greece and a former republic of Yugoslavia concerning the use of the name Macedonia. In this instance, the propriety contest is not merely confined to the name of the Republic but also applies to the character of Alexander the Great and the emblem of the sixteen-pointed star.

Jakubowska (1990) illustrates another example of a similarly disputed claim with reference to the power struggles between the Solidarity movement and the communist authorities in Poland, but in this instance the Polish government failed to appropriate various symbols of Polish nationalism, such as the national colours and anthem. Jakubowska's example suggests that attempts to cloak oneself in the legitimacy of an adopted icon are usually doomed to failure, unless a group is deemed to have a rightful claim to a particular symbol in the first instance.

While my intention in chapters three to five is to query whether the concept of two or three traditions is appropriate, I also give attention to the opposite claim that there is, or could be a single tradition in the Region. In this context I ask whether practices traditionally associated with particular identities are a consequence of cultural piracy and have, in fact, their origins in another tradition. Of course they may also have emerged diachronically from an entirely different source.

When reviewing the perception of cultural traditions in Northern Ireland, it would be easy to slide into a series of essentialisms. 'The perception that culture as a particular way of life is essential helps to explain why the "cultural bases" which underlie seccessionist and irredentist movements are so powerful' (Penrose 1995: 405). But cultural traditions are not homogenous fixed entities. 'Identity must be thought of as shifting, or a process of becoming rather than being' (Lentin 2000: 4). Neither cultures nor traditions have a primordial existence. They are 'not defined by an essence that exists apart from change, a noumenon hidden behind the altering configurations of phenomena' (Modood 1997: 11).

Cultural identities are constructed through change and in recent decades it has become fashionable to speak of the 'invention' of traditions (Hobsbawm and Ranger 1983). Some commentators might see the emergence of an Ulster-Scots tradition, which I examine in the fifth chapter, as a classic example of the generation of a new tradition or what Harrison (1995: 262) calls 'innovation contests'. In these instances groups are engaged in the process of imitation as well as innovation. In my view, re-interpretation is a more appropriate term than invention or innovation as the generation of entirely new customs without resonance has no lasting impact (Handler and Linnekin 1984; Smith 1988). Societies exist in relations of mutual dependence and cultural traditions are changing and uncertain.

Cultures are rarely, if ever, politically neutral and the relationship between culture and politics is a source of great debate (e.g. Gibbons 1996; Mulhearn 1998). 'If we take culture as process producing meanings we must look at power relationships involved in the process' (Spencer and Wollman 1999: 97). In chapters seven and eight, I review Irish and British meta-identities. I examine selected aspects of these traditions, such as Gaelic football, which is deemed to be the prerogative of nationalists, and soccer, which is associated with unionists. But in the seventh chapter I query whether there is anything particularly Irish about Gaelic football. Subsequently I ask whether soccer derives its roots from the Gaelic game of Cad.

In these two chapters I focus on the construction of Irish and British 'webs of significance' or worlds of meaning (Geertz 1973: 5). I examine the politicisation of various cultural activities and sporting rituals and the manner in which these rituals are experienced not just as property owned by various groups but as actual dimensions of self (Harrison 1992: 240). Cultural traditions are not the preserve of particular ethnic groups but in many instances they have been reified and designated as such by a particular emphasis on bounded-ness and mutual distinctiveness. Very often the internal differences within traditions are homogenised in order to construct an impression of uniformity, identity, and significance.

Having already examined the association of particular cultural traditions with distinct political traditions and territories, I review the relevance of state boundaries for the regeneration of cultural symbols. Bauman (1992) argues that the process of identity construction has been 'de-territorialized' in principle and that symbols, rather than spaces, have become increasingly relevant. But sometimes the two are strongly linked. In the case of Orange parades, the itinerary is frequently as significant as the banners and drums, and in some instances re-routing marches fails to appease the participants and serves to devalue the symbol. Marchers experience a sense of loss because their symbolic resources have been tampered with. They may also perceive such interference as a gain for other competing groups.

In symbolic conflicts there is often great concern with the proportion of symbolic capital pertaining to one group as opposed to another. Characteristically such conflicts take the form of a zero-sum game. Proportionality, rather than quantity, is the central issue and the advancement of one particular community is perceived as deprivation by another (Bourdieu 1990; Harrison 1995). Many symbolic contests in Northern Ireland have focused on altering the ratios of cultural capital pertaining to differing groups. Sometimes this has involved the re-evaluation of certain symbols in order to enhance one's own position. On other occasions this has resulted in the appropriation of symbolic capital from another group. It has also led to the generation of a new fund of icons, thereby enlarging the proportion of symbolic capital belonging to particular groups.

But moderates in Northern Ireland are anxious to withdraw from this zero-sum game and cultural discourse sometimes draws on the theme of common heritage. In my final chapter I examine whether politicians should endeavour to promote the concept of an already existing non-threatening common heritage or to generate a new sense of tradition that encompasses the contemporary diversity of the Region. In the context of future peaceful prospects, I query whether politicians should emphasise the significance of a common Northern Irish, Ulster, or supra-national tradition. Ultimately I argue that politicians and communities should adopt a more inclusive discourse of multiculturalism and give greater recognition to minorities, to those on the margins of the two traditions paradigm, and those with hyphenated identities.

With this in mind I draw attention to the concept of 'critical' or 'polycentric' multiculturalism as defined by Turner (1993), which does not predetermine the number of cultural groups in a region, thereby allowing greater expression of a full range of traditions. Gramsci (1971) argues that culture provides the mechanism by which we derive our place in the world. Culture alerts us to the values and norms that reinforce our concept of being, but culture must be placed in a broad social context. For this reason I review Fraser's model of recognition (2000) which places the negotiation of individual circumstances in a social, rather than a cultural context.

Many changes have occurred throughout the world in the present phase of modernity and 'the prefix "post" has become a much used syllable' (Smith D. 1999: 11). It is used to register increasing sentiments of anxiety, emptiness, and uncertainty and is applied in all sorts of contexts 'postmodern, postindustrial, postcolonial, post-Enlightenment, poststructural and so on' (*ibid.*). At the beginning of the new millennium, I believe that it is time for people in Northern Ireland to re-assess or even dispense with the 'certainties' offered by the two traditions context. For this reason I propose the reconceptualisation of the two traditions model and assess the merits and shortcomings of some alternatives.

CHAPTER 1

'WEBS OF SIGNIFICANCE'

*The demise of overarching or meta-identities appears to have allowed
a plurality of new ones to emerge from under the corpse.*
(McCrone 1998: 33)

When writing a personal account of his experiences in Jerusalem, Saul
Bellow (1998: 131) noted that he sometimes thought there were two
Israels. 'The real one is territorially insignificant. The other, the mental
Israel, is immense, a country inestimably important, playing a major role
in the world, as broad as all history – and perhaps as deep as sleep'.
Similarly, it could be argued that there are two Northern Irelands. Territorially the Region is quite small. It is a mere 14,148 square kilometres or
5,463 square miles and incorporates 6 of the 32 counties of Ireland.
Although it could hardly be maintained that Northern Ireland has
played an influential role in world history, it is obvious that its affairs
have absorbed the interest and attention of many politicians, academics,
and readers. This is especially the case with regard to the English-
speaking world in Ireland, the United Kingdom (UK), and the United
States of America (USA).

Like Israel, Northern Ireland emerged as a state in the twentieth century. While some unionists may prefer to call it Ulster, the latter term
actually refers to nine rather than six counties as the Ulster province
includes the counties of Cavan, Donegal, and Monaghan, which are part
of the Republic of Ireland (see Map 1). In this first chapter I examine the
establishment of the six-county Northern Irish State and explore aspects
of its polarised society in the context of its full range of cultural traditions.
While my principal focus is on the two traditions paradigm, I review
this model in the context of the quest for pluralism in international
agreements.

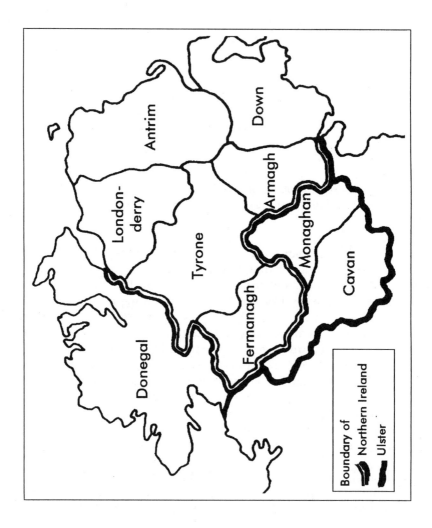

Northern Ireland/Ulster

Establishment of a Northern Irish State

An Act of Union passed in 1800 decreed that the entire island of Ireland should become an integral part of the UK. In January 1801, the Irish Parliament ceased to exist and the British Crown and Parliament at Westminster undertook direct rule of the country. Throughout the following century there were various campaigns for Home Rule. In response, the British government divided the island of Ireland in two in 1920, and 26 of the 32 were no longer under the jurisdiction of Westminster. According to the Government of Ireland Act, the remaining six counties of Antrim, Armagh, Down, Fermanagh, Londonderry, and Tyrone constituted the new state of Northern Ireland (Hennessey 1997; Lyons 1979; McCracken 1967; Moody 1974).

New redrawn boundaries have affected many countries in Europe. Generally speaking, the process was more a consequence of intermittent warfare rather than colonialism. As empires were established, expanded, and dissolved, borders were rearranged. Large empires, such as that of Austria-Hungary, Germany, or the Soviet Union, disintegrated resulting in a conglomeration of diverse peoples and identities. Minorities were created without any form of movement when new borders were arranged. In some instances, these lived in distinct minority communities; in others they survived as isolated individuals. As a consequence of intercommunication, many individuals have mixed parentage and enhanced, or perhaps, confused identities (Eide 1993: 14).

The construction of new borders has resulted in large minorities in a variety of countries. Examples include the Russian community in Estonia (30 percent) and in Latvia (34 percent), the Serbian community in Croatia (12 percent) and the Hungarian minority in Slovakia (12 percent). In contemporary Yugoslavia, Albanians constitute about 8 percent of the national population, although they form a substantial majority in Kosovo, which was the catalyst for the warfare at the end of the twentieth century (Bowers 1994). Nationalists in Northern Ireland acquired an undesired minority status, without any physical movement, when the new Border was implemented. Resulting tensions south of the Border proved the catalyst for a civil war between those who regarded the arrangements as the best possible solution at the time and those who regarded it as a betrayal of the nation.

Generally speaking, the designation of borders is a process that takes account of many elements, such as the ethnic composition of a community or a reward for past loyalty, as is illustrated in the case of Italy. Of particular interest to our Northern Irish case study is the region of Trentino-Alto Adige. This includes the ethnically German population in South Tyrol and the ethnically Italian majority community in Trentino. Following the collapse of the Austro-Hungarian Empire during World War I, this region was given to Italy as a reward for supporting the Allied forces. Ethnic Germans in South Tyrol were hostile to the annexation and demonstrated their antagonism to the new arrangements for many decades. Yet despite the animosities within the region, a largely satisfactory solution was eventually established and tensions here have gradually diminished (Alcock 1991; Coyle 1983; Eide 1996).

Demographics were particularly influential in positioning the Border in Northern Ireland as the state was designed to represent an area with a significant Protestant majority. Although unionists were not entirely happy with this arrangement, they accepted it because it ensured they remained within the framework of the UK. They were anxious 'to disturb the close relationship with Britain as little as possible' (Lyons 1971: 696). They were also aware that this was the largest area possible where they could continue to hold a unionist majority. Likewise, in Lebanon the state boundary was designed to define an area in the Middle East with a significant Christian majority. Since the establishment of these states the demographic proportions have altered. In Lebanon the proportion of Muslims has increased. This trend has been enhanced with the arrival of many Palestinian refugees. In Northern Ireland, a high birth rate has increased the extent of the Catholic community, although this trend has been offset somewhat by Catholic emigration (McNamee 1986).

When the new Northern Irish State was established, a parliament was set up at Stormont with control over local affairs, and the two states, north and south of the Border, began to operate independently. On both sides of the Border there was a great deal of apprehension and ignorance of the other. Boyce (1996b: 223) remarks that for whatever reason 'the north was to most southern Irish historians what Africa had been to the Victorians; a largely blank map, with few guiding features, and inhabited by unknown, and possibly unknowable beings'. Westminster maintained authority over matters concerning the Crown, foreign policy, and military affairs. Politicians in Northern Ireland had a dual mandate. They operated at parliaments in Belfast and in Westminster. Unionists led by Sir James Craig achieved a great victory in the first election held in May. They won 40 of 52 seats, leaving the opposition with less than a quarter of the total number. Nationalists refused to take up their parliamentary positions with the intention of ensuring that the new state became unworkable. King George V formally opened the first parliament at Stormont on 22 June 1921. From that point forward unionists effectively governed the state for many decades (Alcock 1994; Darby 1983; Ruane and Todd 1996; Wichert 1991).

Nationalists and unionists became increasingly polarised during the decades that followed. Government institutions established in the new Northern Irish state were primarily designed to secure power over those areas with nationalist majorities, and the local government 'facilitated exclusivism' which resulted in discrimination with regard to employment policies and the provision of housing (Wright 1987: 114). Many of the larger towns were highly segregated residentially and interfaith marriages were discouraged. Unionists attended state schools and became familiar with British history and literature. Nationalist children acquired their knowledge of Irish history in Catholic schools that were partly funded by the state. They may also have learned the Irish language. Unionists trained in British sports such as cricket, hockey, and rugby, while nationalists enjoyed the traditional games of hurling and Gaelic football.

During the 1950s, the introduction of free secondary education ensured the emergence of a new well-educated Catholic middle-class. Their increasing dissatisfaction with inequality for Catholics sparked a civil rights movement, similar to that led by Martin Luther King in America. In particular, the failure of the Protestant-dominated council in Dungannon to offer adequate housing accommodation for its Catholic population has been identified by Lyons (1971: 762) as 'the spark that was to set the whole province alight'. The Campaign for Social Justice to combat the housing issue was the forerunner of the Northern Ireland Civil Rights Campaign, which was set up in 1967 (Lyons 1971: 762, Wright 1987; 190–2). A variety of protest marches were organised in pursuit of reforms such as the elimination of discrimination not just in the allocation of houses but also with regard to employment opportunities. But the Civil Rights campaigners 'became identified by the Protestant working class as pro-Catholic' (Moore 1973: 31) and there was a great deal of violence as marchers regularly clashed with the Royal Ulster Constabulary (RUC).

In 1969, the British Army arrived in Northern Ireland. While initially Catholics welcomed them, subsequent clashes between these two groups proved the catalyst for the re-emergence of the republican movement. Violence reached a peak in 1972, when 14 civilians were shot during a banned civil rights march in Derry. This occasion became known as 'Bloody Sunday' in memory of the massacre of Russian protestors in January 1905 (Mullan 1998; Walsh 2000). In the years that followed the violence 'was so severe, brutal and prolonged that it would hardly be ignored by anyone involved in Northern Ireland' (Boyce 1996b 224). The terror and destruction that dominated society in the Region augmented the sectarian divide and could hardly be explained as merely the extreme by-product of this polarisation (Guelke 1998: 24).

In consequence of the general instability in the Region, the British government suspended the Stormont Parliament in 1972. Following extensive consultations with local political figures, a Northern Ireland Constitution Act 1973 provided for the transfer of certain powers to a new 78-member assembly. It was intended that representatives from unionist and nationalist communities would participate in this institutional structure. Extreme unionists reacted angrily to the revised arrangements and a general strike was organised in 1974. The ensuing chaos led to the collapse of the new assembly and the post of Secretary of State was established to govern the state of Northern Ireland.

Some 25 years later, power was devolved once again to Northern Ireland. Following talks conducted for a period of two years under the chairmanship of the American senator, George Mitchell, various parties outlined a collective peaceful strategy for the future of the state in a political document known as the Good Friday Agreement (GFA). Voters from Northern Ireland and from the Republic of Ireland overwhelmingly endorsed this document and results of the referenda were declared on 23 May 1998, the bicentenary of the 1798 rebellion. Representatives from a variety of parties were subsequently elected to a new Northern Irish Assembly. Ministers were appointed from the Ulster Unionist Party (UUP), the Social Democratic and Labour Party (SDLP), the Democratic Unionists Party (DUP), and Sinn Féin (SF). While these politicians aim to improve society in Northern Ireland, they operate within the context of a fragile peace in a deeply divided society, a society that is frequently portrayed as plagued with binary oppositions.

The construction of categories

The Northern Irish community is perceived as divided in two, between settlers and natives, Protestants and Catholics, unionists and nationalists. Political and sectarian violence highlights antagonisms between opposing groups, effectively reducing many societies in conflict to binary oppositions of this sort. For example, the conflict in Israel is viewed as simply a contest between Jewish and Palestinian traditions. But of course there is considerable cultural diversity within Jewish and Palestinian populations. In his childhood memoir, *Out of Place*, the Palestinian critic Edward Said speaks of his 'unsettled sense of many identities' (1999: 5). His concealment of his mother tongue in Arabic classes in order to fit in with American classmates in Cairo is a particularly emotive symbol of cultural complexity in society (1999: 82).

Equally complex is the clash of traditions in Kosovo, which is usually simplified as a contest between two traditions, Serbs and Albanians, but a considerable proportion of the population is ethnic Hungarian, or of mixed ethnicity. Moreover, significant numbers of Serbs and Croats in the cities of former Yugoslavia have married so that many describe themselves as Yugoslavian rather than Serbian or Croatian (Fenton 1999). In fact, the cultural attributes they share are at least as significant as that which divides them (Glenny 1990; 1992). And yet, the cultural variations and differences within these traditions are often ignored. Moreover, as I examine in the early chapters of this book, such simplifications lead to the artificial establishment of opposing two traditions 'even where they clearly do not exist' (Rolston 1998: 270).

Sometimes the conflict in Northern Ireland is portrayed as simply a matter of unionists against nationalists. Unionists are largely, but not necessarily, descendants of Scots and English who arrived at various stages in history. In the nineteenth century they vigorously opposed Home Rule. Today they are represented politically by the UUP, which was the only government party from 1921 until 1972. Unionists are also represented by the DUP, which is also popular in electoral terms and more strongly anti-nationalist. Nationalists aspire to the re-unification of the 32 counties of Ireland in a framework that is independent of the UK. The largest nationalist party is the SDLP, although SF has rapidly gained a greater share of electoral support. Most unionists and some nationalists view SF as the political wing of the Irish Republican Army (IRA), although SF continues to insist that these are two separate organisations.

Antagonism in Northern Ireland is also portrayed as a simple contest between Protestants and Catholics but in the two following chapters I investigate whether this has always been the case. It is habitually and incorrectly assumed that all Protestants are unionists and all Catholics are nationalists in political terms. At present Protestants form the larger part of society as a whole, representing 54.1 percent of the population, but this figure is probably falling. On the other hand, Catholics at 41.4 percent are proportionally on the increase. As the number of Catholics born each year since 1978 is greater than that of Protestants, Catholics are in the majority in the younger age groups. Obviously, a greater proportion of deaths in the Region are Protestant because they represent the greater number in older population.

Religious divisions in Northern Ireland are given physical expression in geographical terms. Almost every local authority west of the River Bann has a Catholic majority. Currently Catholics form the majority in three of the six counties in Northern Ireland. As a consequence, there are in fact two majorities or minorities in Northern Ireland. A younger Catholic population is in the majority west of the Bann whereas a more ageing Protestant population represents the majority east of the river. Having had discussions with a variety of school assemblies, the Opsahl commissioners concluded that young Protestants who represent the minority group west of the Bann are more likely to view themselves as British rather than Irish. Those on the other side of the river are more open to the concept of Irishness (Pollock et al 1993). Residential segregation is commonplace in Northern Ireland and research by McKittrick in 1993 established that less than 110,000 people live in a region that has approximately equal numbers of Catholics and Protestants (see Elliott 1997: 158). Of the 51 wards in Belfast, 35 of them represent communities which are 90 percent Protestant or 95 percent Catholic. Tangible religious integration only occurs among two middle-class groups in north and south Belfast (Pollock et al 1993: 44).

Hostility in Northern Ireland is less frequently viewed in age or class terms, although both factors are strongly relevant. For example, the Opsahl commissioners discerned some differences in attitudes towards Britain between younger and older Protestants. While older Protestants

regard the British constitution, the monarch, and his or her religious persuasion as eminently significant, younger Protestants appear to highlight
sport as emblematic of their identity. Catholics in younger age groups
appear to define their Irishness totally in terms of culture (Pollock et al
1993: 99).

As in other countries, there are distinctions between working and middle-class groups. Society in Northern Ireland is not only divided horizon-
tally between Catholics and Protestants, unionists and nationalists. It is
also divided vertically between the financially comfortable and the economically deprived. 'The well-to-do middle classes are protected by their
own mobility. They know that they have the resources to get up and go if
they have to – and more of them are now contemplating it – to a calmer
part of the province, to the Republic, or across to England' (Jackson 1972:
5). In contrast, the less well-off often experience considerable financial
difficulties, and are more aware of tensions and problems. For this reason,
the worst animosities occur at the point where the horizontal and vertical
meet (Pollock et al 1993: 45). One of the added dimensions to class
struggles in Northern Ireland is that they have been stereotyped. In the
past Catholics generally held posts that were lower paid than those of
Protestants, and poorer Catholics were set up against the wealthier Protestants. But not all Catholics were poor and not all Protestants enjoyed
wealth and luxury, and the disparities between these groups have lessened
in recent years.

Identities in opposition

Of the many dualisms perceived as significant in Northern Ireland, the
question of a British or Irish identity is often regarded as the most pertinent – which is as interesting as it is complex, and its patterns of change
have been examined in a variety of surveys taken between 1968 and 1994.
These Northern Ireland Social Attitude Surveys (NISAS) provide considerable detail on the variation in self-ascription among both Protestants
and Catholics, and on the relationship between their identities and political parties. Early surveys conducted in 1968 and 1978 included the categories Irish, British, and Ulster. At the time the term Northern Irish was
not regarded as a valid self-descriptor and implied a suggestion of anti-
Britishness, but as the term was increasingly accepted during the 1970s, it
was introduced as an option in the 1989 survey. Throughout these surveys
the possibility of multiple identities was excluded. For this reason I believe
that the survey technique polarised data and reinforced the perception of
identities in opposition in a divided society. One could choose to be British
or Irish but not both. When Trew (1996) compared the entire data, a distinct pattern emerged.

The first survey indicated that a fifth of the Protestant population regarded itself as Irish. One third was content with an Ulster identity and two fifths were happy with the British category. Within ten years the number who classified themselves as Irish had halved and the percentage of those who considered themselves British had increased considerably. I presume that this change in self-ascription was a consequence of the civil rights struggle – a change which would appear to confirm Renfrew's (1996) perception that an enhanced ethnicity is often a result, rather than a cause of war – a view which affirms the concept of ethnicity as process. Many of those who had previously been attracted by an Ulster identity were now placing themselves in the Northern Irish category. As time passed, the proportion of Protestants identifying themselves as Irish has continued to decrease while numbers in the British category have increased. Although the 1991 and 1993 surveys indicated a growing identification with an Ulster identity, this trend was not sustained in later surveys as outlined in Table 1:1 (Trew 1996: 142):

Table 1:1 Choice of National Identity for Protestants 1968–1994 (single-choice system)

Year	British	Irish	Ulster	N. Irish	Other
1968	39	20	32	–	09
1978	67	08	20	–	05
1989	68	03	10	16	03
1991	66	02	15	14	03
1993	70	02	16	11	03
1994	71	03	11	15	–

(Source: Trew 1996: 142. Figures reproduced with the kind permission of Appletree Press Ltd, Belfast.)

While the concept of an Ulster category appealed to Protestants in the early surveys, it proved largely unattractive to Catholics. But the civil rights struggles did not enhance the numbers opting for an Irish identity, and the percentages in this category dropped from 76 to 69 in the ten years between 1968 and 1978. As soon as the option of Northern Irish became available, a considerable number were happy with this classification, and that figure has remained consistent.

Although these figures are instructive, I would argue that they are not entirely representative. While the categories are not necessarily exclusive to each other, respondents choose a single option when in fact more than one may apply. Moreover, the context in which any survey is taken can seriously affect the results. In particular, perceptions of the intention of the questioner or the latest news can determine the choice made. For this reason I feel it wise to adopt a cautious approach to these surveys. At the same time the tables serve as indicators of changing perceptions among Protestants and Catholics.

Table 1:2 Choice of National Identity for Catholics 1968–1994 (single-choice system)

Year	British	Irish	Ulster	N. Irish	Other
1968	15	76	05	–	04
1978	15	69	06	–	10
1989	10	60	02	25	04
1991	10	62	02	25	01
1993	12	61	01	25	02
1994	10	62	–	28	–

(Source: Trew 1996: 142. Figures reproduced with the kind permission of Appletree Press Ltd, Belfast.)

Overall it appears that Catholics primarily consider themselves Irish, Northern Irish, or British, whereas Protestants prefer the categories of British, Ulster, or Northern Irish. Generally speaking, Catholics who choose to classify themselves as 'Northern Irish' or 'Other' are slightly better educated than their colleagues who opt for the term 'Irish'. They also have a more favourable attitude towards the Union. In common with these, Protestants opting for the 'Northern Irish' category are also well educated and content to remain in the UK. Furthermore they have a very positive attitude to Europe, believing that the UK should align itself more closely with the EU. This group is likely to consist of younger females who support the Alliance Party (Trew 1996: 147).

Trew's results indicated that those who identified most strongly with an Ulster identity were male manual workers. Some years earlier, in 1983, Moxon-Browne had similarly affirmed that the Ulster category was preferred by the working classes. Trew proposes a practical, economic basis for this local preference. As working class groups derive little benefit from the Union, they are more likely to identify with regional rather than national structures. In contrast, upper and middle-class Protestants who reap financial advantage from current arrangements remain very committed to the UK.

Further surveys examined the political allegiances of respondents, and

the results outlined in Table 1:3 are hardly surprising. Those who identified themselves as belonging to British or Ulster categories supported the
Union, whereas those with Irish identities aspired to unity with the
Republic. Over a third of those surveyed regarded themselves as neither
nationalist nor unionist. But there is a fault in this survey of constitutional
preferences. It did not allow respondents to classify themselves as separatists who sought to establish an independent Northern Ireland. I think it
likely that a proportion of those in the 'Ulster' and 'Neither' categories
would have chosen this option had it been available. The responses are
provided in Table 1:3 (Trew 1996: 144):

From this data, it appears unlikely that a sense of Irish, Northern Irish,

Table 1:3 Choice of National Identity for Protestants in Percentage Terms
(single-choice system)

	British	Irish	Ulster	N. Irish	All
Unionist	67	02	75	29	42
Nationalist	02	56	–	25	20
Neither	31	40	22	45	37

(Source: Trew 1996: 144. Figures reproduced with the kind permission of Appletree
Press, Belfast.)

or British identity could ever effectively constitute an overarching identity
for all competing groups although a single identity survey can only give
this result in any case. In a sense, the real question is what identities or traditions were compatible, but this issue was not addressed here. Moreover,
while these results are interesting it should be noted that, between the
years 1912 and 1922, Ulster Protestants supported a variety of positions on
the future of Ireland. It might appear that their attitudes frequently
changed, but one constant remained. They were very determined to
remain separate from Dublin. Everything else was instrumental. Under
such circumstances, surveys of constitutional preferences are less pene-
trating than surveys of constitutional aversions.

Accommodating two traditions

Since the days of the civil rights struggle, the concept of separate British
and Irish traditions has been increasingly incorporated into official discourse into Northern Ireland. In 1983 the Two Traditions Group was estab-

lished as a non-party political group. In its policy document it affirmed that the existence of two traditions and communities 'is indisputable' (in Lambkin 1996: 85). Among its stated aims were 'to stimulate a search for understanding and comprehension of *both traditions and cultures* (their affinities and differences) as may encourage acceptance on "both sides" of the need for a multicultural society' (in Lambkin 1996: 85; original emphasis). This group was the precursor of the Cultural Traditions Group (CTG) established in the late 1980s.

It is interesting to note that the emphasis here was on traditions rather than cultures, although the concept of cultural traditions has also gained a new significance. When these phrases appeared, they were rarely accompanied by a definition of terms. Perhaps that is because they represent notoriously ambiguous concepts and their meanings have changed considerably over time in both academic and commonplace contexts. In this sense the terminology reflects the ambiguity of traditions and cultures themselves. But it is my view that these phrases have not been defined because it is assumed that they are non-problematic – yet this is hardly the case.

'Tradition' and 'culture' are not synonyms although there is a close relationship between the two. While tradition is a term frequently used in folklore, culture has been the preserve of anthropologists. Tradition derives its roots from the Latin term *tradere* and it is used to refer both to inherited material and to the process of transmission. It is often used in contrast to modernity and is associated with cultural conservatism. To say that something is traditional may also imply that it is of value – that it is something to which we should attend, because it has survived several generations. Antiquity in this context validates tradition as authentic and authoritative.

Many books have been written on the concept of culture (e.g. Bauman 1973; Kahn 1995; Thompson 1990) which is infinitely broader in meaning than 'tradition'. Lambkin (1996: 89) defines the distinction between them by suggesting that tradition 'deals mainly with the reproductive process through which a society is constituted'. While culture as a concept includes this process of transmission or reproduction, it also concerns itself with strategies of communication, explanation, and experience. Culture deals with change and innovation. While the definition of culture has been constantly revised since the days of Tylor (1871), in this book I examine the concept in Geertz's terms. He suggested, following Max Weber, that the human being 'is an animal suspended in webs of significance he himself has spun' (1973: 5). Some of the 'webs of significance' that I examine in this book include history, religion, mythology, sport, and language.

In the context of Northern Ireland the concept of two traditions is often assumed to refer to two distinct cultures and two separate communities. The impression of polarity has been further emphasised by violence between opposing groups. In fact, 'the venom and virulence of the men of violence on both sides, the rancour and resentment engendered by them; the murder and maiming of victims; the hurt and heart ache of the bereaved' (Hanna 2000: 36) have contributed to the consolidation of boundaries between the two communities.

Since the mid-1980s British and Irish governments have been anxious to refer inclusively to the British and Irish communities in all official documents. In 1985 these governments declared intentions of respect for expressions of identity from the two traditions of the Region. The Anglo-Irish Agreement issued in November of that year formally permitted the Irish Republic to have a consultative role in the internal affairs of Northern Ireland and the joint statement recognised and respected the rights of both traditions. In Article Five it was affirmed that the administration would concern itself with 'measures to recognise and accommodate the rights and identities of the two traditions in Northern Ireland, to protect human rights and to prevent discrimination' (Department of Foreign Affairs, 1985: 5). Ten years later, the Framework Document asserted that communications within Northern Ireland and those between the two states 'should respect the full and equal legitimacy and worth of the identity' of the two cultural traditions. The British Government pledged that its jurisdiction would be founded 'with emphasis on full respect for, and equality of, civil, political, social and cultural rights'. It would also promote 'just and equal treatment for the identity, ethos and aspirations of both communities' (in O'Day 1997: 203).

The GFA also endorsed two traditions in the Region. Various parties agreed to 'recognise the birthright of all the people of Northern Ireland to identify themselves and be accepted as Irish or British, or both, as they may so choose' (1998: 1). All negotiating parties affirmed a commitment to a policy of equal esteem for British and Irish traditions. This applied to relationships within Northern Ireland and between members of the British Isles. This Agreement contained a pledge to 'reflect the principles of mutual respect for the identity and ethos of both communities' (GFA 1998: 19). Furthermore, it agreed to consider the drafting of a general formula obliging government and public bodies to respect on an equal basis the identity and inherent character of both communities in Northern Ireland (GFA 1998: 20).

While this statement acknowledged disparate identities in Northern Ireland, I believe it unnecessarily restricted the choice to a narrow range reflecting political inclinations towards Westminster or Dublin. Proponents of a distinctly Ulster or Northern Irish identity may have felt that they were disregarded. I think there were several reasons for this neglect. In the first instance, participants may have assumed that concepts of Britishness and Irishness automatically incorporated Ulster or Northern Irish identities. Many critics doubt whether these positions have any significant support at all – except as a desperate fallback if the 'British' position is seen to be failing.

It is probable that supporters of an independent Northern Ireland were under-represented at the multi-party talks and were not inclined to insist on a specific recognition of their preference. Indeed, it is also conceivable that the unionist community did not wish to give any impression of division or weakness. They may have aspired to emphasise the significance of Britishness in the Region as a concept, which might possibly be undermined by the recognition of a separatist perspective. Thus, the lack of reference to a Northern Irish identity may also reflect the desire of the major traditions to remain within the framework of either the British or Irish governments.

But the two traditions paradigm is not the way forward as it essentialises these cultures – generating a perception of cultural traditions as homogenous, fixed qualities. It does not allow for culture shifts or the merging of cultures – but gives the impression of particular traditions being attached to a specific groups – defining them without qualification as the people who lay claim to specific cultures. Yet all cultural standards are contested and 'devotion to specific cultural forms varies across a group and the forms are frequently contested and constantly being defined and redefined' (Fenton 1999: 9).

While the GFA occasionally took account of the range of identities in Northern Ireland, groups such as the Chinese, Indians, or Pakistani were not specifically mentioned. As the primary intention of the GFA was to reconcile the major traditions in the Region, this was unsurprising. Moreover, members of these minority groups had not actively engaged in the 'Troubles' and were not specifically represented by any particular party. Nevertheless I feel that this was an opportunity to draw attention to the actual range of diverse traditions in Northern Ireland. Greater recognition of these minority groups could lessen the relevance of what are perceived to be the two major traditions.

Minority traditions

In this book I intend to focus primarily on the complexities pertaining to British and Irish cultural traditions, but I wish to set these in the context of the spectrum of Northern Irish cultural diversity. For this reason I make occasional references to other cultural traditions often considered too minor to be of any real significance. A recent survey suggested that ethnic minorities constitute less than one percent of the total community of Northern Ireland (Irwin and Dunn 1997), although this proportion is increasing as their rate of growth surpasses that of general population. Some of these ethnic minorities are gaining a real cultural presence.

For example, although merely the seventh largest non-indigenous group in the UK, the Chinese are the largest ethnic minority in Northern Ireland. They began arriving in the early 1960s and their first recorded restaurant, 'The Peacock', opened in Belfast in 1962. By 1989 their number in Northern Ireland had increased to 4,500 and they were primarily coming from the New Territories where people speak the Hakka and Cantonese dialects of southern China. These languages continue to be spoken in the community and many Chinese children do not hear English until they first come to school. Smaller numbers of Chinese emigrants also came from Vietnam, Mainland China, Malaysia, Singapore, and Taiwan.

The size of the contemporary Chinese community is disputed. A survey by Irwin (1996) estimated their numbers at between 3,000 and 5,000; almost 41 percent of this young and growing population had settled in Belfast. Further studies by Irwin and Dunn (1997) suggested that the numbers were perhaps as high as 7,000, an estimate below that of the Chinese Welfare Association, which believes it to be closer to 8,000 (Watson and McKnight 1998). It appears that the majority are first generation Chinese who are primarily engaged in the catering trade. Some 500 outlets are in operation throughout the Region (Lee 1993).

Chinese traditions are observed throughout Northern Ireland. Apart from restaurants, the most obvious symbol of their presence in Northern Ireland is the celebration of the Chinese New Year, which falls between mid-January and mid-February. As well as local parades and ceremonies, the Chinese Chamber of Commerce (NI) organises an annual celebratory dinner. In addition to this, the Chinese women's group in Belfast celebrates a variety of other carnivals such as that of the Dragon Boat or the Moon. These occasions are marked with the preparation of special food and with other activities. As religion is not formally institutionalised in this community there is no special place of worship for practitioners of Confucianism, Buddhism or, Taoism. In 1985 however, overseas students and a local minister initiated a Chinese Christian Fellowship Church in Belfast. Other markers of the Chinese presence in Northern Ireland are a language school, a medical centre, and a children's dance group.

Unlike the Chinese community, Travellers are an indigenous minority (Mac Laughlin 1995; Sheehan 2000). Overall they constitute the second largest ethnic minority in Northern Ireland and are commonly regarded as being deviants in society rather than constituting a distinct ethnicity. Perhaps the fact that they have the same skin colour as the rest of the general population is a contributory factor to this limited perspective – although I should note that the phrase 'yellow Tinker' is a frequent motif in Traveller stereotyping (McVeigh 1998). The size of this community is unclear but recent estimates have suggested that there are approximately 1,100 of them in the Region (Irwin and Dunn 1997). Despite their separate history and cultural traditions, Travellers are under constant pressure to assimilate, and experience considerable racism as a result of their nomadic lifestyle (Mac Laughlin 1996; Joyce and O'Brien 1998; McVeigh 1998). O'Connell (1994: 11–15) has classified the settled community's perceptions of them into five distinct models demonstrating that settled people often regard the failure of 'nomads' to conform as either a problem requiring correction or a deficiency arising out of their perpetual poverty. There is little appreciation of nomadism as an intrinsic element of a culture.

Yet I feel it is important that Travellers are given recognition as a distinct ethnicity and while it is not my intention to explore this here in detail, I would like to draw attention to a few points that I feel clarify the issue. Despite the fact that the settled community may deny this minority a separate cultural identity, there is no doubt that Travellers/Romanies are regarded as different and labelled with a variety of names such as 'tinkers', 'gypsies', and occasionally nomads (Helleiner 1995). Travellers also perceive themselves as constituting a definite group, and the distinction between insiders and outsiders is rather clear: 'We want to identify ourselves as a distinct community and we are seen by others as a distinct community' (Collins 2000: 67). Very definite boundaries separate Travellers from the settled community and it is not a simple matter to move from one group to the other.

The origin of the Travelling community in Northern Ireland is disputed and sometimes reflects a mono-cultural perspective (Noonan 1998). Colonial origins are often ascribed to Travellers, who are portrayed by the settled community as a people dispossessed at the time of the Great Famine. In other words, they were not originally a distinct ethnic group, and their cultural traditions have emerged from poverty and inferiority and are a consequence of British oppression. 'In so far as Travellers are portrayed as products of British oppression their "culture" is deemed to be "inferior" and "undesirable" in the forms in which it exists' (Helleiner 1995: 534). This version of history is rejected by many civil rights activists and Travellers themselves who, sharing their own common myth of origin, trace the distinctiveness of their community back to pre-colonial Gaelic Ireland (McLoughlin 1994; Ní Shúinéar 1994).

Travellers have a strong sense of solidarity and share the cultures and customs usually associated with nomadism. They live in caravans and mobile homes and their identity is expressed in a variety of arts and crafts. They have very high sexual morals and practice a popular form of Catholicism. A strong sense of superstition governs many of their cultural practices, which are often not understood by the settled community. One of the more distinctive markers of the Travelling cultural traditions is also the most guarded. Although the Gammon or Cant language (also known as Shelta) is commonly used by the 25,000 Travellers in Ireland and by their counterparts in Britain and North America, it is not spoken to outsiders (Binchy 1994; Cleeve 1983; Meyer 1909; Ó Baoill 1994). This means that the settled community is largely unaware of it, which may explain their general lack of appreciation of it.

Since 1996 Travellers have been named as a specific minority for protection in the Race Relations Act and there is some indication that there is a new awareness of Traveller identity in Northern Ireland. A few years ago some young Travellers in Andersonstown painted a mural celebrating their separate cultural traditions and ethnic identity and the community also participated in the West Belfast *Féile an Phobail* (Community Festival). Traveller support groups in Armagh, Craigavon, and Derry have organised special events to promote an understanding of nomadic culture. A documentary produced by Northern Visions Television afforded Travellers an opportunity to discuss their own culture and identity. Furthermore, the Department of Education Northern Ireland (DENI) has incorporated aspects of Traveller identity in the development of intercultural materials (Noonan 1998). Public appreciation of the significance of Traveller identity in Northern Ireland is gradually increasing.

Due to the prevalence of Indian restaurants, the public is also increasingly aware of the 1,000 East Indians who have settled in the Region. People have been coming from India to Northern Ireland for over 60 years and many of the original settlers arrived from Punjab and Gujarat. The first Indian high street retailer was established in 1943 in Derry and emphasis within the community is still on the clothing trade. Irwin (1998) suggests that Indians in both Britain and Northern Ireland are losing some of the characteristics they traditionally shared with other ethnic minorities. In part this may be due to the diffusion and the prosperity of the community. A decrease in family size has aided the economic prosperity of this group. Apart from their numerous restaurants, their cultural presence in the Region is strongly symbolised by the establishment of an Indian Community Centre in Belfast in 1982. This is the location of religious worship of the majority of Hindu Indians. South Asian Muslims worship in the Islamic Centre opened in 1986, and some years later the Sikh community converted a former primary school in Derry into a temple or *gurdwara* for their worship.

Pakistani identity in Northern Ireland is less obvious – a factor, which also applies to these individuals in Britain, of whom Lyon (1997:191) noted that they 'will never fit in. They keep themselves to themselves, they are just too different, and they'll never fit in and they don't want to'. These individuals are less visible than other ethnic minorities in Northern Ireland. This is partly in consequence of the fact that the 600–700 Pakistani Muslims live separately rather than in distinct neighbourhoods. While in Britain Pakistani migrants have tended to become employed in the steel mills and other engineering plants, there are no such industries in Northern Ireland and the migrants are mainly involved in the clothing, catering, or grocery business. For many of them Northern Ireland is a secondary rather than a primary area of settlement, their first destination being Britain.

Pakistani Muslims worship in conjunction with others, who are predominantly professionals, wholesalers, and shopkeepers, at the Belfast Mosque and Islamic Centre. In contrast, the Craigavon Mosque and the South Asian Women's and Children's Centre are attended primarily by market trader Pakistanis. Vast cultural differences between Pakistani individuals in Northern Ireland make any consideration of a Pakistani community necessarily simplistic and almost inappropriate, as such a discussion might imply a collective identity which does not exist (Donnan and O'Brien 1998).

Of all the non-indigenous ethnic minorities in Northern Ireland, the Jewish community is the oldest and its numbers have varied considerably over time (Keogh 1998; 1999). Original Jewish settlers were linen makers from Hamburg and arrived in the final decades of the seventeenth century. Two centuries later many Jews arrived from Russia, Lithuania, and other regions in Eastern Europe. Several persecuted Jews found refuge in Northern Ireland prior to World War II, but civil unrest prompted the gradual departure of that community in recent decades. By 1997 there were 230 left in the Region (Warm 1998).

Despite their small numbers Jews have a strong sense of affinity and collective identity. Their heritage has always been communicated through their religious services and the synagogue in North Belfast serves as a focus for Jewish traditions. This institution is central to many other Jewish organisations. *Chevra Kadisha,* the Burial Society, still provides ritual burial services for the deceased members of the community. *Beth Hasepher* (school in Hebrew) is a Hebrew educational establishment, which has been formally in operation since 1908. This provides Jewish education for the younger members of the ethnic minority and reinforces their sense of identity. Other organisations no longer in existence, such as the Belfast Jewish Institute and the Belfast Jewish Ladies Benevolent Society, afforded members in the past an opportunity to socialise with fellow Jews and to forge strong bonds of kinship and loyalty.

When reviewing the circumstances of these minorities such as the Chinese, Jews, or the Travellers, I could easily generate a false impression of permanence or of essential ethnic minority traditions. For this reason it is important to note that many of the terms I have used with regard to the classification of these minorities are in themselves questionable. As pointed out by Lyon (1997: 202), a grouping such as 'Pakistani' can be defined in historical terms – 'a kind of symbolic representation of one's perceived uniqueness'. But, of course, Pakistanis who arrived in Northern Ireland before 1947 are not Pakistanis. 'History is selective: to be "Pakistani" or "Indian" is to ignore most of what makes up one's history' (ibid.).

Moreover, as Rex (1994) asserts, minorities never consist of organised homogenous groups with appointed leaders and committees. As with larger groups, there are inevitably power struggles between those who feel themselves to be genuine representatives of the minority cultural traditions and those who can deal effectively with the institutions of the state. For example, there are elements of tension between Jews with differing degrees of religious orthodoxy in Northern Ireland. But the fact that all worship at a single synagogue helps to maintain the unity of this group. Overall, all these ethnic minorities are gaining a voice in the public sphere, but this is still largely dominated by the two traditions paradigm.

Recognition of diversity

The predominance of the two traditions paradigm reflects the small size of the ethnic minorities that I have just reviewed. It may also be the case that some of these groups are as yet inefficiently organised, but that situation is changing. In 1994 the Northern Ireland Council for Ethnic Minorities (NICEM) was established. This body constitutes a cross-ethnic alliance, defining itself as 'a voluntary sector, membership-based, umbrella organization representative of ethnic minority groups and their support organizations in Northern Ireland' (in McVeigh 1998: 187). This body has deliberately disconnected itself from the question of sectarianism and the tensions regarding equality between Catholics and Protestants. They are gaining a voice in the public sector and although minority traditions did not receive any significant attention in the GFA, they were not entirely ignored.

As a group they were given some recognition in relation to the language question when the text affirmed that all participants 'recognise the importance of respect, understanding and tolerance in relation to linguistic diversity, including in Northern Ireland, the Irish language, Ulster-Scots and the languages of the various ethnic communities, all of which are part of the cultural wealth of the island of Ireland' (GFA 1998: 22). Yet the languages of any of these ethnic minorities were not explicitly named and some groups may have felt genuinely aggrieved at this lack of formal recognition for their cultural traditions (Nic Craith 1999a). Minorities were given similar general recognition with regard to the question of policing and justice when the GFA (1998: 26) affirmed that political parties now had an opportunity to generate new procedures recognising the 'equal legitimacy and worth of the identities . . . of all sections of the community in Northern Ireland'.

That Agreement also bound the governments to bring in new measures to strengthen the protection of human rights and plural identities throughout the British Isles. Such procedures would draw on the European Convention on Human Rights and other international covenants. Examples of such documents include the Universal Declaration of Human Rights drawn up by the United Nations in 1948, which offers provisions on a variety of rights including the freedom of expression, conscience, and religion for all. Article 27 stipulates the legitimacy of every individual to participate in the cultural life of their community – an assertion affirming the entitlement of minority groups to partake in manifestations of their own particular culture.

Some of the later documents issued by the UN focus more on the rights of individuals rather than minorities. Article 27 of the International Covenant on Civil and Political Rights (1966) stipulates that in those states where 'ethnic, religious or linguistic minorities exist, persons belonging to such minorities shall not be denied the right, in community with the other members of their group, to enjoy their own culture, to profess and practice their own religion, or to use their own language' (Eide 1996: 65). The principle was more recently reinforced in 1992 with the United Nations Declaration on the Rights of Persons Belonging to National or Ethnic, Religious and Linguistic Minorities. This document reflected a discernible trend in international law towards greater appreciation of plural identities in society. Article 4, Paragraph 2 requires states to 'create favourable conditions' enabling minorities to articulate their identities and to cultivate their heritage except in cases where such practices constitute an infringement of national law or international standards (Eide 1996: 66).

In the case of Northern Ireland many groups would assert that they have never denied such a principle. It is only in those circumstances where manifestations of one tradition impinge on the other that conflict actually arises. The problem in this particular context is that while the two traditions paradigm is frequently referred to, the identity and ethos of these 'two' sections of community are usually left vaguely defined. As a consequence clashes occur on the boundaries and where cultures are in competition with one another. This applies, for example, in the celebration of historical events, which I address in the next chapter.

At a European level several documents have been issued affirming a commitment to unity within cultural diversity. Article 128 (1) of the Treaty on EU proclaims a community responsibility for the facilitation and promotion of plural identities and minority cultures (Eide 1996: 102). The European Convention for the Protection of Minorities (1991) confirms that 'persons belonging to a minority shall have the right to freely preserve, express and develop their cultural identity in all its aspects, free of any attempts at assimilation against their will' (in Skutnabb-Kangas and Philipson 1995: 401).

I feel that all groups in Northern Ireland would subscribe to these general principles but each would regard itself as the minority requiring affirmation. Nationalists constitute a minority in Northern Ireland but they are the majority in an all-Ireland context. While unionists constitute a majority in Northern Ireland, they are heavily influenced by an all-Ireland minority-mindedness. They are also conscious of Northern Ireland's conditional status within the UK, as the British government has acknowledged the right of this state to secede should a majority desire it. This places Northern Ireland in a different position from that of Scotland or Wales but 'comparable to that of Britain's remaining colonies' (Guelke 1988: 4).

International documents concerning the recognition of minorities are not necessarily legally binding, and states are invited rather than coerced to ratify them. Many countries are still marred by ethnic tension and violence and complaints emerge about a lack of respect for plural identities in various regions. For example, despite the signing of the Dayton Peace Accord in 1995 and the return of 500,000 displaced Serbs, Muslims, and Croats in Bosnia-Herzegovina, the political leaders work towards a hegemonic rather than a multi-ethnic society. In Marseilles, France, where almost 20 percent of the population are immigrants, the municipal government of Vitrolles has drastically reduced grants to culture projects associated with ethnic minorities. This rejection of foreign identities happens on the basis of their apparent incompatibility with French culture. In former East Germany, the city of Magdeburg came to symbolise racism, xenophobia, and a lack of tolerance for plural identities as immigrants and other foreigners were frequently attacked.

Such lack of respect for plural identities is not prevalent everywhere, and many governments have now affirmed a constitutional protection for designated minority identities. For example, section 14 of the Finnish Constitution guarantees that the cultural needs of the Finnish and Swedish-speaking populations will be met by the state (Eide 1996: 11–12). As is the case with the Framework Document and the GFA, these two traditions are rated of equal importance in Finland, and the question of proportionality is not deemed relevant. Constitutions in Norway and Sweden also make explicit provision for the maintenance of the Sámi identity. As a consequence a Sámi Assembly was instituted in 1987.

Conclusion

Unlike all other First World countries except New Zealand and Israel, the UK has not adopted a written constitution. But in the case of Northern Ireland it has committed itself in a series of international documents to the promotion of respect for British and Irish traditions. Furthermore, in contrast to the Irish Republic it has ratified the Council of Europe Convention on National Minorities. As yet the Irish written constitution does not make any specific provision for the variety of traditions within the Republic and the country is struggling to come to terms with the multiplicity of identities now present there (Cullen 2000; Lentin 1999; 2000; Valarasan-Toomey 1998). In the GFA the Republic has affirmed that it will 'continue to take active steps to demonstrate its respect for the different traditions in the island of Ireland' (GFA 1998: 21). At the moment the ethnic minorities of Northern Ireland receive few guarantees of protection for their cultural traditions. Although they get some protection from the Race Relations Act (Northern Ireland), this is primarily designed to prohibit discrimination against them rather than actively promote their cultural traditions.

While the objective of my book is to investigate the polarisation of society in Northern Ireland with particular reference to the two traditions paradigm, I set these traditions in a broader context throughout. In the next chapter I examine the essentialisation of the major traditions in a historical context and query whether the intransigence between them is a twentieth-century phenomenon or whether it actually began much earlier.

CHAPTER 2

DIS-MEMBERING THE PAST

> *Every continuation of tradition is selective, and precisely this selectivity must pass through the filter of critique, of a self-conscious appropriation of history.*
>
> (Habermas 1986: 243)

While unionists and nationalists agree on the contemporary relevance of history in Northern Ireland, they disagree strongly on the interpretation of the past. History has been dis-membered and some episodes are considered of greater importance than others. Selected collective memories have acquired a symbolic consequence. For this reason they have been used as tools in the quest for power, often perpetrating an impression of two traditions constantly at odds with one another. Northern Ireland is not unusual in this regard. Many divided societies explain the past in a simplistic fashion to maintain group boundaries and consolidate solidarity. History has frequently been interpreted as a simple struggle between those with power and those who have been denied it. In the Bible the small tribes of Israel were pitted against the powerful Egyptian pharaohs. Later Romans acted against Carthaginians, American colonists against Native Americans, German Gestapo against Jews (Klima 1994).

In fact, history is usually much more complex and the interpretation of the historical power struggle in Northern Ireland is open to debate. Weber (1978) made a vital distinction between the terms power and authority. While the former is essentially the capacity to force or coerce others into particular actions, the latter constitutes the 'legitimate right and delegated right to command obedience' (Jenkins 1997: 138). Herein lies the root of many of the dual perspectives on the history of the Region. Nationalists view the historical British presence as an assertion of power but unionists regard it as the exercise of a legitimate authority. But investigations into Northern Ireland's past reveal a richly diverse tapestry of traditions. And in many instances sections of the nationalist and unionist communities co-operated rather than vied with one another.

History and hermeneutics

As a term, history has a variety of meanings. It can refer simply to former occurrences, but can also apply to contemporary representations of those events. Revisionist historians are often accused of focusing on the latter at the expense of the facts. Ascherson (1996: 237) has compared the modern concern with the interpretation of the facts to an excessive interest in the label, rather than the contents, of a bottle. 'For many years now, the emphasis of historical discussion has been laid upon the label (its iconography, its target-group of customers) and upon the interesting problems of manufacturing bottle-glass. The contents, on the other hand, are tasted in a knowing, perfunctory way and then spat out again.'

But history as a process is always revisionistic. Moreover, I would argue that it is the contemporary relevance of the past rather than the actual historical details that are of real import for tensions in Northern Ireland. Here I am referring to 'the relationship between a representation (often called the signifier) and that to which it refers (the signified)'. It would be naïve to suggest that 'the latter is more "real", or more substantial, than the former' (Chaney 1994: 67). Yet an awareness of the facts can influence the interpretation and representation of their significance. And many eminent historians have made significant contributions to the common understanding of history in Northern Ireland (e.g. Elliott 1982; 1989; 2000; McBride 1997; Moody 1974).

These historians have heightened public consciousness regarding the collective history of the Region and contributed to a non-partisan awareness of this past. According to Darby (1983: 15), this may be a process in vain: 'Historians keep trying to debunk these myths, but historical scholarship has never had much effect on a folklore socialised into generations of Ulster people.' While I do not entirely agree with this statement, it is true that representations of collective 'memories' frequently engage in a process of dis-membering history mirroring subjective views, although history itself does not exist, except as a reconstruction, which can also be subjective.

Here I am making a certain distinction between history and memory although Tonkin (1992: 119) argues that such a differentiation merely serves to portray false dichotomies. Memory can be treated 'as if it is prehistorical, a distinction which sits all too neatly with traditional versus modern, primitive versus civilised and oral versus literate'. Such distinctions insinuate that memory and history are unequal, that the former is governed by the emotions whereas the latter represents fact and truth. It also suggests that historians can completely separate themselves from their own social identity and prejudices which is almost impossible when one considers the manner in which historians work. While they endeavour objectively to reconstruct the past out of existing historical fragments, these fragments are then interpreted subjectively in order to construct a narrative. This does not mean that objective facts are impossible to establish. Karl Popper (1972) has argued that scientific theories can never be established as fact. They can only be proven untrue. But truth is a guiding ideal and one can always endeavour to get closer to it. Moreover, partisanship in history and in science 'rests on disagreement not about verified facts, but about their selection and combination, and about what may be inferred from them' (Hobsbawm 1997: 166).

The process of selection

In an interesting case study of the social construction of oral history, Tonkin (1992) demonstrates that vivid memories are often less dependent on individual choice that is usually supposed. Society's actions frequently reinforce certain 'memories', and such 'recollections' can strongly influence future social relationships and the interpretation of new experiences. 'People may choose to remember or forget aspects of their past and may choose to venerate some ancestors and discard others' (Fenton 1999: 7). Our understanding of the communal past provides us with a reference point that influences our perception of the present and the future. Memories can inspire us to certain actions. Alternatively they can ensure that particular responses are avoided.

Historians can play a major role in the development of the narrative of a nation. 'In many countries the founders of the historical profession have been leaders of the national revival, concerned to forge on authoritative foundations the claims of their community to an independent and distinctive culture and politics against the sometimes wounding gaps of foreign detractors' (Hobsbawm 1996: 100). This does not mean that historians have fabricated narratives, but sometimes they have been used to legitimate claims to specific territories. Moreover, historians cannot be expected to refrain from acting as political advocates, particularly where they believe there is a case to be made. 'There will inevitably be Bulgarian, Yugoslav and Greek professors who, even without the urging of their governments, parties or churches, are prepared to fight to the last footnote for their interpretation of the Macedonian question' (Hobsbawm 1997: 174).

In homogenous or peaceful context, historical memories are a source of inspiration, commitment, and collective commemoration. Bourdieu (1977) coined the term 'habitus' to describe the usual process of remembering and forgetting. 'Habitus' refers to the common habits and routines of the familiar social world whereby a person or community internalises history.

One's past is internalized and becomes 'second nature', and is almost forgotten. Billig (1995) proposed that such selection procedures pave the path for what he terms a 'banal' form of nationalism that is frequently prevalent among groups portraying themselves as civic, rather than nationalist, in orientation.

This placid interpretation of history does not occur in divided societies where each 'side' usually has its own version of events and fails to understand the experiences or assumptions of the 'other' (Connerton 1989). Sometimes there can be more than 'one memory in action' (Llobera 1998a: 332). This applies particularly to ethnically diverse communities or to instances where the dominant culture vies for precedence with an alternative perspective. Here one must distinguish between history as an effort at objective observation and the subjective interpretation of the past. When talking of the horrors of Auschwitz, for example, Habermas (1986: 237) notes that 'a hermeneutically unreflective procedure is unquestionable'. He argues that 'if one tries simply to project oneself into the situation of the participants, in order to understand the actors and their actions in terms of their own surroundings, then one risks losing sight of the disastrous context of the epoch as a whole'. In Northern Ireland the two traditions use certain historical facts by taking them out of the historical context and instrumentalising them as it seems appropriate for them.

Andric (1995: 17) in his historical novel, *The Bridge*, explains how Serb and Turkish children are so utterly convinced of their version of the past that there is no attempt to communicate with each other. Serb children interpret hoofprints on the banks of the river Drina as 'the prints of the hooves of Sarac, the horse of Kraljevic Marko, which had remained there from the time when Kraljevic Marko himself was in prison up there in the Old Fortress and escaped, flying down the slope and leaping the Drina, for at that time there was no bridge'. Turkish children were certain that this could not have been the case 'nor could it have been (for whence could a bastard Christian dog have had such strength or such a horse!) any but Djerzelez Alija on his winged charger which, as everyone knew, despised ferries and ferrymen and leapt over rivers as if they were watercourses'. Neither group quarrelled about this 'so convinced were both sides in their own belief. And there was never an instance of any one of them being able to convince another, or that any one had changed his belief.'

Remembering the past in Northern Ireland is hardly a 'banal' process. Jackson (1996: 120–1) argues that it is a 'fundamental aspect of Irish tragedy' that 'threads are plucked from past and present and woven into a smothering ideological blanket of a uniform green, or orange'. Opposing groups avail of symbols and rituals such as bonfires and songs to emphasise the significance of certain events as opposed to others (Rolston 1999). Important anniversaries are regularly commemorated in the form of parades, and although the origins of this custom are actually rooted in the Catholic tradition (Jarman and Bryan 1998), parades in Northern Ireland have become predominantly a means of expressing loyalist identity. In the past many of these parades have been conducted in a triumphalist manner. Of the 3,500 parades held in 1995, the police classed 2,581 as loyalist events (Jarman 1997), the majority of which were organised by the Orange Order.

Orange parades place special emphasis on seventeenth-century Ulster, and commemorate events such as the massacre of 1641, the siege of the city of Derry, and the victory of the Protestant king William of Orange at the Battle of the Boyne. In a letter to the *Belfast Telegraph*, a writer suggests that on the 12th July, Orangemen 'not only commemorate a very significant military and political victory, but a great deliverance from Roman slavery, in much the same way as the Jews each year commemorate their deliverance from bondage in Egypt' (in Rose 1971: 258). Some Orange parades also focus on the twentieth century and pay tribute to soldiers who died in the Battle of the Somme in World War I.

Nationalist parades are considerably fewer in number. In 1995 the police identified a mere 302 as specifically nationalist events. Some of these were religious in function while others commemorated the separatist rising in 1916 and the deaths of republican hunger strikers in the early 1980s. Nationalist rituals are primarily held under the auspices of Catholic or republican brotherhoods such as the Ancient Order of Hibernians or the National Irish Foresters. Parades relevant to the entire community are organised by groups like the Salvation Army or the Boys' Brigade.

Murals reinforce the significance of certain events over others (Rolston 1992; 1995; Vannais 1999) and I explore their role in community life in Chapter 8. These paintings are predominantly an expression of unionist, rather than nationalist, culture and were its sole prerogative until the early 1980s. For many decades the paintings concentrated almost entirely on events from the seventeenth century and the victories of King Billy (William of Orange) on his horse provided the central image. But 'the image of a conquering chief on horseback' is an ancient symbol 'adopted by both religion and politics' from prehistoric times (Ó Murchú 1997: 3). In recent years twentieth-century themes, such as the 75th anniversary of the founding of the Ulster Volunteer Force (UVF), and its later decimation at the Battle of the Somme, have figured prominently in murals (Rolston 1992). Historical themes have received less attention in nationalist murals but there has been a strong emphasis on hunger strikes by republican prisoners in the late 1980s. As 1995 was regarded as the 150th anniversary of the Great Famine throughout Ireland, new murals depicted a starved and dispossessed Irish people.

In the nationalist community, symbols of historical significance, such as the Proclamation of Independence in 1916, are exhibited in private rather than in public (Loftus 1994). Many households display emblems that have been handcrafted by republican internees. Paintings and calendar photographs illustrate the wild and natural scenery of Irish rural landscape and picture books focus on national identity as expressed in the countryside. Even though they are confined to the private realm, these symbols are no less significant that those of unionists. Neither does the privacy of these emblems imply that they have been individually chosen. Their lack of exposure is merely a consequence of the restrictions placed on the public display of nationalist emblems in the pre-Civil Rights decades.

Northern Irish communities often interpret significant historical events in a very simplistic manner. Some nationalists regard the Anglo-Norman conquest of 1169–71 as the first invasion of Ireland by the British. From this perspective later historical episodes merely reinforced the distinction between native and the foreigner. In contrast, unionists are more likely to focus on events from the seventeenth century forward to emphasise a variety of dichotomies, such as a distinction between newcomer and native, planter and dispossessed, Protestant and Catholic, unionist and nationalist. Probably the 'two most compelling myths of Northern Irish ethnicity' are the nationalist interpretation of the Plantation and the unionist account of the Siege (Buckley and Kenney 1995: 48). Even though they refer to different events, the two myths are remarkable in their reinforcement of similar dichotomies, such as the distinction between insiders and outsiders, losers and winners.

Contemporary groups use these events to reinforce a sense of two communities with opposing perspectives. In order to understand the significance of historical trajectories for the contemporary two traditions paradigm, it is important to review the narratives rather than the objective facts. With regard to nationalist or unionist interpretations of notable events, this means 'taking seriously *their* ways of structuring experience' (Gibbons 1996: 17). For this reason I will briefly review the competing histories of these groups, focusing primarily on the seventeenth century.

Dispossession or modernisation?

In September 1607 a group of Irish chiefs and their followers, totalling about a hundred persons, set sail for the continent from Lough Swilly in the north of Donegal. The gathering included the two Ulster Earls of Tyrone and Tyrconnell (Donegal) and Cuconnaught Maguire of Fermanagh. 'The exiles had left their people defenceless, and presented the government with an ideal opportunity to solve the problem of Ireland's chief trouble spot' (Clarke 1967: 190). The 'flight of the earls' and the ensuing rebellion of Sir Cahir O'Doherty offered an opportunity to the English Crown to confiscate vast tracts of land. Territories seized included the entire counties of Tyrone and Donegal and half of Fermanagh. As the Gaelic Brehon laws were declared invalid, all non-Church territory in the counties of Tyrone, Armagh, Fermanagh, Donegal, Cavan, and Coleraine were in the hands of the monarch (Robinson 1984).

King James I decided that both English and Scots would benefit from a process of plantation. English money and expertise would provide the craftsmen needed to construct towns and castles in Ulster. More persuasively, the plantation of English here affirmed that Ireland was regarded as an English possession, which had been conquered by English arms and was ruled by English officials. The English would serve as civilising and proselytising influences (Fitzpatrick 1989). Large stretches of land were granted to English and Scottish lords described as undertakers. Further grants were made to English army officers serving in Ireland, called 'servitors', and to compliant Irish chiefs. A new county called Londonderry was created and, as I elaborate in Chapter 6, this territory was presented to London Livery Companies.

By 1611 the King had granted 81,000 acres to 59 Scots, mostly in Donegal and Tyrone. The English largely settled in Armagh and Derry. Individuals from both England and Scotland were planted in Fermanagh and Cavan. Thus Ulster became the meeting point for a variety of peoples including the English, Highland and Lowland Scots, and highland and lowland Irish. Differences between the disposition of the English and the Scottish were quite apparent. Generally speaking, the English settlers were 'plain country gentlemen' who were 'tight-fisted and easily scared' (Foster 1988: 67). The Scottish were of a much tougher disposition and their character and identity aroused many derogatory and insulting comments (Leyburn 1962). Unsympathetic English men drafted almost all descriptions of the Scottish, and their fear of the tenacity of the Scots is detectable in state papers. A memorandum criticising the Restoration Settlement in Ireland in the late 1660s noted that the Scots were so 'numerous, so needy, and so near to Ireland, so cunning, so close and confederated in a common interest that some of our statesmen apprehend that they may soon possess themselves of the whole island, they being at present not only masters of Ulster, but spread over other provinces, and very well armed'. Of particular concern to the English officials was the fact that 'if despair should dictate to the distressed Irish that it is their conveniency to join with the Scotts against the English that possesseth their estates, without question the English interest would be lost in Ireland' (Pentland Mahaffy 1905: 558).

Originally it was intended to segregate the Irish from the newcomers (McCavitt 1994). English and Scottish undertakers would be settled next to rivers, the Irish would live in the lowlands of Ulster, in exposed places where they could be easily overseen (Foster 1988: 64). Some captains and servitors were given lands on the borders and near the Irish. These servitors were permitted to have indigenous occupants but were given an incentive of low rents if instead they attracted British tenants. It was assumed that the introduction of the British would be a civilising influence on the Irish. 'This segregation of the incoming settlers from the native population was to ensure that the colony would take firm root, that the islands of British territory would serve as the leaven of "civility and religion" which would leaven the whole lump of native Irish "barbarism" and "superstition"' (Moody 1939: 60). This philosophy was similar to that of the Middle Kingdom of China in the colonial era, which advocated a theory of cultural assimilation for the transformation of the barbarians (Dikötter 1990).

Although the Plantation occurred in the early seventeenth century, it is still significant in contemporary Northern Ireland. Despite the sheer variety of cultures involved, 'memories' of this episode have proved a catalyst for simplification and polarisation, the most obvious of which is the distinction between coloniser and colonised, between possessor and dispossessed. From the perspective of some nationalists, the British planters stole their land (Buckley and Kenney 1995) and in popular memory it is assumed that all the natives were immediately evacuated from their homes and relocated in barren mountains. British wealth in Ulster was acquired at the expense of the indigenous population and the Plantation is a central symbol of dispossession. The current nationalist ideal constitutes an attempt to regain and reunify territory that rightfully belongs to the Irish and from this perspective the loss of the six counties can be compared with the German loss of East Prussia in 1945 or the Austrian loss of South Tyrol three years later. Of course Europe is a patchwork quilt of lost territories.

In reality the Plantation did not, in itself, constitute an instantaneous process of dispossession. Some of the native chiefs had, in fact, departed prior to the process of Plantation. As only the ruling families had lost their property, many of those who later identified themselves as dispossessed had not actually been deprived of estates (Canny 1989; Ruane and Todd 1996). This does not invalidate the discourse of loss, as natives were no longer in charge of vast tracts of Ulster. As there was a considerable lack of workforce, some of the original tenant farmers continued to work on the land, 'some as labourers, some as tenants, and some even, as landowners' (Clarke 1967: 192). Ultimately, the indigenous inhabitants were largely deprived of the right to own land and many aspects of Irish culture were affected by the loss of property. Poets lost their patrons with the departure of Irish chiefs and the entire Gaelic bardic system was due to collapse, not just in Ulster but in the Highlands of Scotland as well. In many instances worldwide the dispossession of land is 'a central feature of indigenous minorities, invariably accompanied by a demeaning and devaluing of culture and language loss' (Fenton 1999: 42).

From the British perspective the Plantation bears an opposite meaning, and is equated with modernisation and development. Colonisation benefited the land. Because the indigenous population failed to develop the natural resources, the industrious British transformed the territory with carefully cultivated farms and established new urban centres. These arrivals were industrious, enterprising, innovative, and, most importantly, law-abiding (Ulster Young Unionist Council 1986). From this viewpoint the dominant groups brought 'progress' and 'civilisation' in British terms to a land that was being used unproductively by natives. This dualism of civilised settlers versus savage natives also prevailed in the apartheid era in South Africa (Giliomee 1990).

Nandy (1983) has argued that, historically, two distinctive genres of colonisation were at play worldwide and the two types were usually separated chronologically. In the first, the focus was on the simple physical acquisition of new territories. Another force was at play in the second, which was 'more insidious in its commitment to the conquest and occupation of minds, selves, cultures'. Usually greed and a simple desire to expand one's holdings generated the first. In contrast, the second was 'pioneered by rationalists, modernists and liberals who argued that imperialism was really the messianic harbinger of civilisation to the uncivilised world' (Gandhi 1998: 15). While nationalists regard the Plantation of Ulster as an example of the first type of colonisation, unionists place it in the latter category.

But unionists also reject the dichotomy between natives and foreigners on the basis that Ireland was under the jurisdiction of the British Crown. Plantations could be viewed as a form of internal migration, that is the movement of subjects from one part of the Kingdom to another. In later centuries many of those who were identified as 'settlers' were in fact descendants of immigrants rather than planters. Some loyalists have provocatively suggested that the planters were merely returning to the land of their ancestors. 'When the Galloway planters came to Ulster they were only returning to their own lands like emigrants returning home again' (McCausland 1991: 37). I address the concept of the Plantation as return in Chapter 5.

In all of these dichotomies, colonisation works as a lens or a category through which the historic present is assessed. Remembering this event could potentially serve two functions. Firstly, the process could expose the unpalatable past and endeavour to assess more precisely the injustice inflicted. Furthermore, the recollection of past hurts could ultimately lead to a process of reconciliation and appease those who endured suffering, or their descendants. A Forum for Peace and Reconciliation was established in Dublin in 1994 with precisely this intention. A similar forum operated in South Africa in the post-apartheid era. Its intention was to assess and cleanse the hurt endured by the black community under the administration of the Afrikaners. 'This is, of course, another way of saying that postcoloniality has to be made to concede its part or complicity in the terrors – and errors of its own past' (Gandhi 1998: 10). It is doubtful whether either commission achieved its intentions. The location of the Irish Forum in the Republic under the auspices of the Irish Government meant that many unionists refused to acknowledge its relevance.

Insiders or outsiders?

Although nationalists remember the Plantation as the most significant event in Northern Irish history, unionists focus on the Williamite campaign that occurred towards the end of the seventeenth century (Walker, B. 1997), and anniversaries of related episodes are observed annually. Such commemorations reinforce the dichotomy between Protestants and Catholics as essentially they celebrate the deposition of the Catholic king James II who had acceded to the English throne in 1685. His installation was a cause of great celebration for Ulster Catholics. Their new king appointed a Catholic Earl of Donegal, and Protestant officials in the Irish administration were gradually removed.

Three years later in a *coup d'état* which came to be known as the Glorious Revolution, the English Parliament invited the Calvinist and *Staathoulder* of the Netherlands, and husband of James' daughter, William of Orange, to accede to the throne in England. James fled with great haste first to Louis XIV in France and then to Ireland to muster support from his loyal Catholic subjects. When he presented himself on 18 April 1689 before the town of Derry, the Protestants dwellers within fired at him. James' army surrounded the walls with the intention of starving the population, thereby forcing surrender. Derry was under siege for 105 days. In the meantime, William of Orange landed at Larne in County Antrim. Before long, two ships laden with food supplies broke the Jacobite boom that was blocking the Foyle estuary. As this allowed food supplies into Derry, the siege was effectively ended and James fled. Almost a year later, William landed at Carrickfergus in County Antrim and journeyed southwards. He met James at the River Boyne and defeated him in the most fabled battle in Irish history. This Battle of the Boyne is celebrated annually by unionists on 12th July. From this perspective, William's victory was, and is, symbolic of the defeat of Catholics by Protestants. Moreover, it also symbolises the power of the English over the Irish.

In a European context, this battle 'was an important theatre of a war between France and a league of lesser powers' (Simms 1967: 211) and 'helped shape the continent for a century or more afterward' (Doherty 1998: 9). Both armies were international in composition. Regiments of English, Danes, Dutch, French Huguenots, and Germans joined with William in battle. Any Ulster Protestants present were primarily 'skirmishers' and were 'described by one of William's captains as "half-naked with sabre and pistols hanging from their belts . . . like a horde of Tartars"' (Bardon 1997: 12). James' army was primarily French, rather than Ulster Catholic, and any Irish Catholics present were nearly all Old English, rather than Gaelic Irish. At the time of the Orange victory, many Catholics rejoiced. As the Habsburg Empire was Catholic, celebrations in Austria were marked with the singing of *Te Deum* in Vienna. In Rome, Pope Innocent III was particularly pleased.

After the Battle of the Boyne, James fled to Dublin and later sailed for France. Because he had not actually formally abdicated his throne in London, the English parliament announced that he had deserted his kingdom and appointed William and Mary as new joint monarchs. In contrast, the Scottish parliament was unable to depose James, as it officially required the co-operation of the king before it could make any such pronouncement. In this situation, the Dutchman who was proclaimed King of England was also claiming to be monarch of Scotland. In contrast the Catholic king James, living in Catholic France, was claiming kingship of a largely Protestant Scotland. While he had many supporters in the Catholic Highlands, many of the Lowlanders who were Protestant supported William.

Unionists in Northern Ireland enthusiastically celebrate the Siege of Derry and the Battle of the Boyne on an annual basis. The Orange Order and the Apprentice Boys organise a series of parades, primarily in the months of July, August, and December, to commemorate these events. In the late twentieth century some ceremonies have become increasingly contentious, and a Parades Commission has been given official responsibility for the resolution of these matters. Other modes of celebration are less controversial. For example, illustrations of the Siege have been depicted on stained glass windows in St. Columba's Anglican cathedral in Derry. In 1989, Derry City council commissioned a symphony by Shaun Davy to mark the tercentenary of the event.

Many historians (e.g. Akenson 1992) suggest that contemporary Northern Irish Protestants, in common with Afrikaners, display a siege mentality. A mural in a Protestant suburb on the outskirts of the city asserts that 'Londonderry Westbank Loyalists/Still under Siege/No Surrender' (McBride 1997: 75; pictured in Kockel 1994). Unionists are surrounded by natives or 'sons of the soil' and their prestigious position is justified by religious fervour. Others surrounding them fail to acknowledge the true faith and often collaborate with evil forces. Until the collapse of the Soviet Union, Ulster Freedom Fighters believed in a 'secret compact between Old Red Socks in the Vatican and the late Leonid Brezhnev in the Kremlin' (Ascherson 1996: 101). Serbs determined their special connection with God when they decoded the names of international supporters of Bosnia as the encrypted titles of the devil's archangels (Ascherson 1996). Protestants affirmed their special connection with God when they conquered the Catholics at the Battle of the Boyne. For Afrikaners the defeat of the Zulus at Blood River in 1838 is of religious significance. Those victories confirm the fact that they are a chosen people – a concept that I explore in the next chapter.

Commemorations of the Siege in August and December allow loyalists the opportunity 'to recreate the holy city of Protestant legend' (McBride 1997: 77). During these celebrations they often represent themselves as martyrs as well as victors. Ascherson (1996: 100) suggests that these rituals of dominance are a very significant element of identity for an 'outpost' people. Displays of power over 'others' serve to reassure them of their own identity. From their own perspective, Afrikaners, who no longer demonstrate their mastery of the natives, are failing to experience the full extent of their identity. Serb militias practised the ritual gang rape of Muslim women in Bosnia in a similar quest for a confirmation of identity. Similarly, Cossacks, regarding themselves as the authentic Russians, displayed the dominance syndrome 'with gloomy intensity' (Ascherson 1996: 101).

As the victory of William of Orange has become a central myth of ethnic superiority, it has been compared with the Battle of Kosovo. In both cases, the battles represent 'a moment when a small people, in battle with mortal foes, defended Christendom for all of Europe' (Ignatieff 1994: 169). Although Ulster Protestants were the victors at Boyne, and the Serbs were the losers at Kosovo, both cultures developed a concept of themselves as a misunderstood people who heroically defended the faith (Ignatieff 1994; Nordland 1999). From this perspective God rewarded Protestants in Northern Ireland with an ascendancy over the Catholic Irish.

Many cultures commemorate battles with religious significance for identity. Cossacks achieved a victory for Russia and for Christendom when they routed an Ottoman garrison on the Don delta in 1637. In this instance, horsemen from the steppes of Russia defeated the non-Christian enemy within the city walls. A siege of three days was necessary before the Islamic enemy was finally routed. Although the Turks were later to return with reinforcements, the Cossacks had gained an initial victory against them and basked in the glory of Christian success. Later in the century, in 1683, the Polish king John Sobieski relieved the city of Vienna from the onslaught of the Turks. His actions curtailed the threatened Moslem expansion into Central Europe and contributed to the Polish self image as the 'eastward bastion (*przedmurze*) of Christendom' (Ascherson 1996: 168). In reality none of these events were as significant as is often assumed and their contemporary meaning has been allocated to them in retrospect (Hastings 1997).

From a unionist perspective, the Siege of Derry and the Battle of the Boyne reinforce the concepts of liberty and freedom in a religious and political sense. When the English parliament proclaimed William of Orange as King of England, the constant struggles between crown and parliament were over. The concept of king as divinely ordained was held to be invalid and the monarchy became constitutional. Parliamentary democracy was established in Britain (Montgomery and Whitten 1995). From this position, the entire British culture owes a debt to events in Ireland and the 'Twelfth of July is truly an occasion when everyone throughout the UK should be able to celebrate' (Weir 1997: 145).

The story of the Siege also reinforces a dichotomy between insiders and outsiders, although in a manner challenging the nationalist interpretation of themselves as insiders. In the case of the Siege, it is the Protestant, rather than the Catholic, community that is located within the city walls and

Protestants are refusing entry to the Catholic king. McBride (1997) suggests that this event symbolises the closed mind of Protestants incapable of coping with change. A view of Protestants as 'insiders' is reinforced by the regular commemoration of the Williamite conquest. Parades, murals, and other emblems of Orange culture are a discourse of belonging to the Region.

Forgetting to remember

While the Plantation and the Williamite Campaign are the most significant episodes from the seventeenth century, unionists and nationalists have other 'memories' of this period that are mutually exclusive. The episodes of 1641 and 1649 are 'remembered' selectively to reinforce the concept of two distinct traditions. Unionists focus on the massacre of 1641 whereas nationalists concentrate on the dispossessions of 1649 (Darby 1983, Walker, B. 1997). These circumstances are simplified and recounted in terms of simple dichotomies: possessor and dispossessed, persecutor and persecuted, disloyal and loyal.

In 1641 many of the Gaelic and Catholic communities in Ireland rebelled against the English parliament and actively sought the return of territories that had been lost in the previous 50 years (Clarke 1967). Sir Phelim O'Neill and other prominent Ulster landowners led an insurrection against the settlers. Initially they targeted English rather than Scottish settlers. This changed before long and the entire planter community was threatened and many were routed although the precise figures are in dispute. Apprehension and volatility prevailed in Ulster until the arrival in 1649 of Cromwell with a large English army.

As leader of the parliamentary forces, Cromwell had already established the power of parliament over the Crown in England and in 1649, Charles I, King of England and Scotland, was executed. Cromwell was equally intent on restoring law and order in Ireland and immediately conducted a ruthless conquest of the island, the severity of which 'became indelibly impressed upon the folk memory of the land' (Clarke 1967: 202). He also conducted successful battles against the Scots at Dunbar and Worcester in 1650 and 1651. As Cromwell detested Roman Catholics, he ensured that many indigenous Irish were deprived of land, which was then given to the 'New English' planters of the pre-1641 period. They identified themselves as 'Old Protestants' in order to distinguish themselves from the Baptists and Quakers of the Cromwellian army. Catholics owned a mere 22 percent of the land in 1688. This proportion was to fall to 14 percent by 1703 (Foster, R. 1988).

Nationalists and unionists in Northern Ireland 'remember' the events of the mid-seventeenth century, but their memories are mutually exclusive. While unionists recollect the killing in 1641, nationalists remember the

dispossession of 1649. Neither attaches any significance to the other date –
except perhaps to cast aspersions on the 'exaggerations' of the 'other' community. Each group is competitively demonstrating that it has sustained
greater pain that the other. This reclamation of suffering is not unique to
Northern Ireland. Klima (1994: 53) said of the Czech Republic: 'there is a
kind of xenophobia here with respect to the suffering of the past half century. The Czechs are by now rather possessive of their suffering.'

Nationalists vividly recount the slaughter that accompanied the
Cromwellian conquest. Unionists regard themselves as the afflicted rather
than the persecutors and frequently refer to the massacre of 1641 in which
they shed blood in order to redeem the land. Many 'piquant, salted tales –
which included hair-raising narratives of killings and torture, of infants
being ripped from their mothers' wombs, of children being boiled alive
and old people slaughtered – fed the self-righteous vengeance which characterised Cromwell's campaign' (Haddick-Flynn 1999: 34). Contemporary
loyalist perspectives have been outlined by the Ulster Loyalist Association.
In a passage published by the organisation in 1970, the present relevance
of the events of 1641 are established:

> In Ireland our ancestors suffered in the fiendish Romish massacre of 1641,
> and we who are the victors of 1688 are not likely to render tame submission
> to the offspring of the vanquished, for the Protestants of Ireland are com-
> pelled to resist by every means in their power this hated system of Popery,
> which is slavery and the taking away of the freedom of a people. Our fore-
> fathers were encouraged to leave England and Scotland to colonise and hold
> Ireland for Great Britain. They have more than fulfilled that duty; their blood
> has been spilt for freedom, faith, and empire, and in the most trying and per-
> ilous times their loyalty to their country and Protestantism has stood the test.
> They have experienced a massacre more barbarous, and inhuman cruelty,
> than any that characterised the most sanguinary period of the French Revol-
> ution.
>
> (Ulster Loyalist Association 1970: 1)

Loyalism, and its definition, is one of the most interesting aspects of
these mid-seventeenth century episodes. From the perspective of unionists, Northern Ireland is commonly perceived as divided between faithful
and treacherous citizens. It is assumed that the unionist community is
devoted to the Crown whereas nationalists are not. But there is a distinction to be made between loyalty and loyalism. While loyalty may be
defined as the maintenance of allegiance to a monarch and the acceptance
of his or her authority, loyalism implies conditionality. Fidelity is contin-
gent on the fulfilment of certain conditions.

Generally speaking, while loyalism is associated with the unionist community, Catholics have also been faithful (Ruane and Todd 1996). When
Catholics rebelled against parliament, they actively supported the Crown
and this allegiance was not suspended when the Protestant William of
Orange defeated the Catholic king. Ulster Catholics remained devoted to

the Catholic Stuart succession and hoped that its restoration would lead to the recovery of their territory. When Jacobitism finally collapsed, Catholics accepted the legality of the Hannoverian lineage and their demands for reform were accompanied with declarations of fidelity. In this sense Catholics and Protestants were loyal but, like their memories of the mid-seventeenth century, the conditions of their allegiance were mutually incompatible.

Exclusive 'memories' also apply to the twentieth century and are particularly relevant to the year 1916. As Britain was engaged in the First World War, the Irish Volunteers who were agitating for Home Rule split. Their leader John Redmond offered his support to England in this war 'for the defence of "small nations"' (McCartney 1967: 306) and many nationalists along with unionists enlisted in the British Army. In some towns and villages, Ulster and Irish Volunteers marched next to one another in order to send off departing troops. By 1918 some 50,000 had lost their lives but the greatest bloodshed had occurred on the 1st July in 1916 at the Battle of the Somme. On that day, 20,000 British soldiers were killed and another 40,000 were wounded or declared missing. The A and D Companies of the 11th Irish Rifles were completely obliterated, and of particular note was the sacrifice of the 36th Ulster Division. Later on there were severe losses elsewhere on the battlefront, including the soldiers from the 16th Irish Division.

As Ireland had been exempted from conscription, many Irish men did not sign up for active service. Indeed, some volunteers regarded this as an opportune moment to seek independence from Britain and promoted the slogan that 'England's danger is Ireland's opportunity'. 'The Rising took place as the first breach in the world imperialist war front' (Desmond-Greaves 1991: 31–2) and at Easter 1916 separatists seized a number of buildings in Dublin and hoisted the Irish tricolour on the roof of the General Post Office there. Patrick Pearse then read the proclamation of the Irish Republic from the entrance. Leaders of this insurrection were later captured. Their subsequent execution proved the catalyst for the emergence of massive support for the separatist cause. 'Emotion about the executed men quickly reached a high pitch, and the poets and writers reflected the new national spirit' (Dudley Edwards 1990: 335). Outside of Ulster, Sinn Féin received a huge vote in the election after the War. Elected members constituted themselves as Dáil Éireann (the Assembly of Ireland).

1916 is a significant year from the perspective of all communities in Northern Ireland. Unionists remember the bond that was forged between Ulster and Britain at this time. Feeling themselves to be a vital part of the British nation, they had volunteered for slaughter at the Somme. Their Empire was under threat and they fought gallantly for the protection of British civilisation (Cochrane 1997). Though generally speaking the Battle of the Somme is perceived as the grotesque and needless slaughter of the lives of thousands of young soldiers, many in Northern Ireland are proud of their Region's contribution to the action. Parades commemorating the dead heroes are organised annually on 1st July (Brearton 1997). Bell (1976: 144) has remarked of these marchers that they 'are not bitter at the slaughter of their own people in one of the most pointless military battles the world has ever seen, a battle judged necessary at the time by those not of their class, not of their country. They are not angry, they are not bitter, they do not protest; they are proud. That is their tragedy.' Many in Northern Ireland regard Bell's comments as a one-sided view as they believe that the Somme ensured British support for Northern Ireland in any future Irish settlement. For this reason its significance cannot be underestimated and it is regularly commemorated. In Portadown these ceremonies have proved particularly contentious (Kockel 1999c).

Catholics in Northern Ireland remember 1916 as the catalyst for the establishment of the Irish Republic, and it has significant resonance 'as a "recycled" inspiration to would-be revolutionaries, and indeed, to would be constitutionalists as well' (Boyce 1996a: 163). Although Belfast was not actually involved in the rising and at a local level Sinn Féin suffered great defeat in the subsequent election, anniversaries of the rising are marked with celebrations. In 1966 the extent of the 50th commemorations was considerable. As several republicans were on hunger strike during the 65th anniversary in 1981, that anniversary was marked with widespread protest marches. In recent years, the Easter Sunday ceremonies in West Belfast have been quite extensive.

While the Somme is remembered by unionists as an occasion when they shed their blood for the preservation of the union, they often forget that many nationalist Catholics served in the British Army. Nationalists also tend to disregard the Catholic contribution to the British war effort and for many years the sacrifice of Irish soldiers, particularly those from south of the Border, was ignored. There was some sense in which their efforts were regarded as a betrayal of the nationalist cause. These soldiers had mistakenly supported the British Empire instead of mounting a defence for an Irish Republic. They were champions of a British, rather than an Irish goal. Travellers also complain that their contribution to these war efforts is forgotten. 'The reality is that we have contributed in a major way to this society but this contribution has never been recognised' (Cullen et al 2000: 74).

Attitudes regarding the commemoration of the Somme have altered in recent years. Since an IRA bomb exploded at the Remembrance Day ceremonies in Enniskillen in 1987, there have been numerous endeavours to enhance the general appreciation of the contribution of Irish Catholics to the First World War and many veterans feel that their service has at last been recognised. In 1999 a round tower was built in France on a site where unionists and nationalists fought together. Changes in the celebration of rituals are part of the process of commemoration, and the contemporary emphasis on two traditions is primarily a phenomenon that has evolved during the nineteenth and twentieth centuries. The actual diversity of history has been overlooked. Forgetfulness is an art that, according to Ernest Renan, is 'an essential factor in the formation of a nation' (in Hobsbawm 1992: 3).

The polarisation of communities

A variety of factors served to amalgamate this diversity of history into 'two' traditions. In 1800 the Irish parliament, which was dominated by Anglicans, was persuaded to vote for its own dissolution. Although members of the established church were largely to control Irish politics until the end of the century, Ulster-Scottish Presbyterians were greatly relieved by the formal abolition of the Irish parliament. As tensions between these groups eased, they became increasingly identified as one. A similar process had already occurred in Britain when Scottish and English Protestants gradually joined forces against Catholic France. 'The sense of common identity here did not come into being, then, because of an integration and homogenisation of disparate cultures. Instead, Britishness was superimposed over an array of internal differences in response to contact with the Other, and above all in response to conflict with the Other' (Colley 1996: 6). Ordnance survey memoirs by Ligar in 1835 spoke of the division of the Parish of Dungiven in County Londonderry into two distinct races:

> The parishioners are divided into 2 races, the Irish and Scotch. There are some English settlers but their number is so small that they are compounded under the general appellation of Scotch. The distinction between the 2 races is further marked by difference of religions. So completely are the terms Irish and Scotch equivalent to Catholic and Protestant that to call a Protestant an Irishman is considered a high affront, it being in fact an insinuation against his religion. 'Protestant' includes both Presbyterians and Episcopalians, the latter of whom are chiefly from the English settlers.
>
> (Day and McWilliams 1992: 15)

As is apparent from this quotation, the settler-dispossessed dichotomy was strongly associated with religious beliefs. Settlers were identified as primarily, though not of necessity, Protestant, and the natives were Catholic. This distinction is quite dubious in that many Protestants in the eighteenth and nineteenth centuries were Irish converts, rather than migrants from Britain.

The gradual political consolidation of Irish Catholics was aided by the fact that from the 1760s onwards, their relationship with the British government had become more harmonious and many concessions had been made to them. In part this was due to the fact that the Irish were required as recruits for the American War of Independence, for India and, later, for the wars against France (Wall 1967: 231). A risk of invasion from Catholic France was far less likely if the Catholics in Ireland were appeased. Moreover, the indigenous Irish had by and large not supported Bonnie Prince Charlie and the Scottish Jacobite rebellion in 1745, although their lack of assistance was primarily due to a famine that swept Ireland in the 1740s.

A relief bill passed in 1778 eased the constraints on Catholic land ownership, provided they swore allegiance to the British monarch. A second measure in 1793 permitted Catholics to enter military service, to organise religious schools, and to vote in elections, but they were not allowed to sit in parliament. When Ireland was united with Great Britain in 1801 they were subjected to the same restrictions as British Catholics. Many Irishmen became active in the newly formed Irish militia that was primarily a Catholic force, directed by Protestant officers. In 1836 a centralised Royal Irish Constabulary was formed to replace the primarily Protestant County Constabularies. More than half of this force was Catholic in 1851 (Ruane and Todd 1996: 40). Catholics were gradually integrated into the national economy, and the Catholic middle-classes grew.

Irish Catholic advancement in the nineteenth century was given considerable impetus by the establishment of a Catholic Association in 1823 (Whyte 1967: 250). A year later its founder, Daniel O'Connell, introduced the category of associate member at an affordable subscription rate of one penny a month to be collected at Sunday Mass by the local priest. This innovation brought the masses of poorer Irish into politics for the first time (Chenevix-Trench 1986). The collection of the subscription was organised through the network of churches, and the clergy became actively interested in politics. In 1829 the Emancipation Act established the right of British and Irish Catholics to sit as MPs at Westminster without taking the Oath of Supremacy, which was offensive to their Catholic principles. It was given on condition that only individuals with a life interest in either a house or land valued at ten pounds or more would be given a franchise in future elections.

Throughout his campaign, O'Connell had emphasised Catholicism as one of the main factors uniting the dispossessed throughout the country, and his triumph gave them identity and purpose. At the same time his concept of nationality included the Protestant community. He suggested that 'the Protestant alone could not expect to liberate his country – the Roman Catholic alone could not do it – neither could the Presbyterian – but amalgamate the three in the Irishman and the Union is repealed' (in Girvin 1994: 70). Despite such proclamations O'Connell came to be increasingly identified with Catholicism and his unwavering work for repeal of the Union became associated with the aspirations of Irish Catholics.

As time passed, an increase in the knowledge of English ensured greater cultural homogeneity between the lower and middle-class Catholic Irish (Nic Craith 1994). A network of churches provided the infrastructure for a national organisation. Later in the century, another leader, Charles Stuart Parnell, was to reinforce the national unity of the Catholic Irish by demanding home rule for Ireland and by harnessing agrarian support through the organisational structure of the Land League. In 1884 a Franchise Act, which extended the vote to all adult male householders, increased substantially the number of Irish Catholic voters, and the parliamentary returns of 1884–85 confirmed Catholic majorities in the constituencies of Leinster, Connaught, and Munster. Protestants dominated half of the Ulster division (Walker B. 1997).

As the century progressed, Ulster Protestants became increasingly united against the movement for repeal of the Act of Union, and an evangelical movement in the 1820s forged new links across the various denominations. Ulster-Scottish Presbyterians and Anglicans were united in the cause of defence of the Union, although there were still many divisions between unionists in the north and the south of the country. Protestants were divided theologically, but when the Home Rule Bill of 1912 came before Westminster, they immediately rallied under the leadership of Edward Carson – a Dubliner – and James Craig. Their subsequent actions have been compared to God's covenant with the tribes of Israel (Akenson 1992), and were inspired by the Scottish Covenant of centuries earlier. '28 September 1912 was observed as a day of dedication by protestants throughout Ulster.' Religious services were held throughout the Region and a covenant was signed by more than 218,000 men who pledged to use 'all means which may be found necessary to defeat the present conspiracy to set up a home-rule parliament in Ireland' (McCracken 1967). An Ulster Volunteer Force was then enrolled for military and political service against home rule. A variety of tactics, such as the illegal importation of arms, were designed to ensure that unionists would not be subjected to the control of a Dublin-based parliament.

As a consequence of the passing of the Home Rule bill by parliament in September 1914, Redmond, the leader of the Irish Volunteers, pledged the support of nationalist Ireland to the British efforts in the First World War. This decision split the volunteers and, as already outlined, some of them availed of the opportunity to further the separatist cause. When the War ended, the island of Ireland was partitioned. This was 'an attempt to accommodate, rather than to transcend or resolve, the historic conflicts on the island' (Ruane and Todd 1996: 48). Ulster unionists succeeded in their ambition to remain part of the UK. Nationalists in the new Northern Irish State were unhappy with the reinforcement of their British identity while unionists in the Republic of Ireland felt betrayed.

Conclusion

Struggles in Northern Ireland have often been perceived in terms of British in opposition to Irish, and collective memories have served to instil an impression of continuously separate traditions. Unionists remember a British history, whereas nationalists' memories are placed in an Irish context (Roe et al 1999). Each community's self-esteem is enhanced by the celebration of the deeds of dead heroes. Unionists focus on the achievements of King Billy, but they also reinforce the ordinary people's contribution to the survival of the Empire on the anniversary of the Somme. While the Somme in itself is largely a loyalist event, Remembrance Day is more an Ulster British one. Nationalists pay tribute to the Gaelic chieftains who resisted the encroachment of the British and they celebrate the accomplishments of the separatists in 1916.

A variety of rituals are used to reinforce a view of 'us' and 'them'. This use of history is a moral, political phenomenon that has significant contemporary relevance for the people of Northern Ireland. Mythologies are easily constructed on such simple dichotomies. In Brittany, for example, the contemporary Breton movement has gathered any remarks made by French politicians in which they give an impression of perceiving Brittany in colonial terms. In this manner Bretons have generated a discourse of the oppressed and have placed themselves symbolically in a position similar to that of Algeria (McDonald 1989).

Representing the past is a 'purposeful social action' (Tonkin 1992: 3) and history can be dis-membered as 'an exercise in the legitimisation of the present' (McCrone 1998: 51). But memories of past occurrences are not fixed and unchanging and while 'the past is normally considered to be inscribed in stone and irreversible' (Wallerstein 1991: 78), our understanding of history develops and changes as historians unravel its complexities. Whether this actually impacts on the two traditions paradigm depends on the willingness of groups to review their processes of selectivity and to disengage from the practice of exclusivity. Unfortunately religious and social segregation (Harris 1986) both in a historical and contemporary context has entrenched the divide.

CHAPTER 3

DIVIDED BY COMMON COSMOLOGIES

Most of what Catholics and Protestants do is not distinctively either 'Catholic' or 'Protestant'.

(Buckley and Kenney 1995: 201)

For me, the relationship between religion, identity, and cultural tradition is inextricable. Ignatieff (1994: 164) argues that in the cases of Northern Ireland, Croatia, Serbia, and the Ukraine, 'ethnicity, religion and politics are soldered together into identities so total that it takes a defiant individual to escape their clutches'. Hastings (1997: 185) claims that when a sense of nationalism is rooted in religious fervour it is very difficult to destroy or assimilate. In his opinion this accounts for the historical failure of the Communist Stalinist Empire in Catholic Poland or the Protestant British Empire in Catholic Ireland. It is also for this reason that Orthodox Serbia has refused to conform to the political standards of Europe.

In 1996 the Croatian theologian Miroslav Volf called for a review of the relationship between church and culture, arguing that in many instances churches are captives to their cultural traditions. These links are often obscured by a strong sense of self-righteousness. Volf (1996: 37) postulated that Christians should cultivate 'the proper relation between distance from the culture and belonging to it'. This distancing would not in effect remove the Christian from the cultural context but would become internal to the cultural tradition itself. In such circumstances, Christians would respond to life 'with one foot outside their own culture while with the other remaining firmly planted in it'.

Is it possible to stand outside one's own culture and review it from a distance? As an anthropologist I define culture as one's way of life. For this reason I do not think it feasible to have 'one's foot outside one's own culture'. Neither is it possible to separate religion and culture. If the latter is defined as all-embracing, then surely religion is culture and to attempt to separate the two is to set up a false dichotomy that does not correspond to reality. But any individual is capable of acknowledging the cultural dimension to religion and to appreciate that the dilemma of multiculturalism includes the question of multidenominationalism.

In the case of Northern Ireland, different denominations are associated with specific cultural traditions and members of each are assumed to have particular political perspectives. Historically, Protestants and Catholics were regarded as coming from opposing and often competing traditions, and despite the violence and sectarianism of recent decades there has been greater focus on commonalities rather than differences between Christian denominations. Increasingly the question is posed whether Protestantism and Catholicism constitute two genuinely different traditions, or whether they are merely distinct aspects of a common tradition. In essence this is tantamount to asking whether two separate cultural traditions exist or are they simply diverging elements in a common tradition.

A multidemoninational and multicultural region

When writing of religious tensions in Northern Ireland, much of the focus is on Protestant and Catholic denominations. In the first chapter I drew attention to the range of ethnicities in the Region. This is a multicultural society in denial. For many minorities, religion is important and as is the case in Britain, religious identities in Northern Ireland mark 'a significant dimension of cultural difference between the migrants and British society' (Modood 1999: 35).

The census is a useful indicator of the extent of religious diversity in Northern Ireland. According to the published reports for 1991, 38.4 percent of the population were Roman Catholic, representing the single largest denomination (Department of Health and Social Services 1993). This figure demonstrated a substantial increase in the proportion of Catholics, as in the previous census only 28 percent of the population was Catholic. In fact over a hundred years had passed since a proportion of Catholics equivalent to that of the 1991 census had been recorded in these northern counties. The proportional rise of Roman Catholics since the 1981 census had occurred alongside marginal decreases in the numbers registered as Protestant. In 1991, 42.8 percent of the population indicated that they subscribed to one of the main Protestant traditions. Of these, 21.3 percent were categorised as Presbyterian; 17.7 percent belonged to the Church of Ireland; and 3.8 percent was Methodist. All of these figures revealed minor reductions in their respective proportions during the previous decade.

Significantly, almost a fifth of the population could not be categorised as belonging to either of these two main traditions. This substantial minority was subdivided into three categories. Some 7.8 percent of the population classed themselves as belonging to another church while 7.3 percent did not state their religious affiliation, and a further 3.7 percent implied that they had no religious beliefs. The 1991 census was the first occasion when individuals were given the opportunity of recording themselves as having no religion, a fact which is possibly responsible for the dramatic decrease in the figures not stating any religious affiliation. In the previous census, 18.5 percent of the population registered themselves in this category. But given the way these figures add up, I feel it important to note that this change could also be explained in terms of a revival of Catholicism. As indicated earlier, there was a considerable increase in the proportion of those recording themselves as Catholics in the 1991 census.

While these figures give some indication of religious diversity in Northern Ireland, they fail to demonstrate the sheer divergence of beliefs and affiliations that are prevalent. There is a variety of other Christian traditions in contemporary Northern Ireland such as the Baptists (McMillan 1998), the Christian Brethren (Currie 1998), the Elim Church (Smith 1998), the Salvation Army (Smyth, 1998), the Church of the Nazarene (Tarrant 1998), Lutherans (Fritz 1998), Moravians (Cooper 1998), and others. Some groups have been established for centuries. For example, the first settlement of the Religious Society of Friends (Quakers) occurred in 1654 in Lurgan. As time passed, they increasingly settled in the Lagan Valley and in lands south of Lough Neagh. Today there are 14 meetings of Quakers throughout Northern Ireland with a membership of some 900 followers (Chapman 1998: 184). Other Christian traditions, such as the Chinese Christian Fellowship, were established in the late twentieth century (Ryan 1996; Wai Kuen Mo 1998; Watson and McKnight 1998). In fact, the Belfast Chinese Christian Church was not formally established until 1996, but its origins date to 1975 when Rev. T. McCracken and Mr Nai Bob Cham began evangelistic work among the local Chinese.

There is a variety of other ethnic-religious minority communities in Northern Ireland. In the first chapter I referred to the Jewish community, which operates as 'a minority culture existing and interacting with an even larger heterogeneous cultural whole' (Warm 1998: 224). While this Jewish presence dates to the seventeenth century, the community has gradually decreased in size. But the social significance of the synagogue has, if anything, increased and has served to maintain the unity of various Jewish groups who uphold differing degrees of orthodoxy.

There are Buddhists, Hindus, Muslims, and Sikhs in the Region, although to use such generic terms without qualification is to misrepresent the cultural diversity among them. For example, Muslims in Northern Ireland are heterogeneous not only in terms of country of origin, migratory experience, and background, but also in terms of language, sect, age, and location. While there are some 700 Pakistani Muslims in the Region, other Muslims from outside the Indian subcontinent are also resident here (Donnan and O'Brien 1998). But again the term 'Muslim' requires some further qualification to indicate the cultural diversity.

Altogether the census of 1991 indicated that there were 74 different denominations whose congregations numbered at least 10 or more. To refer constantly to the two main traditions in Northern Ireland, in my view, is to ignore the existence of others, many of whom feel that religious consideration within Northern Ireland has focused exclusively on disagreements within the Christian traditions, and has been dominated by sectarian conflict. Very often there is a total lack of understanding of the smaller denominations, and occasionally these can be completely misrepresented. For example, Ryan (1996) points to the fact that one Fair Employment Commission monitoring process mistakenly classified the Baha'i as Protestants, even though the identity of this group is to maintain the unity of all religions. They could not in any sense be regarded as Protestants except that they strongly object to conflicts within religion. In part, the emphasis on Protestant and Catholic traditions derives from the fact that these churches are products of political, as much as historical, forces (McMaster 1995). Religion is associated with a particular perspective, and many political acts have been justified with reference to beliefs and persuasion. But in recent times there have been greater assertions of unity. This shift in emphasis is visible in debates regarding the contemporary significance of the early Celtic church.

The Celtic church

Many Christian groups in Northern Ireland locate their roots in the activities of Saint Patrick and the early Celtic church. Protestant and Catholic cathedrals in the city of Armagh are both dedicated to Saint Patrick, a fact that has not necessarily united these communities. Large numbers of Catholics and smaller numbers of Protestants attend annual church services in honour of the saint in mid-March. Parades in the Falls Road in West Belfast and many Catholic towns mark the occasion with displays that often resemble those of Orange Lodges. Sometimes these commemorations are organised by the Ancient Order of Hibernians or the Irish National Foresters. Some Orangemen also celebrate the day with parades or by wearing the shamrock, which is distributed to members of Irish regiments in the British Army.

Both the Roman Catholic Church and the Church of Ireland have attempted to trace their roots to this figure. For example Crilly (1998: 25) suggests that the Catholic tradition in Ireland 'goes back to the writings of St Patrick'. On the other hand, Clarke (1999: 29) writes that until the 1960s 'the self-understanding of the Church of Ireland, north and south, was that it was the only real and legitimate heir of a Celtic and Catholic church that had blossomed in the time of St. Patrick'.

While the Church of Ireland no longer views itself as the sole inheritor of the Irish Celtic tradition, some Protestant fundamentalists are still keen to disassociate Patrick from the Roman Catholic tradition. In such discourses the intention is to portray Protestant and Catholic denominations as opposing traditions. If this is the case, only one of them can have their roots in the Celtic church. Fundamentalists argue that the association of Patrick with Roman Catholicism is primarily due to his common portrayal in statues in the robes of a contemporary Roman Catholic bishop. On the coins issued by the Roman Catholic Confederation in 1645, Patrick wears a bishop's mitre and crosier (Loftus 1994). However, McCausland (1997: 41) provocatively argues that Patrick was never canonised by Rome, and that his sainthood, like that of many other Celtic figures, is a consequence of popular tradition rather than canonisation.

Implicit in such pronouncements is that Patrick was Protestant rather than Catholic and that the early Celtic Christian Church was the precursor of contemporary Protestantism. According to Ian Paisley Jnr, Saint Patrick was in fact Ireland's first Protestant. 'The early Celtic church was independent and proto-Protestant (a prototype of Protestantism), a matter which has largely been written out of history by sheer ignorance. When Irish Americans celebrate St. Patrick's Day they are celebrating a man who brought Protestantism to this island and effectively developed the idea of religious partition that is separating truth from superstition' (in Lambkin 1994: 281). Alcock (1994: 5), who is an ardent unionist, endorses this perspective, suggesting that 'the Church of St Patrick postulated many of the features of future Protestantism – no appeal to sacramental symbols such as icons or invocation of the Virgin Mary, saints or purgatory, the only mediator being Christ; no requirement of celibacy; the taking of communion in both kinds and rejection of the idea of transubstantiation'.

In these arguments the debate regarding Protestantism and Catholicism is political rather than religious, and from the perspective of many cultural nationalists Saint Patrick is as much a political as a religious figure. His arrival served as the catalyst for the emergence of the Irish Nation. 'Fusing the Christian and Celtic cultures, he pacified the warrior Celts, united the Irish peoples, prepared the way for a national monarchy' (Hutchinson 1987: 124). British fundamentalists take an opposing perspective and are quick to remind nationalists that Patrick's origins were in Britain, and that the patron saint of the Republic of Ireland was probably English (McDowell n.d: 4). Sometimes it is claimed that the contemporary conflict between Protestants and Catholics in Northern Ireland stems from the original antagonism between the Celtic and the Roman Catholic churches (Alcock 1994). I find this a very interesting argument as it places the Roman missionary Patrick entirely in the context of the Celtic church!

In the past two decades the issue of Patrick and the influence of the early Celtic church has lessened in significance. There are probably two reasons for this. In the first instance, there has been a greater focus on the commonality rather than the differences between various Christian denominations. As there is less emphasis on Protestantism and Catholicism as opposites, this allows both to locate their roots in the Celtic church. Moreover, most Protestants and Catholics are aware that before the Reformation, many groups in Western Europe regarded themselves as participating in the same religion. 'They saw a one-religion picture' (Lambkin 1996: 26). While these groups were aware of different perspectives such as those of Islam or Judaism, they regarded those denominations as corrupted versions of their true religion rather than an opposing or alternative system (Bossy 1982; Lambkin 1996). It was not until the sixteenth century that various Christian traditions began to view themselves as distinctively different and opposite to one another.

Politically distinct traditions

Roman Catholicism in Ireland is associated with changes that occurred in the twelfth century. Prior to this, Celtic Ireland was a fragmented society with no central unity. Although the Celtic church professed loyalty to the Pope in Rome, adherents of Catholicism in Ireland were largely independent of the structure of the Roman church as the country had never been part of the Roman Empire. A synod held in AD 1111 established two ecclesiastical provinces in the country (Corish 1985: 32) and gave the church a national structure. In 1132 St Malachy was installed as archbishop of Armagh. The naming of a papal legate some eight years later strengthened the infrastructure of Roman Catholicism. A synod in Kells in 1152 redrew the diocesan boundaries. Ireland was divided into four church provinces: Armagh, Dublin, Cashel, and Tuam.

In 1155 the English Pope Adrian IV in Rome issued *Laudabiliter* which exhorted the English king Henry II to reform the church in Ireland. In effect 'the pope gave Ireland a king'. Ironically that king was English and the pope was 'the only Englishman ever to have occupied the chair of Peter' (Corish 1985: 36). This factor contributed to the subsequent arrival of the Anglo-Normans and the twin processes of Anglicisation and Romanisation began. By the end of the twelfth century a church that complied with the Roman tradition had superseded the Celtic church in the Norman-dominated parts of the country. It is somewhat ironic that the church most associated with Irishness today was initiated in part by the arrival of the Normans! But the Normans did not succeed in conquering the entire island and Gaelic chieftains controlled many regions in the north and west of the country. In these regions the power of the monasteries was formidable for many centuries.

Four centuries later the English king Henry VIII severed the link with Rome and declared himself head of the church in England. The Irish Reformation Parliament of 1536–37 asserted the primacy of the king's authority over that of the pope and marked the formal arrival of Anglicanism in Ireland. English supporters of religious change were quickly appointed to senior positions within the Irish Church. An Act of Supremacy decreed that Henry and his successors were supreme heads of the church in Ireland and prescribed a range of penalties for any public criticism of this position. A revised power structure accommodated the transferral of power from the papal curia to the English royal administration. While the reign of Mary, Henry's daughter, re-established Roman Catholicism for a temporary period, Elizabeth was soon to revive the Church of Ireland as the religion of the state. A second Irish Reformation Parliament held in 1560 approved the Elizabethan Church settlement for Ireland and consolidated the social and legal dominance of Anglicanism. Legislation ensured that all appointments within the royal service acknowledged the monarch as head of the church.

From 1537 until its disestablishment in 1870, the English ruled the Anglican Church in Ireland – one of the facts that ensured it was associated with foreign rule. Although a mere 10 percent of the population in Ireland identified with this denomination, Anglicans dominated the power structure. This generated considerable resentment not only among the Catholic community, but also among other denominations that arrived subsequently (Ruane and Todd 1996: 31). Because Anglican preachers frequently came from England and spoke the English language, the church was further perceived as unfamiliar and foreign.

The reformed or Calvinist version of the Reformation arrived in Ulster during the reign of King James VI and I. This religion was, and is, primarily associated with the Scottish settlers who were planted in Ulster, although many Scots who had settled in the Region from the thirteenth century onwards were Catholic. Presbyterian Scots were heavily concentrated in the counties of Antrim and Down and particularly along the Ards peninsula. Although based in Ulster, many of them regularly travelled the sea route from Donaghdee to Portpatrick in order to attend Sunday worship and particularly the celebration of the Lord's Supper. This link with Scotland was to prove significant during the years of persecution that followed (Brooke 1986).

The Catholic rising of 1641 was examined in the previous chapter from a political perspective. The British government at the time responded with an army of 10,000 soldiers under the leadership of General Robert Monro. This army included several chaplains and officers who were elders of the Presbyterian Church, and the following summer a presbytery was formed at Carrickfergus (Brooke 1986: 29; Westerkamp 1988: 38). Fifteen congregations opted to join this first presbytery and the event was regarded as the formal commencement of the Presbyterian Church in Ireland, although several congregations had been in operation for a number of decades (Robinson 1988). In 1992 the General Presbyterian Assembly convened for a day in Carrickfergus to commemorate this significant event in their church history. Presbyterians placed a key emphasis on the concept of a covenant and in 1643 that community affirmed its commitment to a

Solemn League and Covenant pledging the removal of popery from Britain and Ireland. This action had far-reaching consequences.

Towards the end of the seventeenth century, Catholic hopes were revived temporarily with the accession of James II, a Catholic convert to the throne. As outlined in the previous chapter, James appointed a Catholic viceroy and called for religious toleration. However, his reign on the British throne was quickly ended when the Protestant William of Orange was installed as monarch (Haddick-Flynn 1999). By the end of the century, Roman Catholicism, Anglicanism, and Presbyterianism had firmly established themselves but it is practically impossible to know with any degree of certainty the proportion of each at any particular period. Census figures for religious denominations were notoriously unreliable. While a survey conducted in 1732–33 gave some details on religious denominations, it made no distinction between Anglicans, Calvinists and others. It merely classed all these groups as Protestant and suggested that their numbers to Catholics in some northerly counties was in the region of 3:2. Figures for each county are given in table 3:1 (Braidwood 1964: 7). These figures are, however, regarded as unreliable, principally because they do not give any account of family size nor do they indicate whether some or any of these figures represent single adults.

Table 3:1. Catholics and Protestants in Ulster in 1732

County	Protestant Families	Catholic Families	Ratio
Antrim	14,899	3,641	4.5:1
Down	14,060	5,210	3:1
Derry	8,751	2,782	3:1
Armagh	6,064	3,279	2:1
Fermanagh	2,913	2,122	1.4:1
Donegal	5,543	4,144	1.3:1

(Source: Braidwood 1964: 7. Reproduced with the kind permission of the Ulster Folk and Transport Museum, Holywood, Co. Down.)

As time passed, the proportions of each denomination altered and there was great diversity both within and between traditions. For example, a schism within the Synod of Ulster in the 1830s proved the catalyst for the emergence of the Non-Subscribing Presbyterian Church. The remaining members of the Synod of Ulster joined with the Secession Synod in 1840 in order to form the General Assembly of the Presbyterian Church in Ireland which is still in place. A revival in 1859 renewed many Presbyterian Churches (Dunlop 1999: 43).

Soon after the Anglican Church in Ireland faced a crisis, and at the time of its disestablishment it almost disintegrated. According to Clarke (1999: 36), 'the fact was that the Church of Ireland was a divided church in terms of doctrinal stance and what is loosely called churchmanship'. A great deal of tension focused on the meaning of the terms 'Catholic' and 'Reformed' and the Anglican Church in Ireland had to decide whether it would continue to represent a broad comprehensive church or become 'a Protestant sect with carefully delineated edges'. It decided on the former and the intention henceforth was to avoid extremism of all sorts. In the preface to the Book of Common Prayer, revised in the 1870s, it stated that 'what is imperfect, with peace, is often better than what is otherwise more excellent, without it' (in Clarke 1999: 38).

Censuses taken from the mid-nineteenth century onwards give a greater insight into the diversity of traditions. In 1861 the proportion of Roman Catholics, Presbyterians, and Church of Ireland were 40.9, 32.7, and 23 percent respectively. While the proportion of Catholics at the end of the last millennium is similar to that recorded in 1861, the size of the Presbyterian and Church of Ireland communities has declined whereas the proportion of Methodists has increased from 2 percent in 1861 to 3.8 in 1991. Increases have also occurred in other classifications such as 'other denominations', 'none', and 'not stated'. Of course such figures don't reveal the impact of migration and other factors on various traditions.

Diversity within denominations

Although many in Northern Ireland are aware of the tensions between denominations, the diversity within them is often disregarded. For example, Catholics in the eighteenth century could hardly be regarded as a cohesive community (Ruane and Todd 1996). Descendants of the Anglo-Normans and the 'indigenous' Irish all subscribed to the Catholic tradition but there were very clear cultural and political distinctions between them in terms of social class and education. Members of the Catholic middle class spoke English, whereas the destitute classes communicated through Irish. Political activity among Catholics was conducted in English. In rural Ireland, there were divisions between Catholics who owned land and those who rented it. While urban and rural elite may have formed some networks at a regional level, the underprivileged operated primarily at a local level. Although the small number of wealthy landowners participated to some extent in the political process, poorer Catholics had no franchise and little access to any commercial infrastructure. This would have also applied to poorer Protestants, of whom Ulster had plenty.

Catholics throughout Ireland suffered under the imposition of a series of restrictive Penal Laws that were passed in the eighteenth century. British Catholics also suffered legislative repression at this time (Colley 1996: 20). Even though Catholics owned a mere 10 percent of the territory of Ireland, the Penal statutes aimed at a further reduction of Catholic-owned property. Catholics were also prohibited from holding public office, practising law, or bearing arms. While all Catholics grieved at the treatment of their religious community, there was a great variation in their sense of dispossession and displacement. Many gentry families sought positions in the armies of France and Spain after the 'flight of the earls' and they became known as the 'wild geese' (Wall 1967).

Protestants did not form a distinctive group either at this stage. As Anglicans, often of English descent, were members of the established church and largely controlled the institutions of the state, they formed a distinct but greatly stratified group. Impoverished Anglicans worked on land owned by their richer counterparts and depended on them to provide employment and other forms of support. The middle classes, often relatives of the rich, operated as privileged tenants or instructors or clergy. Common worship and participation in shared annual celebrations regularly consolidated the mutual bond between the various classes of Anglicans. This sense of solidarity reinforced an impression of distinction from other Protestants (Ruane and Todd 1996: 34).

Unlike these descendants of the English who lived throughout the country, the Scottish Presbyterians were concentrated in East Ulster. Many of them were speakers of Scots, rather than English, and regarded Scotland as their mother country (Brooke 1986). They remained in constant contact with fellow Scotsmen across the water, and regularly travelled by boat to services in Scotland. Their opposition to the Anglican Church was due to its privileged position, and they were fully aware of their own disadvantaged status. 'The so-called "Protestant Ascendancy" was in reality an Anglican Ascendancy' (Hanna 2000: 27). Although they suffered less than Catholic Irish under the imposition of the Penal Laws, they were excluded from public office and subjected to other forms of discrimination (De Paor 1990: 24). For example, their marriages were regarded as invalid. More seriously, the Trust Act of 1704 prevented them from entering public life unless they produced a certificate affirming that they had partaken of the Eucharist according to the Anglican tradition. As a consequence they could no longer work as members of corporations or hold military commissions. For a time this led to 'Catholic-Presbyterian relationship which was in some ways closer than that between the Protestant sects' (Darby 1983: 16). A Toleration Act in 1719 eased some restrictions on Presbyterians but many of them migrated to the USA where their descendants have become known as the Scotch-Irish. Many were given the impetus to leave by James McGregor, a dissenting minister of the Aghadowney congregation in County Londonderry who 'saw himself as the Scots-Irish Moses' (Fitzpatrick 1989: 53).

There were many other distinctive traditions in Ulster at this time. Baptists and Quakers had arrived with the Cromwellian army (Chapman 1998; McMillan 1998). They were called the 'new' Protestants in order to distinguish themselves from the Anglicans and Presbyterians. A French Huguenot community had been introduced with government support at the end of the seventeenth century when a colony of linen-makers was founded in Lisburn. Their first pastor arrived in 1704, and government support of a French pastor continued until 1819 (Lisburn Museum, 1985). Huguenots formed a distinct group for a time. 'They clung together, associated and worshipped together, frequenting their own Huguenot church in which they had a long succession of French pastors. They carefully educated their children in the French language, and in the Huguenot faith ... But ... eventually mingled with the families of the Irish, and became part and parcel of the British nation' (Smiles 1870: 284–5) – a statement that provides a very interesting comment on the process of becoming British!

Popular memory reinforces an image of two traditions, Catholic and Protestant, in constant conflict. Such simplification ignores the variety of allegiances and the three primary religious denominations in eighteenth-century Ireland – Catholic, Protestant, and dissenter or Presbyterian (Canavan 1994). Tensions between Protestants groups were high. Although Anglicans and Ulster-Scottish Presbyterians were loyal to the British Crown, a king of Scottish descent had been deposed with the help of the English Parliament in favour of a Dutchman. The image of the Siege became a source of conflict rather than unity as it marked the triumph of the English Parliament over a British king of Scottish descent. It also represented a power struggle between Anglicans and Ulster-Scottish Presbyterians (McBride 1997).

Moreover, this simplification of history ignored the co-existence and co-operation between Catholics and Protestants at the end of the eighteenth and the beginning of the nineteenth centuries. Irish Catholics participated in the celebration of the centenary of the Siege in 1789. The Catholic bishop, Philip Mac Devitt, and a number of his clergy joined in the procession to the Anglican Cathedral in Derry. Catholics and Presbyterians were politically united in a struggle for reform in 1798. Radical Presbyterians in Antrim and Down rose briefly with a number of Irish Catholics to create an entirely new social order (Elliott 1982).

Wolfe Tone, one of the primary instigators of this insurrection, believed that resentment between different denominations could be dissolved and replaced with a harmonious sense of Irish identity (Dunne 1982: Elliott 1989). Tone proposed the co-operation of Irish Catholics and Protestant radicals in order to achieve Catholic emancipation and the reform of parliament (McDowell 1967: 239). He suggested that 'the odious distinction of Protestant and Presbyterian and Catholic' should be abolished. If 'the three great sects blended together, under the common and sacred title of Irishman, what interest could a Catholic member of Parliament have, distinct from his Protestant brother sitting on the same bench, exercising the same function, bound by the same ties: Would liberty be less dear to him, justice less sacred, property less valuable, infamy less dreadful?' (in Girvin 1994: 56).

Despite such aspirations, a concept of common identity did not exist and the Act of Union was passed in 1800. Following this, Presbyterians and Catholics remained allied forces in an endeavour to achieve land reform in the first half of the nineteenth century (Walker B. 1997). But factors such as the disestablishment of the Church of Ireland in the latter half of the century and the growth of industry convinced many Protestants of the economic benefits of union with Britain. Although there were – and are – deep social divisions between them, 'the things which divided Protestants from each other had come to be less important than the things which united them against Catholics' (Lyons 1971: 719). Akenson (1988: 127) proposes that their belief systems were so strong and overarching that they could be called 'cosmologies'. While there may have been local differences in the interpretation of these cosmologies, variations were still perceived as belonging distinctly to one group or the other, to either Protestants or Catholics. Their two worlds were regarded as separate, different, and opposite.

The two religions paradigm

This partition of minds and worlds has been carefully nurtured over several hundred years. Lambkin (1996: 27) suggests that as early as 1600 'a point had been reached where Catholicism and Protestantism were mutually understood to be separate heretical and schismatic religious systems in violent opposition to each other'. Many statements from senior clerics had encouraged this picture of opposite religions. In 1562 Anglican bishops in London stated that the pope had absolutely no jurisdiction over English territories. But the pope subsequently excommunicated Queen Elizabeth I and publicly denounced her for prohibiting the practice of the one true religion (Lambkin 1996: 27).

Fragmentation within the Protestant community intensified this picture of opposing religions. While Anglicans denied the role of the papacy, Presbyterians identified the pope with the Antichrist declaring that Jesus Christ was the sole head of the Church. No pope could depose Christ as the head of the Church. Those who exalted themselves in the Church in this manner were in fact Antichrists. In the centuries that followed the partition of minds was maintained especially in the areas of marriage and education.

'Mixed marriages' is the term commonly used in Northern Ireland to denote an alliance between a Catholic and a Protestant, and the term reflects the sense of defilement with which these unions are sometimes regarded. Many involved in such relationships are unhappy with the term 'mixed', because they do not wish to be identified on a religious basis. But it is difficult to suggest a more appropriate term and phrases such as 'cross-community', 'interfaith', or interracial' are equally divisive and often inappropriate (Morgan et al 1996).

Laws inhibiting interfaith marriages were passed in the eighteenth century with the intention of protecting Protestants, and Anglicans in particular, from the corruption of Catholicism. Protestants who entered into these marriages were deprived of land and inheritance in accordance with the Penal code, and legislation condemned Catholic priests who officiated such marriages to a penalty of death. In 1726 one priest was executed for conducting such a ceremony. An act passed in 1745 specified that any interfaith marriage conducted by Catholic clergy was invalid. This legislation was not repealed until 1879 (Akenson 1988).

Towards the end of the eighteenth century priests officiating mixed marriages were subjected to fines of £500, and between 1820 and 1832 six clergymen were penalised accordingly. This statute was repealed the following year. From the mid-nineteenth century onwards the Catholic Church regularly castigated mixed marriages. Paul Cullen, the Archbishop of Armagh from 1849 until 1852 and subsequently of Dublin for a further 26 years, was particularly hostile to such unions. While the Protestant churches were less public in their opposition to mixed marriages in the nineteenth and twentieth centuries, it is probable that individual clergymen counselled their communities against it (Akenson 1988).

At the beginning of the twentieth century the Sacred Congregation of Propagation of Faith drafted a declaration on interfaith marriages. In April 1908 Pope Pius X officially approved this *Ne Temere* decree which had serious implications for the non-Catholic partners in interfaith marriages, as couples could henceforth only present themselves for a marriage ceremony before a Catholic clergyman. While the Catholic partner should continue to practise his or her religion in an uninhibited fashion, he or she should make every attempt to convert their spouse. Any children should be baptised as Catholic and could only attend Catholic schools. This *Ne Temere* decree had a strong impact in Northern Ireland.

Not only were mixed marriages perceived as a loss to the Protestant community that could ultimately lead to a decline in overall numbers of Protestants, but many Protestants felt that they were now on the receiving end of Roman Catholic imperialism. A response to this decree by J.A.F. Gregg, the Church of Ireland Archbishop of Armagh, indicated that Protestants should avoid marrying Catholics in any circumstances. He noted that it was shameful for men from Protestant families to marry Catholics and allow their children to be raised as Roman Catholics. Such Protestants were draining the strength of their own group and were fortifying a Roman Catholic community who would expel Protestants from their land if it were at all possible (Gregg 1943: 9).

Boundaries between the Catholic and Protestant communities have also been maintained in the education sector and it was 'in the matter of schooling that sectarian influences exerted some of their strongest pressures on the pattern of social relationships' (Harris 1986: 137). Northern Ireland was not a particularly unusual example in this regard as most religions 'promote and foster sectarian institutions' (Ó Murchú 1997: 9). In the early nineteenth century the Catholic clergy vigorously opposed the establishment of proselytising schools in parts of Ulster and the rest of the country (Nic Craith 1994). They were particularly keen to ensure that no member of the Catholic community attended the schools set up by the Hibernian Society for Establishing Schools and Circulating the Holy Scriptures in Ireland that was instituted in 1806. Yet by 1824 this society had instigated 639 schools in Ulster with an enrolment of 54,288 pupils.

Published reports of these societies give an account of the reactions of the local Catholic clergy, although they are careful not to give precise details regarding the locations of such conflicts. In 1825 the society reported that 'the Priest of this place [in Ulster] is a most determined opposer of the Schools. Whenever any accident happens to either man or beast, he declares from the altar that it is a mark of God's anger against them for permitting the existence of Free Schools; stating that gross ignorance is far preferable to knowledge derived through such means' (London Hibernian Society 1825: 46).

According to these published reports, which were written by members of the society itself, any Catholic interest in education in these schools met with serious opposition from the local priest. 'The Priest not only goes to their houses to keep them at home, but stands in the road, and threatens to curse them and their parents if they go to the Free Schools' (London Hibernian Society 1825: 47). Clerical opposition to these schools stemmed from the fact that the Protestant Bible in Irish was the text used to teach reading. No Catholic Bible was available in Irish at this time and members of the Catholic congregation were often anxious to get a copy of the Book in their own language (see Nic Craith 1994: Ch 2). Those who obtained such copies were subjected to serious condemnation. In one instance the 'Priest poured out all the invective he could against him, threatened that he would mark him, and have him hunted like a hare; but if he would return to his duty, he would be his friend, and serve him' (London Hibernian Society 1825: 48).

In 1831 a national scheme of education was established in Ireland (Akenson 1969; Coolahan 1981). Its instigator, Lord Stanley, had intended that this system would be non-denominational but non-secular. This ambition would be simply achieved. Catholics and Protestants would attend the same schools controlled at a local level by individuals of different faiths. Children of different denominations would receive their secular education together. For their religious instruction they would separate and be taught by their respective clergymen. This was deemed to be a 'united education' (Dowling 1971: 16).

As the Commissioners of Education were keen to ensure the rapid expansion of this system, they ignored the ideal of Lord Stanley in many instances and by 1850 over three-quarters of the schools were under sole Catholic management and the rest were often jointly controlled. In 1862 more than half of the schools in the country were officially mixed but this figure includes schools with very minute numbers of Protestant children. By 1900 only a third of the schools in the country were officially regarded as mixed and children of different denominations remained segregated throughout their formative years, although attendance at school was not compulsory at this time.

As I have already noted in the first chapter, many changes occurred in the education sector after partition. The Government of Northern Ireland quickly arranged local rate aid for education and ensured a greater input into schools by parents and locals. The government also continued to contribute a substantial proportion of the expenditure of Catholic schools. In 1923 the Londonderry Act proposed that sectarian religious instruction be prohibited in schools and that teachers be appointed on the basis of merit without regard for their religious orientation. Although several aspects of this Act were effective, the Protestant churches and the Orange Order succeeded in modifying some of its central features and schools continued to operate as either Protestant or Catholic. In 1977 almost three-quarters of the schools in Northern Ireland were either completely Catholic or wholly Protestant (Darby et al 1977).

Partition in the sectors of education and marriage ensured that Protestants and Catholics remained strangers to one another and continued to view themselves for decades as members of opposite religions. Akenson (1988: 147) suggests that the partition of Ireland in the early 1920s was merely 'an outward and visible sign of the partition of the Irish people, one sort from the other, that long had existed in their hearts and minds'. Many fundamentalist Protestants still identify Catholicism as a system of slavery. This view was strongly advocated in the 1860s by William Johnston of Ballykilbeg, the leader of the Orange movement in Belfast. In contemporary times it is reinforced by churchmen, such as Dr Ian Paisley, who equate Catholicism with tyranny and Protestantism with liberty. This perspective emphasises the alleged clerical control of the Catholic political and social community. As a consequence, Catholicism is seen as inherently political. The implication is that Protestantism must become political purely for defensive reasons (Wright 1973: 224).

The historical separation of Protestants and Catholics also led to emergence of stereotypes reinforcing differences between communities. From a Protestant perspective such stereotypes portray their own community as clean, industrious, loyal, and democratic whereas Catholics are lazy, dirty, and priest-ridden. The Catholic stereotype is equally biased. According to this, Catholics are tolerant, open, and appreciative of their culture whereas Protestants are money-grabbing, narrow-minded bigots (Buckley and

Kenney 1995). Both sets of stereotypes reinforce an impression of two different traditions, yet each regarded itself as the bearer of the true traditions, as fulfilling God's wishes. For this reason both groups at one time or another regarded themselves as chosen people.

Chosen peoples

While the Israelites are normally identified as a chosen people, this concept is more commonly associated with Protestant fundamentalists rather than the Jewish community in Northern Ireland. But myths of ethnic election were prevalent among many groups throughout Ireland and Britain, especially from the seventeenth century onwards. When Issac Watts translated the Psalms in 1719 he replaced the word 'Israel' with 'Great Britain'. The defeat of the Highlanders at Culloden was celebrated with the performance of a new composition by G.F. Händel entitled *Judas Maccabaeus*. This compared the Duke of Cumberland to a Jewish leader who defeated an invading tribe of Seleucids, in this instance representing the Scots. Zadok, the founder of the priesthood of Jerusalem, has been commemorated at every British coronation since 1727. According to Swedenborg, an eighteenth-century mystical writer, a special heaven was designated for the English. In a lecture given by Edward Hine in Chelsea in 1879, Great Britain was the Promised Land of Israel and the stone of Jacob was housed in Westminster Abbey, having been stolen from the Scots by Edward Longshanks. In many instances William Blake's Hymn 'Jerusalem' serves as England's national anthem (Paxman 1998; Thompson 1991). This is not to imply that Blake was a British Israelite. To Blake, the term 'Jerusalem' simply denoted a land that was free of corruption, narrow-mindedness, and materialism.

Welsh and Scots communities have also regarded themselves as the lost tribes of Israel and Scottish Calvinists arriving in Ulster in the early seventeenth century were motivated by a form of persecuted righteousness. A concept of ethnic election was not necessarily particular to Presbyterians and is associated with the entire Protestant community in varying degrees. Generally speaking, it is assumed that identification with Israel is a Protestant phenomenon, and an attribute primarily of Protestant discourse. Colley (1996) proposes that both English puritans and Scottish covenanters understood that God's favour was a direct consequence of their Protestant faith. English-speaking Protestants in New England also regarded themselves as part of this chosen group. Some of these communities viewed the pope as the anti-Christ and conceived of Catholics as clinging to a false ideal. From this perspective, Catholic countries such as France compared poorly with England.

Yet Catholics in Ulster also portrayed themselves as God's chosen at this time, and Gaels have their own myth of origin identifying Ireland as a

Promised Land. According to this myth the Gaels are descended from the Israelite Goidel Glas, a contemporary of Moses in Egypt. Just before their escape from slavery, Goidel Glas received a snakebite in his thigh but Moses cured his suffering with his staff. However, the spot where he had been bitten by a snake remained green – hence the Irish term 'Glas', denoting the colour green. Moses prophesised that the descendants of Goidel Glas would inhabit an island in the north in a territory that would be free from snakes. According to Moses, the Gaels would maintain control of the island until the end of time (MacAlister and Mac Neill 1916).

Throughout the centuries the status of the Catholic Irish as a 'chosen people' has been re-affirmed in various fashions. In the seventeenth century many literati throughout Europe used Biblical analogies in their writings, and Ireland was no exception. In 1720 Aogán Ó Rathille welcomed the new chieftain of the Brown clan with a poem 'The Good Omen', which implied that God's favour had been transferred from the Jews to the indigenous Irish (see Hartnett 1998: 68). Ó Rathille's good faith in the Brown clan was not maintained, and later poems reflect the poverty of the poet's circumstances. Many Irish bardic poets in the mid-seventeenth century also grieved their own personal loss of status and prestige and lamented the extraordinary devastation of Ireland. Poets such as Aindrias MacMarcuis bewailed the fact that Ireland had no figure such as Moses to lead the people from their current despair (see Montague 1974: 123).

Several political poems written in the mid-seventeenth century compared the behaviour of the Irish with that of the wayward Israelites. This theme was especially prevalent in poetry written about the state of Irish churches after the trauma of the reformation and the post-reformation. In '*Músgail do mhisneach*' (Waken your courage)' the poet Haicéad likens the disobedience of certain Catholics to the defiance of the Israelites in the desert. Apparently the behaviour of some Gaelic and Old English Catholics in Ireland was not unlike that of the Israelites in the desert, who grieved for the debauchery and false indulgences of life in Egypt (Ní Cheallacháin 1962).

The suggestion that the Irish were a chosen people was further reinforced in later centuries when many writers encouraged scholars and poets towards the 'restoration of an original Irish community in its *insula sacra*, its sacred island home' (Smith 1992: 447). Sometimes it was implied that Irish was one of the purest languages in the world. One writer argued in 1753 that the Irish language was 'near as old as the deluge' (O'Conor 1753: xi). A century later it was suggested that the *Iliad* had originally been composed in Irish and was subsequently translated into Greek (Crowley 1996). In fact, it was translated into Irish in 1844.

By the mid-nineteenth century some writers were claiming that Irish was the language spoken in Eden. A writer in the newspaper *The Nation* suggested that the very name of Adam was Irish:

Its importance need not be questioned, even if we begin with the Garden of Eden – and in doing so I do not for a moment think we assume too high a position. We find the meaning of the first word that necessarily had been spoken by the Creator to his creature pure Irish – Adam, that is *Ead, am – As yet fresh*, which was very appropriately addressed by the object he had just created in his own likeness and hence was our first father called Adam . . . I believe that most, if not all the names in Scripture will be found to be pure Irish, or, at least, a more satisfactory radix than any other language we know affords them, will be found in the Irish language.

(in Crowley 1996: 108-9)

The Irish were not the only group to suggest that their language enjoyed this particular favour. About the year 1500 an anonymous writer known as the 'Revolutionary of the Upper Rhine' wrote in *The Book of a Hundred Chapters* that 'the German people had been the genuine Chosen People, not merely since Charlemagne but since the creation; that before the Tower of Babel, the language spoken by the human race had been German' (O'Brien 1988: 24). In South Africa the Boers believed they were God's chosen race. 'As God has selected them, then Afrikaans was logically the language of God' (Phillipson and Skutnabb-Kangas 1995: 337). Similarly in the Arab world, the language of the Koran is presumed to be that of the creator.

The concept of a chosen people is still relevant in contemporary Northern Ireland. Since its foundation in 1795 the Orange Order has placed a strong emphasis on loyalty to the Crown and to Protestant religious traditions. God has given these Protestants a foreign home where they are surrounded by Catholics, just as the Israelites in Canaan were threatened by Midianites (Buckley and Kenney 1995). Many of the contemporary symbols of the Orange Order reflect the appeal of the theme of a chosen people. Emblems such as Noah's Ark or the burning bush reinforce the special relationship of these people with God (Loftus 1994). Loyalty to the Monarch and to the Creator is marked by representations of the Crown, the Bible, and lips of silence. Biblical stories are an essential component of the initiation rites of the Arch Purple and Black Institutions. Prescribed tales invariably have a central theme of conflict in which an individual or group enjoying God's favour confronts an alien people, usually sinners (Buckley 1986; 1989; 1991). Sometimes the contest is between the virtuous and the wicked as exemplified in the contrast between Elijah and the prophets of Baal or David and Goliath. Protestant leaders are often compared with Biblical heroes as is implied in the following passage from the *Orange Standard* (June 1976: 6):

God spoke once to an old man, a political refugee, his career finished, hiding in the mountains, tending sheep.

He said "Moses, go down to Egypt and get my people". Moses obeyed, and the history of the world was changed. God spoke to Gideon at the winepress, to Samuel in the Temple, to Saul on the road to Damascus. These men heard and obeyed and the world has benefited from their influence.

Through the ages we find inspired voices leading people from the depths of despair to the heights of joy, happiness and prosperity. Voices right down to our own time. Churchill, Carson and James Craig. All this is our goodly heritage.

Occasionally Protestant leaders compare themselves with such biblical heroes. For example, in a cassette recording released in 1980 Ian Paisley compared himself with Moses who is bringing his community out of tyranny (Paulin 1984). Moses has rejected the comforts of Egypt in order to lead God's people to the Promised Land. Metaphorically, the implication of any of these Biblical stories is that Northern Irish Protestants are God's People and the Region can be compared with Israel or Judah.

A variety of small Protestant denominations in the contemporary Loyalist community could be regarded as fundamentalist and some of the numerically more significant churches also attract fundamentalist individuals. In the 1991 census, only fourteen people classified themselves as British Israelites although many more may have refrained from classifying themselves accordingly. This number appears minuscule and possibly represents a small grouping whose influence on Northern Irish affairs is minimal. On the other hand it is possible that the cultural or political significance of British Israelites could have great potential particularly if they are activists steering the course of events that are then followed by others.

For example MacDonald (2000: 29–30) reported that the leader of the loyalist terrorist group, the Red Hand Defenders, is a British Israelite. According to MacDonald this character 'is a highly intelligent self-appointed Preacher who belongs to a branch of British-Israelism, a hard-line Christian sect that believes the Ulster Protestants rather than the Jews are the true lost tribe of Israel'. Their myth of origin provides a Biblical justification for British control of Ireland. It affirms that the British are God's chosen people with a responsibility to bring civilisation and salvation to the Irish. The British Isles are the lands promised to Abraham and Jacob. Smith (1992) has identified this myth of ethnic election as typical of an emigrant colonist who has left his own homeland and is intent on establishing a new community without any regard for the original residents.

While some may regard such myths as risible, the concept of a chosen people is still prevalent in many contemporary societies. These myths operate primarily as narratives of a nation and are not necessarily believed in a literal sense. However, Ethiopians do believe that Menelik I, a son of Solomon, carried the Ark of the Covenant from Jerusalem to their homeland. Accordingly, this myth confers a special status on their nation. Similar myths can be found elsewhere (Akenson 1992; Hastings 1997). South Africans, Germans, and French have all at one time or another regarded their country as the 'new Jerusalem'. As the greatest number of crusaders had originated in France, that country was perceived as God's new Israel for many centuries. The Puritan fathers also saw America as the Promised Land, and after the revolution, George Washington was compared with Joshua who conquered Canaan (O'Brien 1988).

A variety of recent fictional publications in Northern Ireland have reinforced the theme of Northern Irish Protestants as God's people. *The Sons of Levi* (MacDonald 1998) is an allegory that presents this community as the Lost Tribe of Israel. They are a holy priesthood destined to build a New Jerusalem in Ulster. A novel in the Ulster-Scots style, *Wake the Tribe O' Dan* (Robinson 1998), explores Ulster-Scottish heritage in Ulster, implying that this community is a tribe of Israel. *Esther, Quaen o tha Ulidian Pechts* (Robinson 1997), a bilingual Ulster-Scots novel is based on the biblical Book of Esther. Although the concept of a chosen people is primarily identified with the Protestant community, all communities in the past two decades have believed it of themselves in varying degrees. Protestants and Catholics have shared a variety of symbols in the past and are gradually recognising their common beliefs. This has led in some instances to a drive towards ecumenism, although some groups are less open than others to the concept of a shared religion.

Towards a paradigm shift

Since the beginning of the twentieth century in particular there has been a paradigm shift within various Christian denominations which involves viewing Catholics and Protestants as members of one rather than opposite religions, although violence and the sectarian divide has ensured that this is a slow process in Northern Ireland. Lambkin (1996: 28) cites a conference in Edinburgh in 1910 as one of the most significant initiatives in this Western European drive for ecumenism, although he recognises other earlier developments as contributory factors. Concerns regarding the fragmentation of Protestant groups led to the establishment of the World Council of Churches in 1948. The intention was to emphasise the shared beliefs and traditions among various Protestant denominations. While, generally speaking, great progress has been made, the Presbyterian Church in Ireland formally withdrew from the Council in 1980 (Holmes 1985).

Relations between Protestant and Catholic groups have also improved following this drive towards ecumenism. Since the Second Vatican Council, official church policy endorses the view of Protestants and Catholics as members, although separated, of one religion and there is far greater recognition of the fact that 'both sides are guilty of the sins of division' (Brown 1969: 67). It is increasingly recognised that members of different denominations should acquire an understanding of their differing perspectives. Education would eradicate prejudices, which are often consequences of ignorance and misunderstanding.

The changing emphasis in relationships between Catholics and Protestants in Northern Ireland has been reflected in the activities of the Clonard Mission to Non-Catholics, which operated in Belfast between 1947 and 1968. In its initial years this organisation emphasised its role as a provider of information on Catholic doctrine. Services consisted simply of the explanation of Catholic teaching on various topics. Questions were then invited from the audience, which was subsequently urged to view the Catholic premises. After the Second Vatican Council, the name of the Mission was altered on a variety of occasions, each change reflecting greater empathy with the beliefs of non-Catholics. The final name change occurred in 1967 when the lecture series was billed as lectures for all communions (Lambkin 1996: 30).

Whether such efforts have made any real impact is questionable. Social segregation over several centuries and the violence endured by all groups has hardened the sectarian divide. While the *Ne Temere* decree no longer officially applies, a range of surveys has established that mixed marriages are still a relatively rare occurrence in Northern Ireland. Research by Lee (1981) concluded that the incidence of cross-community marriage was possibly as low as 1.54 percent in Belfast and even less for the Region as a whole. According to data from the NISAS taken between the years 1989 and 1994, the overall figure is 6 percent but there is considerable variation according to locality. Information from the Catholic Diocesan Office indicates that whereas a fifth of marriages in 1990 in the diocese of Down and Connor were interfaith, less than a tenth of those in the Derry diocese were mixed. In Armagh the comparable figure was 4 percent (Robinson 1992). A more detailed analysis of data from the 1993 NISAS demonstrated that the highest proportion of these marriages occurs in Belfast. While the figure here was 8.4 percent, and the east of the Region was 6.2 percent, a mere 2.2 percent of marriages in the west is mixed (Morgan et al 1996). The Protestant–Catholic divide is still apparent and O'Connor (1993: 172) records the fact that many Catholics clearly remember being taught that other denominations were 'lesser Christians, lacking the fullness of truth'.

In the education sector, integrated schools have been established in a number of locations but as yet there is little co-operation between the Churches regarding the work of these schools. In 1994 the British-Irish Inter-Parliamentary Body reported that the 'main established Churches were not prepared to support the development of integrated education'. The Body detected a sense of fear regarding a loss of control over religious education. Some clergymen expressed the view that 'education should develop within the two communities before one "opened up" to the other' (British-Irish Inter-Parliamentary Body 1994: 5).

In 1989 an education reform order introduced a selection of cross-curricular themes into formal education throughout the community. Some of these, notably *Education for Mutual Understanding* and *Cultural Heritage*, intended to promote and foster a respect for the different traditions in

Northern Ireland (Northern Ireland Council for the Curriculum, Examination and Assessment 1997). But these educational changes provoked controversy particularly among the unionist community, who reacted by comparing themselves with the Israelites. Brian Mawhinney, the education minister responsible for the introduction of cross-curricular themes, was denounced as a pharaoh who was attempting to indoctrinate Protestant children: 'it would appear that the strategy that Pharaoh adopted, because he feared the growing strength of the Israelites, and felt that it would not suit his purpose just to mount a massacre against the adults, he decided to control them through their children' (in Cochrane 1997: 53).

However, some cross-community initiatives have been favourably received. In May 1993 the Northern Ireland Inter-Faith Forum was formed. This draws its membership from Roman Catholic and Protestant Churches. It also includes representatives from other communities and churches such as the Baha'i, Buddhists, Chinese, Jews, and Muslims. The forum in Northern Ireland has linked up with the Inter-Faith organisation in the UK, representing some 70 communities in Britain. A primary motivation of the network is to generate an increasing understanding of the diversity of beliefs and to establish dialogue between groups. Members of the forum are not official representatives of their communities and do not necessarily represent the majority opinion of their group, but they have made genuine progress towards an enhanced understanding of differing perspectives. In addition, the Evangelical Contribution on Northern Ireland (ECONI) has made a significant contribution to addressing sectarianism in modern society (Liechty 1999: 95).

Conclusion

Roman Catholicism and the various Protestant denominations in Northern Ireland have emerged at different times and from differing political circumstances. Yet all groups retain common features. In the past, members of these denominations perceived the other as opposite and different. The world consisted of a series of contrasts or dualisms such as light and darkness, good and evil. Protestants defined themselves as the opposite of Catholics. Although Catholics tended to refer to the other in terms of nationality, that is as British (Pringle 1997), their Catholicism as strictly defined as the absence of the negative attributes of the Protestant faith. Each group needed the other in order to arrive at a positive self-definition.

Catholic and Protestant denominations in Northern Ireland are still 'heroically pre-modern' (Akenson 1988: 132) and display characteristics that are associated with past rather than current generations. They implicitly believe in the subordination of the material world by spiritual forces and have proved remarkably devout and intense for this reason. Each group is convinced that it has endured great persecution. Despite their privileged position in Irish society for several centuries, Anglicans have often felt under siege. Contemporary Presbyterians are aware of the discrimination of their members under the Penal code. According to Dunlop (1999: 43), 'Presbyterians were second class citizens in Ulster' for much of this time. And the Catholic theme of dispossession and martyrdom is also preserved in song, poetry, and iconography.

At both political and religious levels there has been a great determination for centuries to merge the Protestant traditions and emphasise their difference from Catholicism. Yet many of the rituals, such as parades, which are regarded as distinctively Protestant have their roots in Catholicism (Jarman and Bryan 1998). Associations in both communities mirror one another in their implementation of secrecy and rituals (Robinson 1986). And at an individual level there is recognition that some Protestant denominations are closer to Catholicism than others. The renowned Anglican poet, Michael Longley (1996: 75), records the taunts he received as a child from his Presbyterian friends: 'Sure you might as well be Roman Catholic'.

In the past two decades Catholics and Anglicans alike are beginning to view one another. as members of the same Christian tradition, although social segregation and violence has ensured that these groups still view one another with great suspicion. Ideally they believe in the 'one catholic church' and theologically they are committed to a paradigm of a single Christian religion. A shift to a one-Christian religion paradigm is ongoing in many regions in the world but it is far from complete. This new ecumenism may in part derive from a general decline in church attendance and a growing recognition of the presence of other non-Christian faiths.

Despite these efforts at intercultural exchange, religious tension has not dissipated and there is still a sense in which the Protestant/Catholic dichotomy dominates any discussion of religious conflict in Northern Ireland. Perhaps there is an increasing appreciation of the fact that divisions between groups are not solely a consequence of theological differences, but have been fostered and maintained particularly by violence but also by the artificial partition of the population at large into separate schools, secret societies, and marriage alliances. Dunlop (1999: 47) explains that this 'demographic disaster' has deprived people in Northern Ireland of the 'experience of living together with people of the "other" community'. For this reason, the shift from the opposite religions paradigm to the single tradition paradigm has been slow. But the changing emphasis in the religious sector is also reflected in many other aspects of cultural traditions.

CHAPTER 4

A DISCOURSE OF DIFFERENCE

For as long as Irish people think of themselves as Celtic Crusoes on a sequestered island, they ignore not only their own diaspora but the basic cultural truth that cultural creation comes from hybridization not purity, contamination not immunity, polyphony not monologue.
(Kearney 1997: 101)

Before the Plantation of the early seventeenth century, Ulster was considered the most Celtic province in Ireland (Darby 1983: 14). But the term 'Celtic' is not always clearly defined. Historically it refers to a number of tribes such as Britons, Celtiberi, Gauls, and Helvetii, whose presence in Europe was testified by the Romans. In modern times the term can refer to a speaker of one of the recognised Celtic languages or merely to claim kinship with a region, such as Scotland or Wales, where Celtic languages are spoken. It is sometimes used in a much more general sense to imply spirituality, anti-materialism, and romanticism. In this chapter my focus is on Celticism – a term which, Leerssen (1996: 3) suggests, refers to an analysis of the reputation of Celts and of the meanings and connotations ascribed to Celtic identities. Here I wish to explore the shift in paradigm that has occurred in Celtic discourse, not just in Northern Ireland but with reference to the British Isles as whole.

In the past the concept of Celticity has been largely associated with the nationalist community in Northern Ireland. In a letter written in the twentieth century, the unionist leader Edward Carson stated that 'the Celts have done nothing in Ireland but create trouble and disorder'. Moreover, 'Irishmen who turned out successful are not in any case that I know of true Celtic origin' (in Colvin 1936: 441). In this context Celticism has operated in racial terms and set up a dichotomy between nationalists and unionists. But some loyalists are currently re-claiming their Celtic heritage and re-defining themselves as Celts, postulating two separate Celtic traditions in the Region. Whether or not unionists actually believe this revised discourse of Celticity is not the subject of my chapter. I am quite sure that it is hardly as significant a discourse as that of Orangeism. But it is important to recognise that Celticity as a useful polemic. In redefining a Celtic heritage, unionists may simply be establishing their credentials as Celts in the British tradition and claiming their share of this cultural pool or some may wish to promote the concept of a single tradition or a shared common heritage in Northern Ireland. But the loyalist discourse of Celticity may have more sinister implications. Some may wish to detract from the cultural significance of the Celt for nationalists and lessen its value as a symbol of opposition, thereby rendering it irrelevant.

Emblems of Celticity

Northern Ireland retains several markers of Celticity and this applies particularly to territorial matters. Smith (1992: 447) suggests that in Wales and Ireland, Celtic communities pay special attention to what he terms 'their sacred land'. This pattern of ethnic survival, denoted as the 'communal-demotic', claims that members of the community are the original occupants, and that their culture is the true one. Such a tradition associates groups with particular territories and endorses their abode in a particular homeland (Brow 1990). Perhaps this claim to the land is best exemplified in the Welsh language. According to the English speaker, the people living in Wales are 'Welsh', which is derived from the Anglo-Saxon word *wealth*, meaning 'foreigner'. In the Welsh language, however, they are the '*Cymry*', the 'kinsfolk', who live not in the 'land of strangers' (Wales), but the 'land of fellow countrymen/women' (*Cymru*) (Bowie 1993: 186).

There are several symbols of Celticity in the landscape of Northern Ireland. An impressive geological formation on the Antrim coast is strongly associated with Celtic heroes such as Fionn mac Cumhail. Some islands on various lakes in the Region are in fact *crannógs*, early Celtic artificial island settlements. Celtic crosses are further reminders of the possible presence of these early peoples. It is generally accepted that the earthworks and sites around the townland of Navan in County Armagh represent Ireland's most important pre-historic Celtic monument. They constitute the remains of *Emain Macha*, the Camelot, or legendary capital of the Ulster cycle of tales (Warner 1994). An interpretative centre, opened here in July 1993, examines the mythology and archaeology associated with a variety of local late Bronze and early Iron Age Celtic sites. Its archaeological section explains that local excavations revealed what is believed to be a Celtic temple which, upon completion, was burnt in sacrifice to the gods. Thereafter it acquired a special significance as the crowning place of the kings of the Region.

Many contemporary placenames in Northern Ireland are imbued with a Celtic significance. For example, the term *Dún*, the Irish for Down, can refer to a fort or fortress and was commonly employed for the homes of chieftains and kings. According to the heroic literature of Ireland, Cú Chulainn was instructed in the names of all the chief forts between Tara and Kells on the day that he took up arms. In early historic times, there was a royal stronghold in *Dún Sobhairce*, meaning Sobhairce's fort, which is now known as Dunseverick in County Antrim. Its devastation by Queen Maeve was mentioned in the *Táin Bó Cuailgne*, the Cattle Raid of Cooley (Flanagan and Flanagan 1994: 75).

Doire, the Irish for Derry, denotes an oak grove, and features commonly in a variety of Irish placenames. The original oak grove in Derry, known as *Doire Calgaich*, meaning Caglach's oak-grove, was positioned on a little hill that was once an island in the River Foyle (Flanagan and Flanagan 1994: 70). As the water that ran past the western side of the island gradually dried up, it left a marshy, boggy territory, which is now known as the Bogside. Oak groves were regarded as sacred places by the Celts and 'Oak placenames' occur throughout Europe. The regularity of these placenames reflects the prevalence of oak forests, and the significance of their position in Celtic culture. It is almost certain that Celtic rituals were held in Derry and several superstitions regarding the trees in the area survived until the sixteenth century.

Place lore, or *dinnshenchus*, as it is known in Irish, plays an important role in the ancient Gaelic tradition. For example, the remarkable length of the Ulster tale *Táin Bó Cuailgne, Cattle Raid of Cooley* (Strachan and O'Keefe 1912; Kinsella 1969), is primarily achieved by the lists of names which are often given in a descriptive context, and by the onomastic legends of the *dinnshenchus* type, which are designed to explain the origin of certain placenames (Ó hUiginn 1992). Baumgarten (1990: 122) described this genre of material as a 'major source of Irish literary creation'. Many of the placenames in the *Cattle Raid of Cooley* reflect the journey by the men of Connaught to Ulster and the duels fought en route.

Much Irish placelore was lost with the Anglicisation of Irish placenames, particularly in the nineteenth century, and many Northern Irish writers have lamented this loss. Brian Friel's celebrated play *Translations* (1981), first produced in Derry, deals with the decline of the Irish language and pays particular attention to the ordnance survey of Ireland, carried out by the British Army Engineer Corps in the 1830s. Owen, the son of the hedge-school master, who aids the British army with the mapping and renaming of places in Donegal, is portrayed as betraying his ancestral Gaelic domain for a modern English world. *Translations* devotes considerable attention to the historical significance of placenames and to the legends associated with them.

Now You're Talking, a BBC (Northern Ireland) course in the Irish language (Ó Dónaill 1995), devoted a proportion of each programme to an interesting explanation of placenames in Northern Ireland. Of course, there is always a problem with the presentation of such data, as it can be misconstrued as an attempted reclamation of the territory, as implying, correctly or incorrectly, that the land originally belonged to the Gaels or Celts. However, the fact that many loyalists are aware of their Celtic heritage may lessen the divisive potential of such information. For nationalists and unionists a sensitivity regarding placenames is a reflection of the significance which they attach to land, particularly in Northern Ireland, where ownership of the territory is often in dispute.

Some loyalists and many nationalists have been familiarising themselves with the Irish language in the past two decades (e.g. Mac Giolla Chríost and Aitchison 1998; Mac Póilin 1997; Maguire 1991; O'Reilly 1999). Speaking a Celtic language remains one of the more popularly accepted symbols of belonging to a Celtic tradition. Throughout Ireland as a whole the name of the language, Irish Gaelic, acquired a racial resonance and became the signifier of a great proportion of the population. This process has been replete with contradictions as language is essentially a cultural rather than a racial phenomenon (Akenson 1988: 135). But it is probably related to the fact that people in the eighteenth century sought their racial credentials primarily through language. Yet despite an apparent desire to be perceived as Gaelic, the great majority of people opted in the nineteenth century to acquire English and use it as their sole medium of communication. Their knowledge of Irish was suppressed and silenced (Crowley 1996; 2000; De Fréine 1978; Hindley 1990; Nic Craith 1994). Contemporary archaeologists are increasingly discounting the existence of an original culturally homogenous group speaking one of the Celtic languages (Renfrew 1996).

The symbolism of Celtic languages is increasingly interesting if one takes account of some of the arguments, regarding the construction of linguistic familial relationships. McDonald (1989) questions the definitional reality of Breton and notes that its similarities with Welsh are considered systematic and natural and are accepted as proof of its Celticity. Where differences occur between Breton and Welsh, they are explained as 'corruptions' or 'intrusions' and are deemed to be irrelevant or random. Controversially, McDonald suggests that there are potentially many parallels between Breton and French, and that it would not be impossible to posit a relationship between those two languages. But the Breton desire to be different from the Gaul, particularly in the nineteenth century, has led to the elimination of many French terms from Breton and the inclusion of many Welsh, Gaelic, and Cornish words.

Although Irish has tended to absorb some English terms in the last century, the two languages are markedly different and the use of the Irish language has increased significantly in Northern Ireland in the past two or three decades. According to the published reports of the 1991 census, 142,003 people, that is 9.5 percent of the population, claim knowledge of the language (Nic Craith and Shuttleworth 1996; Nic Craith 1999b; O'Reilly 1999). While these figures are often disputed, the language has gained a definite presence in the public sector. In particular the setting up of a formal Cultural Traditions Group (CTG) in 1988 and the subsequent establishment of the ULTACH Trust agency indicated recognition of this Celtic language as a significant element in the heritage of Northern Ireland.

While individuals across Northern Ireland are increasing their knowledge of the language, only the nationalist community plays Gaelic sport and I explore the reasons for this exclusivity in Chapter 7. Hurling is a particularly ancient game resonating with Celticity. According to Sugden and Bairner (1995: 25), the earliest match dates from 1272 BC. While it seems virtually impossible to assign such a precise early date to a game of hurling, the game features in a variety of early Celtic tales. For example, Cú Chulainn's original name was Setanta, but it was changed after he was invited to a feast at the house of Culann the Smith. As Setanta was playing a game of hurling, he arrived late for the banquet. He was attacked by Culann's guard-dog, but he killed him by shoving the *sliotar* (hurley ball) down his throat. Subsequently the druid, Cathbad renamed the warrior Cú Chulainn, meaning the hound of Culann, and he served as a guard for the smith, until a replacement dog was found.

Although hurling is assumed to represent an unbroken link with Ireland's ancient Celtic past, Gaelic football is by far the more popular Irish sport. Many Northern Irish Catholics also play association football although they originally branded its arrival as an element of foreign culture. Belfast once boasted its own Celtic Football Club (FC) which originated from a largely Catholic/nationalist setting (Coyle 1999). Celtic Park was the home of Belfast Celtic FC, which played football until a series of political controversies led to its closure in 1949.

In Ireland, the term 'Celtic' is pronounced with a hard 'C' or 'K' sound but the name of the Belfast FC was conspicuous in that it sounded more like an 'S'. (In this it is similar to Glasgow Celtic FC.) According to one internet source, the British pronunciation of 'Celtic' with a soft 'c' developed in the Roman Era. It was decided at this time that the Latin spoken by the British should contrast with that spoken in other parts of the Roman Empire and many of the previously hard 'k' sounds were softened. The aim of these changes was to demonstrate that the British were different from other Roman subjects. Whether or not this is an accurate reflection of history, I believe that the different pronunciation of Celtic remains a powerful symbol of a common, yet divided, heritage.

Nationalist groups in Northern Ireland regularly support the Celtic team in Scotland, and their reasons are sometimes political as well as cultural. Overall, 93 percent of Celtic supporters are Catholic and Celtic football jerseys are often worn in Catholic, nationalist areas. This gesture is interpreted as having a religious and cultural significance (Bradley 1995:

62). For example, at a march in London in 1989, which called for a British withdrawal from Northern Ireland, two ladies wearing Celtic FC jerseys strode at the front with Labour MPs Ken Livingstone and Jeremy Corbyn. In many ways the success of Celtic FC in Scotland contributed to the demise of other markers of Celticity. Bradley (1995) notes that as the focus of attention on the Celtic team increased, it provided the primary manifestation of Irish identity. Any interest in Gaelic music and language fluctuated.

Narrative of the nation

Interest in Celtic sports, music, and language is largely the prerogative of nationalists, many of whom assume that they are Celtic. Most of them are vaguely familiar with the medieval chronicle *Lebor Gabhála Érenn* (Book of the Conquests of Ireland; see MacAlister and MacNeill 1916). This legendary history purports to narrate the story of the Irish people from creation to the twelfth century. While the Book of Conquests does not assume a cultural hegemony in Ireland's prehistory and acknowledges diverse ethnic peoples in Ireland's ancient past, it is vague with regard to the arrival of various groups. In a manner consistent with mythologies of other nations, the principal characters are gods on some occasions and kings or heroes on others.

The Book of Conquests attributes an ancient ancestry to the Gaels, recounting their original journey from Scythia to Babel. These Celts were reputed to have arrived in Egypt at the time of Moses and migrated from there to Spain. An association between Ireland and Spain was possibly facilitated by an apparent correspondence between [H]ibernia and [H]iberia. It was suggested that the Milesians, the sons of Míl Espáine, conquered the land of Ireland at the time of Alexander the Great. Then these last colonists, the ancestors of the Gaels, established themselves as the dominant class despite their limited numbers. They defeated the Tuatha Dé Danann in two battles, one at Slieve Mis in County Kerry and another at Taillte in Leinster. A late addition suggests that part of Ulster was given to the followers of Ir, one of the sons of Míl.

Very few have ever given credence to this mythological history and it has been described as 'a deliberate work of fiction', although there is no doubt that the compilers 'could not afford "entirely" to ignore the popular traditions which were current' (O'Rahilly 1946: 194). Yet the existence of a distinct group of ancient Celts has largely remained undisputed until recently. The fact that very little is known regarding the ancient Celts in Europe has merely contributed to their appeal and mystique. A strong emphasis within Celtic society on the importance of the oral tradition has deprived modern scholars of internal written accounts of these people and the Celtic tradition in Europe became 'known almost exclusively from outside reports' (Leerssen 1996: 3). Classical authors ascribed the term *Keltoi* to various transalpine people. They rendered accounts of their physical characteristics and behavioural patterns, and described the social practices of these groups.

Modern scholars have examined the records of classical writers and have ascertained archaeological and historical characteristics typical of regions dominated by the Celts. They have classified art styles, artefacts, and social practices cultivated in those locations as Celtic (Raftery 1964: 49). Much of *La Téne* culture is regarded as Celtic. Furthermore, there has been a presumed co-relation between Celts and a specific family of Indo-European languages (Greene 1964), but it is possible that many of those with a material culture of *La Téne* character were unfamiliar with Celtic languages. Similarly not everyone who drinks Coca-Cola from classic bottles speaks American English. Any similarities between diverse Celtic practices may have been confined simply to the warrior or wealthier classes (Chapman 1992: 32–3).

It is generally accepted that the earliest Celtic influence in Ireland occurred in the Iron Age period – probably during the second half of the first millennium BC. Raftery (1964: 50) dates the Celtic influence in Ireland from about 300 BC to about 450 AD. The nature of the arrival of elements of Celtic culture on the island of Ireland is much debated. Although there is no evidence to suggest that any large-scale invasion took place, it has traditionally been accepted that the Celts arrived by boat, and that a physical invasion or intrusion actually occurred (Clark 1966). In fact the primary source of contention was the origin rather than the arrival of these Celts (Wagner 1987). This invasion hypothesis was supported by the fact that a Celtic language is spoken in Ireland and that its arrival required the migration of a number of tribes or communities (Mac Eoin 1986: 167).

While the precise historical details of Celtic peoples are unclear, their significance has been immense in all Celtic regions. When the concept of the Celt as ethnonym or self-defining term was first established on the continent with the publication in 1703 of *L'Antiquitié de la Nation et de la Languge des Celtes,* its author Pezron offered the Bretons and Welsh a discourse of difference and constructed new imagined communities. He traced their roots back to the ancients Celts, who once had a mighty empire, and had fiercely resisted Greeks and Romans over many centuries. Moreover, he asserted that Celts themselves were descendants of imaginary heroes in patriarchal times. Though his volume presented an unsubstantiated version of history, it was received with enthusiasm, especially when David Jones, a Welsh historian, translated it into English in 1706 (Morgan 1983).

The following year saw the publication of Lhuyd's *Archaeologia Britannica* (1707), which proposed that the Welsh had descended from the British, whose ancestors were the glorious Celts. It is doubtful whether many of Lhuyd's readers actually understood the logic of Lhuyd's elaborate linguistic methodology but its implications were obvious enough. A dichotomy was set up between Welsh and English and the Welsh had acquired a separate history, which was distinct from that of England. The Welsh were using a discourse of race as distinct from racism. ' "Race" and associated words suggesting commonality of descent or character were developed into popular modes of thought and expression in many European languages in the eighteenth century' (Banton 2000: 51). As a concept, race bears the traces of its roots in biological discourses and emphasises alleged (rather than real) physical characteristics, the most obvious of which is skin pigmentation.

By sheer coincidence, an Act of Union between England and Scotland officially established the term 'British' in year 1707. It is possible that the state usurpation of the term 'British' was a major impetus for a widespread acceptance of the term 'Celt' as an ethnonym, although of course the Bretons were happy with a variation of this term, as it established their difference from the Gauls! Popular tradition in Brittany claims that a considerable number of British Celts were forced by the Anglo-Saxons to flee to the Armorican peninsula (Brittany) in the fifth century where they quickly established a British (Breton) presence (McDonald 1989). This history affirms an opposition between Bretons and Gauls and establishes the Bretons as a distinct race, both genetically and culturally. A dichotomy between the Cornish and the British was enhanced by Borlase 's work in the mid-century, when he made a connection between the stone monuments in Cornwall and the ancient religion of the Celts (Hale 1997).

By this time Scottish-Gaelic Highlanders were also establishing their authenticity as Celts and had created a legend distinguishing them from their English neighbours. In this account their ancestors were Caledonians, who had resisted the Romans. This version of history was given further credence in the 1760s when James Macpherson published a series of prose poems that he claimed were translations of ancient Scottish-Gaelic material (see Gaskill 1991). Despite generating a major literary controversy regarding their authenticity, these forgeries were enthusiastically received on the continent and established a receptivity towards a romantic image of the Gael (Chapman 1978; Trevor-Roper 1983).

These controversies regarding Macpherson's forgeries did not dampen the overall enthusiasm for indigenous culture and literature in the Celtic languages, and in 1789 Charlotte Brooke published her *Reliques of Irish Poetry* in Dublin. This volume, essentially a translation of ancient Irish poetry, served as a catalyst for the first Celtic revival in Ireland. Three years later a harp festival celebrating Celtic music was organised by Edward Bunting in Belfast. His volume, *The Ancient Music of Ireland*, was first published in 1796. (A recent edition has been published in Cork in 1983.) Subsequently many Ulster personalities, such as Samuel Ferguson, contributed to the construction of Irish identity as Gaelic and Celtic.

The writings of Standish O'Grady (e.g. 1857; 1892) provided the catalyst for the second Celtic revival in Ireland. His works in the last decades of the nineteenth century devoted considerable attention to the character of Cú Chulainn and the Ulster Cycle of Tales. This group of heroic stories explains how the name Ulster was derived from a powerful tribe who lived in the north of Ireland in prehistoric times. These people's territory extended from Donegal to the mouth of the Boyne and their seat of power was located in *Emain Macha*, now Navan Fort near Armagh. The tales recount the continuing conflict and dynastic struggle between the Uliad of Ulster and the people of Connaught. Groups in Northern Ireland still celebrates the hero of Cú Chulainn who features primarily in the central tale of *The Táin* (Cattle Raid of Cooley), although his character remains a divisive rather than an uniting factor between competing Celtic communities.

When Lhuyd and his counterparts offered evidence that the Celtic communities differed from the industrial regions, they established a historic two traditions model. They were creating images of themselves as earthy characters, resisting policies of urbanisation and machination. Such dreamy figures stood in opposition to rationality and a series of contrasts were set up between Celt and Anglo-Saxon, Caledonian and Roman, Breton and Gaul. In this regard the Bretons had a particular problem, as the ancestral Gaul, or French Celt, had survived in French consciousness. Bretons were attempting to develop a distinctly British form of the Celtic metaphor, that was unrelated either biologically or culturally to the Gauls who could also claim to be Celtic (McDonald 1989). Insular Celts did not encounter this dilemma. Whereas the French were not prepared to view themselves simply as Franks or as Germanic invaders in a Celtic realm, the majority English were content to construe themselves as Anglo-Saxons.

Racialisation of the Irish

Opposition between the Celts and Anglo-Saxons was given a strong biological slant in the nineteenth century and the emphasis now was on racism rather than race. 'By the late nineteenth and early twentieth centuries imperialist ideologies had developed a racial notion of national identity to refer to other European nations as well as colonial people' (Back and Solomos 2000: 15). At this time the British press seized on the alleged physical characteristics of the Celts and linked them to attributes such as incompetence and imbecility. Essentialising categories of biology and culture, this racialisation of the Irish was a process of power control. The media representation of the Celts as a distinct and subordinate race was a social and political power struggle. It was also a process of race formation or racialisation. As Gilroy (1987: 38–9) has argued in another context:

> Accepting that skin 'colour', however meaningless we know it to be, has a strictly limited material basis in biology, opens up the possibility of engaging with theories of signification which can highlight the elasticity and emptiness of 'racial' signifiers as well as the ideological work which has to be done

in order to turn them into signifiers of 'race' as an open political category, for it is struggle that determines which definitions of 'race' will prevail and the conditions under which they will endure or wither away.

The racialisation of the Irish in nineteenth-century Britain has received some attention at the end of the last century (e.g. Curtis 1971; Curtis 1991). These books focus on the deliberate attempts to portray the Irishman in Britain as subhuman and the evidence they provide is strong and convincing. Various sources at this time pointed to alleged physiological differences between the Anglo-Saxons and the Irish Celts. For example, Fraser's magazine in 1847 stated that the English were 'naturally industrious' – preferring 'a life of honest labour to one of idleness'. In contrast, the Celts were 'famous everywhere for their indolence, and fickleness', of which 'the Irish are admitted to be the most idle and the most fickle' (in Lebow 1976: 40).

In 1862 the journal *Punch* suggested that 'a creature manifestly between the gorilla and the negro is to be met with, in some of the lowest districts of London and Liverpool'. The journal affirmed that this creature 'belongs to a tribe of Irish savages' and when 'conversing with its kind it talks a sort of gibberish. It is, moreover, a climbing animal and may sometimes be seen ascending a ladder laden with a hod of bricks' (in Swift 1990: 28). At this time the historian Lord Acton expounded on the benefits of Anglo-Saxons authority for the Celts who 'waited for a foreign influence to set in action the rich treasures which in their own hands could be of no avail' (in Curtis 1991: 57). Three years later the *Times* noted in an editorial that the Celts were emigrating from Ireland and 'a Catholic Celt will soon be as rare on the banks of the Shannon as a Red Indian on the shores of Manhattan' (in Curtis 1991: 58).

But to rely solely on any number of these quotations is to present an incomplete picture. The journal *Punch,* which is regarded as the chief medium of anti-Irish racism in the nineteenth century, sometimes portrayed English peasants in an equally degrading fashion and was often as 'anti-medical students, or anti-politicans or anti-income tax' as it was anti-Irish' (Foster 1993: 174). This is not in any sense to detract from the racialisation of the Celt. It merely demonstrates that *Punch* did not single out the Celts in particular for its racist comments.

But it also appears at this time that there was a certain ambiguity on the part of the English with regard to the distinctiveness of the Irish as a separate race. Occasionally the Irish were included in the concept of a common British identity. In 1849, for example, the Anglo-Saxon magazine argued that the term Anglo-Saxon 'does not exclude the Celt, whether Irish, Scottish or Welsh; the two families rapidly blending into one, and it is only natural to retain the name of the predominating element' (in O'Toole 2000: 21).

But generally speaking Celtic cultures in Britain were perceived as obstructing progress and modernity (Hutchinson 1987; Kiberd 1996; Williams 1994). Opposition between the Celts and Anglo-Saxons was given prominence in the second half of the nineteenth century with the work of Mathew Arnold. In his Oxford lectures *The Study of Celtic Literature* (1867), Arnold gave the minority a precise metaphorical portrait. He defined this character as a dreamy, illogical and spiritual figure whose psyche was possibly feminine. This set the character in direct opposition to the typical Victorian who was construed as diligent, industrial, practical, and in many senses dominated by what were regarded as essentially male characteristics. Arnold availed of the term 'Celtic' particularly to denote the Irish and to differentiate between them and the English. He intimated that as they were ill-matched ideologically, the tedious English could never properly legislate for the dreamy, wild Irish. His endorsement of the Celts ultimately led to the romanticisation of the Irish Catholic.

I am convinced that this nineteenth-century dichotomy between Celt and Anglo-Saxon was the precursor of the opposition between Irish and English, which still pertains in a vague sense in contemporary Northern Ireland. From the perspective of some English, everyone in Northern Ireland is Irish – an issue that I explore in Chapter 6. Contrasts between Irish and English are construed in terms of Celt versus Anglo-Saxon or barbarian against civilian. In this context the Irish stereotype still retains many of the characteristics of the barbaric Celt. According to Deane (1986), the greatest imperfection of this stereotype is that he is Irish and probably Catholic. If not Roman Catholic, such individuals are generally extreme ranting Protestants, usually dissenters in the Calvinistic tradition. Deane (1986: 40) suggests that this Northern Irish stereotype is construed as suffering from further imperfections. Usually,

> he is from a working-class background and is unemployed (unemployable); therefore he draws money from the benevolent state which he wishes to subvert and by which he is oppressed as he was also educated and fed free milk by it. He is from an area of dirt and desolation, not to be equalled in Western Europe, a blot on the fair face of the United Kingdom. He drinks a lot, for since the Fenians, it has been a standard piece of English lore that all Irish guerrilla groups meet in pubs when they are not blowing them up. Sometimes, they manage to do both. Finally, and worst of all, he is sometimes a she . . . Most important of all, they are not only barbarians, they are criminals.

Stereotyping is a mechanism for control 'another strategy of maintaining the social order' (Lentin 2000: 8). It usually happens in the context of unequal power relations and as the balance of power has shifted in Northern Ireland, its impact has lessened. But the sense of difference between Irish and English still represents a battle for supremacy between discourses and political attitudes.

Within Northern Ireland the sense of difference between Irish and

English is sometimes expressed as a form of antagonism between nationalists and unionists. The nineteenth-century sense of opposition between the Celts and Anglo-Saxons has remained, but the terminology has changed. It is now construed as a conflict between Gaels and primarily English (occasionally British) people. Celts, or Gaels, had always been portrayed as the Other in society, and in the past this has provided a very powerful and meaningful symbol for the general Northern Irish Catholic community whose former lack of civil rights was sometimes portrayed as an attempted eradication of Celtic, Gaelic culture:

> The Gaelic way of life is a major threat to the English plan for Ireland. Before the Brits can ever hope to control the Irish, the Gaelic way of life must completely disappear. Since they first set foot in Ireland they have relentlessly tried to destroy the old order. They have mis-spelt our names and place-names, and they have broken the old laws of our land. They suggest that only fools speak Irish. They drove the Gaels from the land and to the mountains.
>
> (MacCormaic 1986: 15)

But the situation in Northern Ireland has improved radically since the 1960s and the discourse of oppression has lessened substantially. While the narrative of Celticism is not explicit, its symbolism is understood and remains a powerful communal factor. There is a sense in which the nationalist community is composed of Gaels, who are still experiencing the marginalisation endured by their ancestors in the nineteenth century and by the ancient Celts during the expansion of the Roman Empire – except, of course, Ireland was not part of the Roman Empire.

Contemporary Northern Ireland is not unique in reviving its Celtic past in modern political discourse. In Padania, Italy's separatist Northern League is currently redefining itself as a Celtic community, whose difficulties with the Italian government are represented as being largely due to the latter's imperialistic, Roman instincts. This Padanian 'Celtic versus Roman' controversy has been given an added impetus with the revision of early history which lays great emphasis on the contribution of the heroic, civilised Celts to Padanian society before the arrival of the pedantic, imperialist, and decadent Romans (Kennedy 1998).

A separate Celtic tradition

While nationalists may view themselves as natural descendants of Celts, loyalists have begun the reclamation of their British Celtic heritage and increasingly challenge the Celtic discourse of nationalists. This, I would argue, constitutes an example of 'reverse assimilation'. In an analysis of this process, Levine (1990) points to the example of white sheep farming communities in new Zealand that have cultivated concepts of spiritual and emotional connections with the land. Maori groups resent the development of these ideologies, as they believe that it represents an appropriation of Maori values and beliefs concerning territory that rightfully belongs to them. But there are significant differences between this example and the evolution of Celtic discourse in Northern Ireland. In the case of the latter, unionists are referring to a sense of Britishness, which formerly embraced the concept of the Celt – a fact that I return to in Chapter 8.

Many elements of this debate revolve around the language question, and proponents of Northern Ireland's British Celtic heritage refer to historical sources to enhance their arguments. Surviving Celtic languages are grouped into two families, the British (Brythonic) or 'P' Celtic languages – Welsh, Breton, and Cornish – and the Gaelic (Goidelic) or 'Q' Celtic languages – Irish, Scottish Gaelic, and Manx. As this debate is intricate, complex, and challenging I am merely presenting a simplified account of some of its main tenets here. If there were any differences at all between early versions of British and Gaelic Celtic, and it is unlikely that there were sharp variations between them (De Búrca 1966: 134), then it is probable that both were spoken in Celtic Ireland. But it is generally assumed that speakers of Gaelic reached Ireland before their British counterparts. Subsequently, the superior strength and social importance of the Gaels ensured the assimilation of British Celts.

Contradicting this theory, loyalists point to classical sources that indicate that early Celtic Ireland was British rather than Gaelic in character. Adamson (1991a) explains that the Gaelic Celtic language developed earlier than its British counterpart. For this reason he claims that it has been assumed in error that speakers of Gaelic Celtic arrived in Ireland before their fellow British Celts. Reference to the British as Ireland's original Celts has been given prominence in some loyalist journals. The *Combat* magazine of 25 April 1974 suggested that

> The majority of Ulster Protestants equate Gaelic and Irish culture with Roman Catholicism and are of the opinion that no 'good Prod' would have anything to do with such Popish traditions. The truth of the matter is, Ulster Protestants have as much claim, if not more in some cases, to the Gaelic culture as the Roman Catholic population. Someone once said that the Irish language was stolen from the Protestant people by the Papists. It would be more correct to say that the Protestant people gave their culture away to the Roman Catholics.
>
> (in Ó Glaisne 1981: 870)

While this debate may seem largely irrelevant today, I believe that the earlier arrival of either tribe is being used to confer a territorial claim on their descendants. This is particularly pertinent in the case of Northern Ireland where ownership of land has always proved contentious. In Chapter 2 I noted that the Plantation episode is often used to establish a dichotomy between native and settler and that the 'indigenous' Irish have traditionally assumed that their ancestors were the first significant inhabitants of the country. A suggestion that British Celts may have lived in certain territories prior to the Gaels is highly controversial. If true, it would redefine the 'native-settler' dichotomy in terms of 'invaders-natives' and those who now regard themselves as the original owners would be viewed as incomers.

This may explain the vociferous reaction to Adamson's assertion that the *Dal Riati* tribe of north Antrim and the *Dal Fiatiach* or Uliad tribe were probably British Celts. According to him these groups, which he collectively calls the *Uliad,* resisted the control of Gaelic Celts for a thousand years. From this perspective the diversity of society in Iron-Age Ireland was later disguised by the Book of Conquests which was 'a medieval scholarly attempt to give Gaelic ancestry to all the peoples of Ireland of that age, while maintaining the older origin legends' (Adamson 1995: 11). This view is endorsed by a variety of sources including Mac Póilin (1994a: 3) who argues that 'everyone in Ireland knew that the country was full of non-Goidels, pre-Goidels, and anti-Goidels, all of whom took a very dim view of the Goidels. The consensus-seekers, however, put their trust in the long view. They buried past differences by proving beyond reasonable doubt that all pre-Goidelic people in Ireland had either perished or been banished.'

Many groups of people have similarly presented a picture of unity and obscured former diverse realities. For example, Eriksen (1993: 70–71) draws attention to the pan-native American tradition of Quebec. Here the Huron people present themselves as a group who has been marginalised by forces of European colonisation whereas their real persecutors from the mid-seventeenth century onwards were the Iroquis, another native American group. Contemporary influential native American historians fail to recount the tension between these indigenous peoples and where such enmities are acknowledged they are represented as being incited by the European colonists. In the case of the Book of Conquests there was possibly an attempt to present a united Celtic front against a common Other and any diversity in early Irish society was ignored. But when one considers the modest numbers of any Celtic arrivals, especially in proportion to earlier pre-Celtic inhabitants, it is possible that if they occurred, none was particularly momentous.

In support of their claim to a Celtic lineage, many loyalists point out that Highland Scottish migrants in Ulster spoke Scottish Gaelic for centuries. Such migrants included the Gallowglass soldiers who were hired by Irish chieftains from the thirteenth to the sixteenth centuries (Perceval-Maxwell 1973: 2). Loyalists speak of these as 'mercenary warriors, speaking a Celtic tongue but of Viking blood, who were much in demand as hired fighters amongst the clan chiefs of Ireland' (McDowell n.d: 5).

A proportion of the Scottish communities who arrived during the Plantation period in the early seventeenth century were speakers of Scottish-Gaelic but others were speakers of Scots. Heslinga (1962: 159) suggests that 'it is fairly certain that many colonists of the first three decades of the seventeenth century who came from Galloway were Gaelic speakers'. The presence of Scottish Gaelic speakers in Ireland continued for many decades. State papers in 1661 recorded of some prisoners in Antrim that a Captain Campbell spoke 'the Highland Irish with divers of them' (Pentland Mahaffy 1905: 457).

There was possibly little difference between spoken Scottish-Gaelic and Ulster Irish in the early seventeenth century (Thomson 1977) and Scottish and Irish Celts would certainly have been capable of communicating with one another, leading to a blend of cultures between them and contributing to a common Celtic heritage across the Region. According to Hill (1993), the great majority of English and Lowland Scottish settlers probably found Ulster barbaric and perhaps, according to their standards, uncivilisable. On the other hand, the Highlanders intermixed with the 'indigenous' Irish, generating a cultural fusion that was neither distinctively Irish and Catholic nor British and Protestant.

In the latter half of the seventeenth-century Gaelic-speaking Episcopalians arrived in North Antrim. After the Siege of Derry, two Church of Ireland clergy attended to a congregation of some four or five hundred from the Highlands of Scotland. John Richardson states that many of these were ignorant of English. He submits an extract of a letter sent to him as proof of same: 'Soon after the late War in *Ireland*, when a great Part of the Country was waste and uninhabited, several Families, who could neither speak nor understand any Language but *Irish*, found their Account in coming from the Western Isles of Scotland, and settling in the Northern Parts of the County of *Antrim*' (original emphasis in Richardson 1712: 101–2).

At the beginning of the nineteenth century Dubourdieu (1802: 492–3) noted a divergence between the Scottish Gaelic and Irish spoken in Ulster. In the Ordnance Survey Memoirs he wrote that '[a]ll speak English; and the descendants of the first Scotch settlers speak also a dialect of the Celtic, said to be a mixture of the Highland language and that, which the ancient Irish inhabitants spoke; but it is not easily understood by those, who speak Erse or Irish well'.

Contemporary Loyalist journals urge their readers to reclaim this Celtic heritage and to speak Irish in order to ensure that it does not become incorrectly associated with a single community. 'Don't be afraid to quote Gaelic, use Gaelic names and speak the language if you wish. Don't allow the Provos and their ilk to hijack the language and transform it into a weapon against all Ulsterfolk. Don't listen to ignorant unionist politicians who brand it a "foreign language". Reclaim this vital part of these islands' common British heritage' (*Ulster Nation*, 2(3) 1991: 1). They are very keen to emphasise the Celtic dimension of the British character:

Not of course that there is anything unBritish about the Irish Language. In Roman times the Irish Language was widely spoken in the North of England

and throughout Scotland. Queen Boadicca, that personification of British resistance to the Roman Legions in the early years of the conquests might well have screamed as her battle cry 'Fág an Bealach' as she led her army to Colchester. That is not to say that she commanded the Dublin Fusiliers, the Connaght Rangers or the Royal Inniskilling Fusiliers, only that she, like they, raised a battle cry in Irish. But what is so strange in that? Under that later day namesake of Boadicca – her name means 'Victorious' – Queen Victoria, the Inniskillings and the Connaught Rangers helped to spread the British empire right around the globe. And, for many of them, Irish was their Mother Tongue.

(Napier 1989: 41)

The reclamation of a British Celtic identity by loyalists in Northern Ireland differs from the adoption of a Cornish identity by in-migrants in Cornwall who may learn the Cornish language in order to demonstrate that, 'in their hearts', they are Cornish (Ivey and Payton 1994). While such in-migrants eventually become one with the indigenous Cornish in terms of attitudes, clothing, and speech, they do not compete with them regarding the historical claim to 'Cornishness', although many in-migrants engage in genealogical research in order to establish the presence of any Cornish ancestry.

In the case of Northern Ireland some loyalists are reclaiming Celticity as an assertion of their British rather than their Irish identity. Moreover, their use of Irish, which they call 'Ulster Gaelic', is an affirmation of their historical claim to the Region. (It may also be a matter of not letting the devil have all the good tunes!) In the past some republicans manipulated the language in an equally political fashion. For some of them Irish is an attestation of difference from the British and similarity with the Irish speakers in the Republic of Ireland.

Some unionist academics encourage loyalists to conceive of Northern Irish place-lore as an essential element of a British Celtic heritage. 'No cultured person in Northern Ireland ought to be ignorant of the linguistic influences – in place-names, in figures of speech – of their own land' (Aughey 1995a: 15). While, generally speaking, loyalists set their discourse of Celticity in opposition to that of nationalists, they occasionally speak of the Celtic tradition as being common to all and loyalist journals remind readers that the evolution of placenames is a central element of a common, albeit British, Celtic heritage (it is interesting in this context that English is defined as part of the Celtic heritage): 'Yet Irish is just as much a part of our common British heritage as Welsh, Scots Gaelic, Manx, Cornish, Breton and of course English. Many Ulster towns have names taken from Gaelic–Ballymena, Straid and Belfast to name but a few. Irish and Scots Gaelic only really separated in the Sixteenth Century (*Ulster Nation* 2 (3) 1991: 1).

Many loyalists viewed the opening of the Interpretative Centre at Navan Fort as an affirmation of a common Celtic tradition in Northern

Ireland. In one journal it was noted that the Centre demonstrated that loyalist 'history and culture pre-dates the religious, cultural and ideological arguments so crudely abused by the "culture vultures", who claim our [loyalist] heritage as their [Gaelic] exclusive property'. The writer maintains that this 'heritage belongs to everyone in Ulster today, and it should not be abandoned by the loyalist tradition or allowed to be hijacked by republicans for propaganda purposes' (*New Ulster Defender* 1994, in Lambkin 1994: 282). Loyalists are particularly keen to reinforce the fact that they have a common claim to this Celtic heritage. 'For hundreds of years the Gael has stolen our heritage and because they claimed it for their own we refused to identify ourselves with it' (Alexander 1985: 9).

Negation of the discourse

While nationalists may find the loyalist reclamation of a Celtic tradition formidable, both groups may be disturbed by challenges to the discourse at the wider level of the British Isles and particularly from archaeologists in England. The focus of contemporary argument seems to have shifted from the question of when various groups disembarked to the issue of whether any Celts arrived at all! Some archaeologists believe that the actual numbers of Celts who migrated to the British Isles were minute and barely discernible. A variety of immobilisation theories assumes that prehistoric groups were generally static and infer that perhaps only traders moved. Renfrew (1987), for example, attempted to combine trends in language studies and archaeology when he proposed that Celtic languages spread with the development of new methods of farming, and the movement of agricultural populations across Europe. His 'wave of advance model' implies that the Celtic languages of Europe developed in mutual contact with one another from an early date, and that there was no original central Celtic homeland.

Such revisions imply that the spread of Celtic influences to Ireland was not necessarily a consequence of any physical movement. Chapman (1992) claims that as Celtic languages, fashions, and styles of craftsmanship gained popularity, non-Celtic peoples may have adopted them. He asserts that one should give credence to the 'possibility that what was moving across the map were names and fashions, not people at all' (1992: 43–4). This idea is supported by James (1999: 99) who states 'that it was mainly ideas and ideologies – religious, socio-political, material – that were moving, rather than people'. Such proposals do not entirely preclude some minor demographic changes, but they do eliminate them as prerequisites for change.

Part of the problem appears to lie in our conception of primitive peoples. Prehistoric societies were construed as being culturally homogenous and severely deficient in logic and reason. It was often presumed that ancient society was childlike, responding primarily to nature and society. Anthropologists, such as Malinowski, postulated that prehistoric communities were motivated chiefly by the primal needs for food and sex, while Lévy-Bruhl (1975) believed that primitive peoples were governed principally by emotions. Such simple tribes were surely incapable of any self-advancement. New innovations presupposed migration. Changes were a consequence of exposure to new or 'higher' civilisations and could not be explained from within. Of course, these theories fail to explain the existence of any higher civilisations.

It is more commonly accepted now that empirical societies were in some sense socially stratified and displayed some cultural diversity (Leach, 1982). Variations in language, dress, and food patterns were often the norm and, as is the case today, there was probably no clear delineation between one cultural group and another. Differences within societies may have prompted innovations and improvements. Some archaeologists have proposed that a natural desire to improve one's physical environment may have paved the path of progress from the Bronze to the Iron Age (James 1999). Perhaps these advances could have occurred without the influx of significant numbers of a new tribe.

How do such theories relate to a Celtic theory of ethnogenesis? Some academics argue that the migration of large numbers of Celts to Ireland is, in fact, an implausible theory. Aware of the offence that such an opinion may cause, Raftery (1994) intimated that it was almost tantamount to heresy to postulate that Ireland had never been invaded by the Celts. Yet James (1999) argues precisely this case suggesting that the Celtic invasions in Ireland never actually occurred. He suggests that 'the early peoples of the archipelago, then, were overwhelmingly of local Bronze Age origin, not invaders from the continental homeland of the "real" Celts in Gaul. They were actually very diverse, and the physical remains of many communities do not correspond with the standard model of a "Celtic society"'. In his opinion early British and Irish society was diverse and complex. 'We cannot even discern a distinctive common "Britishness" or "Irishness": rather, some groups in each island were in contact with, and influencing, each other while, especially in the late Iron Age, some southern and eastern British groups were sharing more and more in common with Gauls'.

If true, the implications of this hypothesis are that the concept of the 'ancient British' or 'ancient Irish' as a culturally unified and distinct people is no longer tenable, although few would give credence to such concepts in any instance. In the case of Northern Ireland, this hypothesis implies that the two traditions paradigm is not the natural consequence of an ancient state of affairs but is an artificial construction belonging to a later stage of history. Of course, even if two separate traditions coexisted in the Iron Age, it is reasonable to assume that they only acquired an awareness of their own identity when confronted with foreign people. In the case of Northern Ireland this could have occurred during the Viking invasions and settlements. Yet even then, a vague awareness of one's own identity would not necessarily have generated homogeneity throughout the country.

Obviously those who endorse the existence of historical Celts have reacted vigorously to these theories and some have set these arguments in a political context. According to Siân Jones (1997: 142), 'the critical scrutiny of a minority group's identity and history by the dominant society rather than vice versa' is unacceptable in that it ultimately perpetuates hierarchical relations between the communities. Megaw and Megaw (1999: 47) have connected the denial of past Celtic identity with English dominance suggesting that such archaeologists 'are participants in the redefining and restating and extending backwards of a traditional English identity, by laying claim to ethnic, even racial, continuity for the English'. They propose further sinister reasons for the negation of this Celtic discourse relating it to recession and 'government pressures on tertiary institutions', all of which apparently make it imperative for English archaeologists to assert English primacy over the Celts!

While some newspapers have exaggerated such political points with provocative headlines as 'Irish Eyes are English not Celtic' (*The Sunday Times,* 14 November 1999: 8), I agree with Sims-Williams (1998: 5) who writes that English archaeologists are hardly motivated by endeavours for political advantage. In any case, scepticism regarding the historical existence of the Celts is not necessarily confined to English archaeologists and there is a vague suspicion even in Celtic regions that 'pan-Celticism is as much of a foreign creation as the Union or the French Republic' (Sims-Williams 1998: 5). Moreover, I believe that in the present context, historical facts regarding the arrivals of the Celts are irrelevant. My concern is with the significance and interpretation of this discourse rather than its historical accuracy.

But there is a problem with this entire discourse of Celticity – that is its link with racial discourse. It is not totally surprising that the Celts were often viewed in distinctly racial terms, as the racialisation of the Celts was prominent in nineteenth-century Britain. Celts themselves in the eighteenth century had emphasised their difference from the Anglo-Saxons. Breton history had emphasised the migration of British Celts to Aremorica in order to affirm their physical separateness from the Gauls. Over time the meanings of 'Celt' and that of 'race' as discursive concepts have changed and the representation of the Celts as different led, during the dictatorship of Franco (1939–75), to the conception of Celts as the primary racial group of Spain. In this instance such a strategy was designed to strengthen national identity and to affirm the unity of the Spanish nation from 'Celtic times' (Zapatero 1996).

Celticity in Northern Ireland is frequently associated with fragmentation rather than unity. As nationalist groups have clearly indicated their preference of withdrawal from the UK, there is an unfounded concern that some groups might use the discourse of Celticity to promote violence (Megaw and Megaw 1999: 44). When contemporary Celts engage in oppositional relationships, they frequently acquire the moral advantage by adopting, whether accurately or inaccurately, a discourse of disadvantage. According to McDonald (1989), this permits them to feel exempt from moral responsibility for their own violence. Chapman (1992: 253) was concerned that it might 'provide a place in world opinion for the IRA and the protestant paramilitary groups, casting a curious glamour upon the former and vulgarising and debasing the latter in contrast'. However, since both loyalists and nationalists lay claim to a Celtic heritage, I believe, its promotion would not necessarily benefit either.

Since the endorsement of the GFA, there has been a significant reduction in terrorist activities in Northern Ireland and the concerns of Collis and Chapman may no longer apply. But I have no doubt that the Celtic narrative has implications for warfare generally. Celts have traditionally been viewed as an heroic society and there are numerous classical and Irish portrayals of warriors who were skilled in battles and superb duellists. Such champions were particularly disdainful of death – a fact that may be related to the Celtic belief in the otherworld. Death was not to be feared, as it simply heralded the beginning of a new era. Violence has long prevailed in Northern Ireland, and some murals depict current leaders as the contemporary reincarnation of ancient Celtic warriors. In particular, the character of Cú Chulainn has proved relevant for the IRA and the UDA, although the latter propose that this hero was a Cruthin rather than a Celt. Many Hollywood films produced in the past decade, such as *Braveheart*, *Rob Roy* and *Michael Collins*, have further reinforced the image of Celts as romantic fearless warriors who are not easily defeated.

The horrors of Nazism and eugenics, and the decline of fascism have ensured that discourses of race have been discredited (Miles 1989). Moreover, there is a greater awareness that the concept of race does not exist outside of representation. Instead, it is formed in and by representation, usually in the context of political and/or social power struggles. Modern Celts in Northern Ireland often appeal to ideological, rather than biological differences. Although some contemporary militants speak in 'racial' terms, there is a general awareness that it is neither analytically nor politically correct to do so. While many nations claim an ethnic base, they are not necessarily speaking in genetic terms. Balibar (1991) has applied the term 'fictive ethnicity' to the community or group that is instituted by the nation-state. He believes that no nation possesses a natural ethnic base. Instead, social formations become nationalised and the populations within them are ethnicised. These are then represented in the past or in the future as if they formed a natural community, possessing its own unique identity of origins, culture, and interests (Balibar 1991: 96).

Conclusion

As society changes, symbols are invested with new meaning. Whereas the term 'Celtic' may have particular resonances in Northern Ireland, its implications elsewhere may be entirely different or may have no significance at all. A 'map of meaning' or 'web of significance' has a variety of functions but essentially it provides people with a framework, allowing them to make sense of reality. Northern Irish traditions are often interpreted as wholly distinct, fixed entities that are competing with one another. Yet an exploration of the Celtic dimension illustrates that the heritage of the Region is often shared and sometimes divided. Rapid changes over the last two decades have resulted in the redefinition, reclamation, and re-assertion of various elements of the cultural life of Northern Ireland. A renewed interest in the Celtic tradition is a natural consequence of these changes (Deacon and Payton 1993).

CHAPTER 5

THE PROCESS OF 'CRUTHINITUDE'

But an outline of a general theory of power and violence cannot ignore the fact that the fiercest struggles often take place between individuals, groups, and communities that differ very little—or between which the differences have greatly diminished.

(Blok 1998: 33)

In this chapter I review the emergence of an Ulster-Scottish cultural identity, which is sometimes viewed as an alternative to that of the Celt. The renaissance of Ulster-Scots culture at the end of last millennium has generated its own myth of ethnic descent. 'No aspirant ethnic group can be without its myth of ethnic descent, if it is to secure any recognition from its competitors' (Smith A. 1999: 60). Frequently such myths have become 'a charter for revolution, for turning established arrangements upside-down, and creating new political communities' on the basis of a feeling of commonality that is largely derived from historic memories and a myth of common descent (ibid. 1999: 61). Ulster-Scots culture is not merely confined to the emergence of the myth of the Cruthin, but is expressed in various ways in contemporary Northern Ireland.

Scottish theory of ethnogenesis

As with the Celts, the loyalist theory of ethnogenesis resorts to the Book of Conquests and proposes that the original invaders, described as Parthalons, are in fact the Pretani or the tribe of the Cruthin. Greeks used the term Pretani (proto-Pictish) for Northern peoples prior to the Celtic era (e.g. Adamson 1991b). This hypothesis implies that the Cruthin were a distinct, pagan group who spoke an ancestral pre-Celtic tongue and were largely uninfluenced by the Celtic culture that would later dominate Irish society. Apparently, the Cruthin were a substantial tribe whose territory consisted of most of the counties of Antrim and Down and also extended from Loch Foyle to Dundalk Bay. After the final defeat of their king in the Battle of Moira, 637 AD, they migrated to Lowland Scotland (Adamson 1995; 1991a; Hall 1994; 1995).

Proponents of the Cruthin theory of ethnogenesis are essentially generating a new tradition or a new fund of cultural symbols in Northern Ireland. As part of establishing a distinct Ulster-Scottish identity, they are inventing a new combination of motifs, designed to enhance their own cultural repertoire and lessen the significance of cultural symbols of nationalists. In one sense this process of innovation is designed in a spirit of emulation of nationalists whose ancestors are deemed to constitute some of the earliest inhabitants of Northern Ireland. Ulster-Scots groups are involved in a process of mutual identification. They are making claims to equality with, if not superiority over nationalists, and augmenting their own share of the cultural pool (Harrison 1995: 269). As yet the Cruthin theory of ethnogenesis has failed to attract large numbers of supporters.

Scholars question the difference between the Cruthin and the Gaels and attack this theory at many levels. Archaeologists dispute their pre-Indo-European origins and point to the fact that there is no archaeological evidence to suggest that the Cruthin were an ethnically distinct group. The region in Northern Ireland where they have been deemed to survive is as culturally mixed as any other (Mallory and McNeill 1991). At a more general level it could be argued that the Cruthin theory of ethnogenesis, like that of the Celts, ignores the nature of mythology. As with the Celts, the principal problem with this interpretation of the Book of Conquests is that it applies analytical reasoning to primitive and essentially 'wild' thinking. Its proponents are applying Cartesian logic to metaphorical thought as they are reviewing a myth analytically and examining each invasion separately in order to arrive at an understanding of Ulster's prehistory. But early Irish mythology did not aim to provide a detailed account of history. Its overriding concern was to establish, by the shortest means possible, a total understanding of Irish prehistory. It never intended to verify historical fact.

This theory of ethnogenesis gives primacy to Ulster-Scots traditions and challenges the assumption that the ancient culture of Ireland is solely, or primarily, Gaelic. Its particular relevance is that it implies that the Cruthin arrived in Ulster prior to the Gaels. 'Ethnic myths are vital "evidence" for territorial "title-deeds" . . . for a recognised "home-land" ' (Smith A. 1999: 69). From a loyalist perspective it establishes an identifiable, pre-Indo-European Cruthin tribe as the original inhabitants in Ulster. Following their migration to Scotland in the seventh century the descendants of the Cruthin returned a thousand years later during the Plantation of Ulster (Day and McWilliams 1991). According to this myth, contemporary Ulster-Scots are descendants of non-Celtic peoples, living in tracts formerly possessed by their ancestors. They cannot be regarded as Outsiders.

Furthermore, the Irish with their Gaelic heritage can no longer reasonably claim to be indigenous to the Region. In fact this theory proposes that many of those who purport to be Irish are really themselves descendants of the Cruthin. This view is endorsed in the publications of the Ulster Heritage Agency (1991: 13), which affirms that 'once down the road of Cultural enlightenment the clouds of time dispel to reveal an ancient people – The Cruthin (Pretani). A people who have suffered for thousands of years at the hand of successive invaders. The most successful being the Gael who to this present day continues to enforce its will on the ancient people of Ulster.' Such a view suggests that unionists have been misled by the pseudo-history of the Gael and that the true facts have been obscured by the false claims of the Gaels. It proposes that even the modern Gaels are descendants of the Cruthin:

> The ancient people of Ulster – the Cruthin – began a migration to Lowland Scotland after their defeat at the hands of the Gaels at the battle of Moira in 637 AD. The Lowland Scots who migrated to Ulster in the seventeenth century came from precisely those areas inhabited by the Cruthin. In short the lowland Scots are the descendants of the Cruthin. Also of the ancient Cruthin are those who remained in Ulster after 637 AD and were absorbed by the invading Gaels.
>
> (Hume, D. 1986: 12)

The claim of some Ulster-Scots to be descendants of the original occupants of Ulster can be compared in some ways with that of the Serbs who maintain that the territory of Kosovo originally belonged to them. Serbs suggest that from the seventeenth century onwards, Albanians immigrated in a series of waves to Kosovo and gradually outnumbered the original inhabitants (Eide 1996). Biberaj (1993) rejects this theory of movement, arguing that it is highly improbable that significantly large numbers would emerge from a country as underpopulated as Albania. Such propositions are also condemned by Albanians themselves who maintain that they are descendants of the Illyrians who lived in the territory prior to the arrival of Serbs and other Slavs from northern Europe.

The concept of return has been extremely important for a variety of other cultures and the desire of a community to return to its homeland is identified with groups such as Armenians, Black Africans, Greeks, Jews, and many post-Soviet groups. Adamantios Korais, a Greek educator, argued that the concept of return must be understood in a physical and spiritual manner. It involves both the actual recovery of an ancestral homeland and a spiritual regeneration of identity (Smith 1992). Supporters of the Cruthin theory would argue that the revitalisation of certain emblems of Scottishness in Northern Ireland could be interpreted as the part of the process of return.

Cú Chulainn: Cruthin or Celt?

In the last chapter, I referred to the fact that the character of Cú Chulainn provides the classic example of a proprietary contest over symbols in Northern Ireland as the Ulster-Scottish theory of ethnogenesis appropriates him to the Cruthin (Buckley 1989; 1991). This appropriation is significant in that Cú Chulainn is a sacred emblem of Northern Irish nationalist culture and has figured centrally in many nationalist murals. A painting executed in 1988 in Belfast depicted the dying Cú Chulainn surrounded by etchings of heroes who had signed the proclamation of Irish independence in 1916. A further mural erected in Armagh in 1991 displayed the hero on a background of a map of Ireland, surrounded by shields of the four provinces and other symbols of Irish nationalism, such as the wolfhound and the Irish harp. Although the triangular harp is primarily regarded as a symbol of Ireland, it was originally recorded on Scottish stone crosses in the eighth century and only appeared in an Irish context three centuries later (Loftus 1994). Such murals emphasise the link between the growth of the Gaelic ideal at the turn of the twentieth century and the separatist rising in 1916, which had introduced a new strand into Irish nationalist thought – that 'of the warrior-prince, Cúchulainn, valiant, noble, and willing to sacrifice himself for his people – and for eternal fame and glory' (Boyce 1996a: 170).

According to the loyalist interpretation of the *Táin Bó Cuailgne* or the Cattle Raid of Cooley, the most celebrated saga of Irish nationalist culture, Cú Chulainn fought against, rather than for the Gaels. Cú Chulainn, who has for centuries represented the heroic ideal of the native Irish, is now portrayed as shedding his lifeblood defending the Cruthin while preventing Gaels from entering Ulster. Proponents of the non-Celtic character of Cú Chulainn point to a tradition which reports that the hero was a member of the Tuath Tabhairn, a non-Gaelic tribe. They also point out that this warrior was exempt from the sleeping sickness of Ulstermen, who had been cursed to experience the pangs of childbirth in times of danger. According to the Ulster-Scots, the curse did not apply to Cú Chulainn simply because he was not an Ulster Gael. This anomaly is explained by the Celtic tradition with reference to the youthful age of the warrior. Cú Chulainn was excluded, as he had not yet fully matured.

Supporters of the Cruthin theory refer to the physical characteristics of Cú Chulainn as further evidence that he was not a member of a Gaelic tribe. According to this theory the Celtic physique was generally regarded as tall, with long flowing hair, whereas Cú Chulainn is described as rather short in stature with dark cropped hair. These physical attributes may have been more indicative of the pre-Celtic inhabitants of Ireland. But references to such biological characteristics cannot be regarded as valid as the previous chapter has established our lack of knowledge regarding the physique and other traits of the Celts.

Some Ulster-Scots speculate that the tract on which the *Táin Bó Cuailgne*, the Cattle Raid of Cooley, was fought was the plain of Muirthemne – a designated Cruthin territory. This view is supported by Rhys (1990) who explains that the epic tale recounts the manner in which Queen Maeve marched past Slieve Gualann (County Armagh) and raided Dunseverick (near the Giant's Causeway) in her approach on the Uliad and the Cruthin. Rhys suggests that the epic implies that one, or perhaps both, of these localities were Cruthin territories. If the epic originated in a distinct Cruthin territory it would probably laud a Cruthin, rather than a Celtic hero. However, the distinctive non-Gaelic nature of the Cruthin tribe is a controversial issue and its significance is questionable.

Perhaps its authenticity is irrelevant. Weber (1978) proposes that this kind of belief in a common ancestry is far more likely to be a consequence rather than a catalyst of collective actions. Because people act together in some way they come to regard themselves as belonging together. Whether there is any objective basis for the hypothesis of belonging together is immaterial but the subjective belief in kinship is highly significant for the reinforcement of the group. The efficacy of any myth of origin depends upon the belief in it. However, the extent to which the contemporary community gives credence to the hero of Cú Chulainn or the Cruthin hypothesis is debatable.

It appears that the narrative has had a certain impact on views espoused by the Ulster Defence Association (UDA) and stories regarding Cú Chulainn have appeared regularly in its monthly edition, *Ulster* (McAuley 1995). Paulin (1986: 13) suggests that the interpretation and appeal of this myth is a 'significant influence on the UDA's Ulster nationalism and forms an influential part of that organisation's hostility to the British state'. Finlayson (1996) recounts the manner in which John McMichael, the now deceased head of the UDA, displayed maps of the prehistoric Cruthin Ulster in his headquarters and argues that its influence is potent. He feels that the myth is part of a discourse that informs Protestants that they are different and that they should take pride in their unique heritage. It also offers a discourse of opposition to the Celts.

At a more general level some commentators propose that the hypothesis is merely a propaganda exercise designed to incite loyalist sentiment. In a particularly virulent attack on this narrative, Morgan (original emphasis in 1993: 36) suggests that the claim:

> answers the deep-seated needs of the Protestant community – it gives that community a claim to be native so that no one can upbraid them with the term 'colonist': it actually asserts an original claim *prior* to the Gaelic one. It gives Ulster Protestants in the story of the Cruthin, going to and then returning from Britain, a continuing link with 'the mainland'. It also underwrites their claim that Ulster is culturally distinct from the rest of Ireland by claiming that it always has been. Basically, Adamson has concocted an origin-myth for the Protestants of Ulster and trumped up Cú Chulainn as their earliest hero.

The same author suggests that the Irish have similarly used the Cattle Raid of Cooley for propaganda purposes. He notes that in the Middle Ages the O'Neills referred to the saga to support their claim to provincial supremacy. Their poets applauded the O'Neill chieftains with particular reference to Cú Chulainn, Conchobar, and the knights of red branch. From this perspective Ulster-Scots are merely repeating a pattern of desecration that was formerly practised by the Irish.

Adamson, one of the principal proponents of this thesis, rejects such a claim and denies that his theory gives credence to the idea of a 'Protestant Ascendancy'. In cultural terms this assertion of superiority reflects itself in the form of a 'we were here first' mentality. Adamson's view (1991a: xiii) is that he has endeavoured to promote a theme of common identity among the Protestant community, which many members are keen to share with Catholics. He advocates 'the complete expression of the native Ulster tradition, broader than Irish Protestantism and Catholicism, and populist in sentiment'. His conciliatory stance has not been widely accepted (Kockel 1999b), but this is hardly surprising as the Cruthin myth of origin reinforces historical antagonism. The fact that it results in difference rather than unity between unionists and nationalists can probably be regarded as a reflection of contemporary reality.

Overall it appears that the general unionist community has never widely accepted the myth of origin (Rolston 1995). This is almost certainly the case among middle-class unionists and adherents of the civic dimensions of unionist ideology, which I explore in Chapter 8. The symbolic value of the character is far more likely to appeal to loyalists and those minorities who advocate an independent Northern Ireland. According to Harkness (1990), contemporary loyalists are acting in a similar fashion to nationalists. Just as the Irish community developed the theory of Celts in the nineteenth century, loyalists generated the Cruthin hypothesis in the twentieth. 'Today we seem to be witnessing the process of Cruthinitude: understandable, perhaps, but lamentable if it implies yet another exclusive club for the chosen few, and equally dependent upon ancient mythology to bolster present insecurity' (Harkness 1990: 48–9).

Bruce (1992: 235–6) speculates that the fact that the Cruthin draws on traditional Irish sources is a source of discomfort for many unionists who would prefer a Protestant version of history that would disassociate itself entirely from any reference to Celtic mythology. Any such narrative would have to rely largely on invention as it is not possible to distinguish entirely separate histories for Northern Irish Protestants and Catholics. The two groups are merely reconstructing aspects of a history that can be viewed through different lenses. Although this past can be construed in different ways it cannot be entirely fabricated. It is constrained by certain facts of history that must be incorporated into the narrative.

A shared narrative

Although there is strong disagreement regarding the Cruthin/Celtic traditions, there is no doubt that Scotland and Ireland have had many points of contact from early times. Archaeologists often speak of these regions as forming a 'culture-province', as the sea operated as a unifying, rather than a divisive, factor (Hall 1993: 15). Trevor-Roper (1983: 15) suggests that in earlier centuries the Highlands constituted a *de facto* colony of Ireland:

> Before the late years of the seventeenth century, the Highlanders of Scotland did not form a distinct people. They were simply the overflow of Ireland. On that broken and inhospitable coast, in that archipelago of islands large and small, the sea unites rather than divides and from the late fifth century, when the Scots of Ulster landed in Argyll, until the mid-eighteenth century, when it was 'opened up' after the Jacobite revolts, the West of Scotland, cut off by mountains from the East, was always linked rather to Ireland than to the Saxon Lowlands. Racially and culturally, it was a colony of Ireland.

The Romans used the term Scotia to describe fifth-century Irish raiders to Scotland. According to Tranter (1987), these migrants called themselves Scots as they believed they were descendants of Scota, a pharaoh's daughter who had eloped with a Celtic prince to Ireland, carrying with her Jacob's pillow of stone, which later became the Stone of Destiny, on which Scottish kings were crowned. This is possibly a modern myth masquerading as an ancient one although Evans (2000) claims to have used mythological, archaeological, linguistic, and DNA evidence to argue that Irish and English descended from the Egyptians! Early Irish settlers in Scotland were Gaelic speakers and the language spread throughout the territories of Scotland, further enhancing the link with Ulster (Hall 1993).

One of the more remarkable of these Scoti was the Irish saint Columba whose legacy for Celtic Christianity in Scotland has been well documented (e.g. Bradley 1996; Devine and McMillan 1999; Herbert 1988; Lacey 1997; Mari MacArthur 1995; Whitside 1997). Following a quarrel regarding the copying of a manuscript, Columba arrived in north-west Britain in 563. He established his church on Iona, an island that was divided by a disputed border between Dalriada and Pictdom. The frontier on Iona was marked by a cairn that was known as *Cul Ri Alba* (back to Alba). Ownership of the entire island was also the subject of controversy. In the early Irish annals, Tigernach wrote that the Scottish (Irish) king Conall had bequeathed the island to Columba, whereas the Venerable Bede maintained that it belonged to the realm of Britain (Williams 1997). In this sense the island could be regarded as symbolic of contemporary Northern Ireland as both Irish and British have, at different times, laid claim to it. Columba's influence in Scotland was immense but when his monastery on Iona later became the target of Viking raids, many of the gospels, vessels, and other treasures were carried to Ireland for safe-keeping, indicating that the church in Ireland, rather than Scotland, was still perceived as the mother-church.

The relationship between the Scottish and the Irish continued over the centuries and in May 1316, the Scottish Edward Bruce, brother of Robert, was crowned King of Ireland in the presence of a large gathering of Scottish and Irish noblemen. His death in 1318 halted any Scottish invasion of Ireland and 'the attempt to create a kingdom of Ireland and drive out the settlers came to an end' (Lydon 1967: 153). But as I noted in the previous chapter, Irish clan chiefs continued to hire fierce Scottish mercenaries, known as Gallowglasses, from the thirteenth to the sixteenth centuries (Perceval-Maxwell 1973: 2). These Gaelic speaking soldiers were in particular demand in Ulster and ensured a strong, though fluctuating, Highland Scottish presence in the Region prior to the Plantation. For many centuries 'Gaelic Scotland shared the form and matter of its literary and cultural life with Ireland; the sea was less of an obstacle to communication than the land, and the whole Gaelic world formed one cultural unit with a common literary language, and with a mobile literary class to spread its standards and maintain a remarkable degree of linguistic uniformity over so large an area' (Thomson 1977: 127).

Opposing Scottish traditions

In 1607, Sir Arthur Chichester had suggested to King James VI and I that Scots be brought to Ulster as part of the Plantation. Although this could be interpreted as an attempt to flatter the then Scottish king, it is more likely that Chichester hoped it would alleviate England of some of the burdens of ruling the Scots as he had spoken of Scotland and Ireland as 'weaklynges' suckling at England (Perceval-Maxwell 1973: 77). King James decided that the Scots would benefit from the Plantation and by 1611 some 59 Scots had acquired 81,000 acres. Donegal and Tyrone were given almost entirely to them, though some were also planted in Fermanagh and Cavan. Down was also the destination of Scots brought by Hugh Montgomery and James Hamilton (Robinson 1988).

Many of the English servitors viewed themselves as being in competition with the Scots and were incensed at the allocation of land to them. English and Scots represented differing traditions. English money and manpower had supported the Crown's suppression of rebellion in Ulster and the servitors felt 'they had been cheated of their rightful rewards as conquerors' (McCavitt 1994: 31). It is probable that Celtic and Lowland Scots also regarded themselves in terms of opposing traditions as the Reformation had intensified differences between them (Perceval-Maxwell 1973). While Highlanders retained their oral traditions, Lowlanders, with their Puritan emphasis on Bible reading, had become highly literate. Highlanders were loyal to their Clan chiefs whereas Lowlanders were devoted to their religious persuasions. Although the Scots language of Lowlanders was the subject of derision it had not been the subject of discriminatory legislation. The Statutes of Icolmkill issued in Scotland in 1609 had banned the patronage of Gaelic bards and had intimated that *Inglis,* the language of the Lowlands, should become the sole language of Scotland. Highlander Gaelic had become identified with barbarity. It is probable the Highland Scots were far closer in culture and temperament to the Irish than to Lowlanders and that differences between the Scottish communities were as great if not greater than those between the Scottish and Irish.

In the previous chapter I explored the Celtic Highland traditions in Northern Ireland but of course many of the Scots who arrived during the Plantation were speakers of Lowland Scots. Herbison (1992: 55–6) notes that the 'Scots brought with them the most distinctive and highly developed regional form of English. *Inglis,* as they called it ... was derived from the Northumbrian dialect of Old English ... It possessed many of the distinguishing characteristics of a separate national language ... not only in pronunciation, but also in orthography, vocabulary and syntax.' The precise difference between Scots and English, both then and now, remains a matter for some debate. McClure (1981: 59) has argued that 'Scots and English, like many pairs of tongues then and since, exhibited that degree of similarity which makes it possible to *assert* either an essential identity or an essential distinctiveness, but to *assume* neither' (original emphasis). Buchanan (1982) has proposed that the differences between the two languages would have inhibited relations between the English and Scottish immigrants. Indeed, in 1624 an extra Clerk of the Council was appointed to deal with the requests from Scotsmen in Ireland. His function was to deal with the Scots correspondence from Ulster (Robinson 1989). Not all of the planters were speakers of Scots. As noted in previous chapter, some were also speakers of Scottish Gaelic, although the proportion remains a matter for debate (Heslinga 1962; Hill 1993; Rushe 1921).

Despite an ambitious plan for the segregation of the Irish, it proved impossible to achieve and the integration and assimilation of the Irish and Scottish communities soon proved a matter of angst. State officials were concerned that the Scots and Irish would merge to constitute a force that would eventually oppose the English. In June 1614 Lord Chichester received the following instructions:

> Being informed that divers of the undertakers, especially the Scottish, marry with the Irish, by which they will degenerate and in a short time become altogether Irish, His Majesty requires him to restrain all the undertakers from marrying with the Irish, and to call before him such as have already offended therein, and reprove them severely for the same until order may be taken for their further punishment.
>
> (Russell and Prendergast 1877: 482–3)

But the pattern of the Plantation was constantly modified and under-takers themselves were often responsible for changes. As a consequence of their persecution in the years between 1636 and 1639, many Presbyterian Ulster-Scots returned to the west of Scotland. A great proportion came back again to Ulster and remained until the introduction of penal laws in the eighteenth century resulted in their migration to America and Canada. The Diaspora was gradually to develop considerable interest in the char-acter of the Ulster-Scot, and Ulster emigrants founded the Scotch-Irish Society of America in 1889. Over a decade later the research and scholar-ship stimulated by this society resulted in *The Scotch-Irish or The Scot in North-Britain, North Ireland and North America* (1902) by Charles Hanna, a work that was welcomed in Northern Ireland.

Many literati attempted to depict the stereotypical Ulsterman at the turn of the century, and cultural constructions of the Ulster-Scot were often politically motivated. Hill, a librarian at Queen's College, conducted historical research which emphasised the role and achievements of the Scots in the Ulster Plantation. Harrison's *The Scot in Ulster* (1888) asserted the inalienable right of the Ulster-Scot to resist the demise of the Act of Union. Other new books produced at this time, including Woodburn's *The Ulster-Scot* (1914), gave prominence to the singularity of the Scots in Ulster and invoked their historical ties with Scotland. The archetypal fig-ure, which emerged from these books, was 'dour but hospitable, shrewd, self-reliant, steadfast and industrious, blunt of speech, and gifted with the capacity to govern less fortunate people' (McBride 1996: 7). This image or stereotype directly opposed that of the Catholic Irish who were assumed to be charming but unreliable, disorganised, and lazy. Unlike the plain-spoken Presbyterian, Catholics were suspiciously good at words but could not be trusted. Of course the Catholic Irish were also perceived as drunkards.

Presbyterianism and the covenantal mentality

Certain emblems of Scottishness are particularly relevant in contem-porary Northern Ireland. Many of these markers have originally been associated with Lowland, rather than Highland, Scottish identity. In Chap-ter 3 I outlined the introduction of Presbyterianism to seventeenth-century Ulster. Its ministers were primarily Scotsmen until the Williamite wars at the end of the century. Throughout the following century many from Ulster opted for the ministry, and of the 175 Presbyterian clerics in Ulster between the years 1691 and 1720, 129 were actually born in the Region (Gailey 1975). As they were denied entry to Trinity College, Dublin, they trained in their mother country and returned to serve the Ulster com-munity. (Presumably there would have been a definite preference for train-ing in Glasgow or Edinburgh anyway.)

A similar pattern applied to Presbyterians who wished to become lawyers or doctors. Many of these trained in Glasgow until higher education for Presbyterians became available in Belfast at the beginning of the nineteenth century. Culturally the influence of the Presbyterian Church was immense as it established that all members should be capable of reading the Bible for themselves. Its emphasis on literacy proved a catalyst for the emergence of an Ulster-Scots written tradition, particularly in Scottish settlements in Antrim and Down.

A continuing interaction with Scotland reinforced the covenantal mentality in Ulster, a phenomenon that originated with the sixteenth-century tradition of entering into groups or 'bands' for mutual protection. In Scotland the Kirk had embarked on such an arrangement in order to combat the anti-Presbyterian disposition of the Crown. Groups such as the National Covenant of 1638, established in opposition to the new prayer book, came to be viewed as a contract between God, the monarch, and the people (Miller 1978). Ulster's distinctive Presbyterian culture was particularly enhanced by the Home Rule crises at the turn of the twentieth century. As I noted in Chapter 2, a Scottish Presbyterian original of the late sixteenth century was the prototype for Ulster's Solemn League and Covenant, signed in 1912 by more than 400,000 Protestants. This action indicates that a covenantal culture was not the sole prerogative of the Ulster-Scot but applied to a large proportion of the British community.

Scottish culture in the Region has been particularly influenced by Presbyterianism, and Akenson (1992) suggests that this is still one of the primary components of Ulster-Scottish covenantal mentality. In his seminal study, Miller (1978) examined the mind-set of loyalists in Northern Ireland and concluded that many viewed themselves as virtuous people who are honourable in their dealings with government, but are frustrated when it appears that double standards are applied. In Presbyterian fashion, they resist an authority that has betrayed their trust (Alcock 1994). Their interpretation of loyalty is expressed in the form of a contract with the monarch, rather than the government. The king is their 'guarantee of Protestant liberties'. Having yielded some of their freedom to the Crown, the people 'receive back, under that guarantee, their full liberty of conscience, full petitionary access to the Throne, and the capacity to make their own laws subject to – and in partnership with – the crown' (De Paor 1990: 55–6). This principle has regularly been re-iterated in journals and booklets such as those of the Ulster Vanguard Publications which propose that:

> Ulster's loyalty is primarily to her Queen, and not to ministers or governments that fill in their duty to give loyal subjects the blessing of the Queen's Peace. It is no disloyalty to the Queen to refuse to accord to them a transferred loyalty they have not deserved. There are respectable British precedents for successful mutiny against ministers who have served the people as

badly as the loyal Ulster people have been served by Her Majesty's Government in recent years.

(*Ulster – A Nation*, April 1972: 7)

The extent to which contractarianism influences contemporary Northern Irish society is debatable and to some extent there appears to be confusion relating to the contractual partners. Northern Ireland maintains allegiance to the Crown but despairs when Westminster does not reciprocate this loyalty. In a revision of Miller's conclusions of 1978, Aughey (1991) proposes that it is the British government, rather than the loyalist in Northern Ireland, that has been conditionally loyal to the Union. From this perspective, if there is any crisis of conditionality in Northern Ireland, and many are keen to suggest that this is the case, it arises from an ambiguity on the part of Westminster, rather than the people of Northern Ireland. In this context devolution in Scotland and Wales raises some interesting questions and appears to have enhanced, rather than detracted from, the commitment of Westminster to the UK. Although part of the UK, Northern Ireland is not officially part of Britain. Loyalists are uncomfortable with any prospect of desertion by the British government.

This discomfort largely arises from the fact that despite their numerical superiority, many Ulster-Scots and those who perceive themselves as British generally fear their eventual engulfment by the Catholic population. In common with Afrikaners in the apartheid era, they defend the status quo on the basis of the discrimination that would occur, were alternative arrangements in place. All unionists are familiar with the predominance of Catholics in the Republic of Ireland (95 percent) and throughout the Island as a whole. They berate the Republic as a homogenous state that does not facilitate its Protestant minority. Yet, it was the very insistence of unionists on partition that more or less guaranteed that the Republic evolved as a hegemonic state. Had unionists chosen otherwise, the sheer numbers of Protestants would have ensured that they could not be ignored (Johnson 1990).

Unionist anxieties regarding Westminster and nationalists have led to them being construed as a 'double minority', and it is possible to detect similarities between the circumstances of the Quebecois and those of Northern Irish Protestants. Both communities have developed a 'siege' mentality and perceive themselves as surrounded by a foreign culture. Francophones make up a majority within the Canadian province of Quebec, yet they are conscious of the overwhelming prevalence of Anglophones in Canada and North America and constantly strive to reinforce symbols of French identity within their own province (Williams 1994).

Similarly, German language speakers who are a majority within the province of South Tyrol/Alto Adige, are reduced to minority status within the larger region of Trentino-Alto Adige, Italy. The fact that principal economic decisions have been entrusted to the regional, rather than the provincial level, reinforces their sense of disempowerment. Although control over cultural concerns, housing, and handicrafts is maintained at provincial level, regions retain legislative powers over matters relating to industry, forestry, and tourism. Consequentially, German speakers have a minor input into affairs of central economic significance. Moreover, ethnic Germans are cognisant of their proportionally marginal numbers within the state of Italy, thereby constituting a genuinely 'double minority', a term that 'has actual currency in the Italian case but merely potential currency in the Irish case' (McNamee 1986: 23).

Despite their siege mentality, loyalists and unionists are keen to affirm that any sense of total commitment has been eroded. After all, what government or state at the end of the twentieth century can be absolutely certain of the unqualified support of its citizens in all circumstances? Unconditional loyalty is a pre-modern ideology, which assumes that people are incapable of reflection or judgement. To presume that contemporary loyalists would remain unquestioningly loyal to Westminster, or even the Monarch, regardless of the actions of either, would be to infer that somehow they were a naïve people who are completely influenced by a sense of covenantal culture (Aughey 1991; Coulter 1994).

Not everyone agrees with this perspective and politicians, such as Enoch Powell, have argued that it is a contradiction in terms to express a desire to remain an integral part of the UK while refusing to co-operate with its laws. Powell (1989) suggested that the desire for citizenship implies respect and toleration of a state's laws. But it is sometimes more loyal to question rather than remain silent: 'the time might come when Ulstermen would have to become Queen's rebels in order to remain citizens of any kind' (Miller 1978: 1).

Although covenantal culture in Northern Ireland may have its roots in Scottish Presbyterianism, it has gradually influenced the British community at large. Contractarianism has become a feature of the Britishness, rather than the Scottishness of contemporary Northern Ireland. But I believe it is also more typical of the nationalist community than is generally realised. Perhaps Catholics or nationalists maintain a similar type of relationship with the Dublin government (Aughey 1991). Certain extreme groups have not recognised the referendum in the Republic renouncing the constitutional claim over the six counties. While citizens in the Irish Republic voted overwhelmingly in favour of the removal of the claim to the Northern counties, certain groups, such as the continuity IRA, refuse to accept anything less than a 32-county Éire. Extreme republicans have never approved of the legitimacy of the 26-county state and in that sense cannot maintain loyalty to a government they do not recognise (Cochrane 1997). To a certain extent, conditionality is a feature of all modern society but is perhaps visible in a more extreme form in the case of the Northern Irish population generally.

Glasgow Rangers football club

I noted in the previous chapter that football is not the only reason for the rivalry between Glasgow Rangers and Celtic. Fans of these two teams are divided by political as much as sporting allegiances. Rangers is a Protestant team whose identity is primarily anti-Catholic and anti-Irish. Its character has developed in opposition to Celtic. As a consequence it has been infused with some strong anti-Catholic and anti-Irish elements in Scottish society. Bradley (1995: 37–8) suggests that 'because of the over-riding anti or negative element in the club and its support, and as a reflection of much of the larger society's attitude towards the Catholic Irish in general, forthwith, Rangers football club were perceived by many people as being one of the most overt anti-Catholic institutions in society'.

Fans of both Rangers and Celtic regularly sing songs alluding to the violence in Northern Ireland. Both clubs have numerous fans and supporters clubs in the Region and their emblems are commonplace. For example, when ITV broadcast a series of programmes on the John Stalker affair, the initial street scenes portrayed children from east Belfast wearing the jerseys of Glasgow Rangers while playing football. These jerseys are commonly worn at matches featuring the Protestant Linfield FC. There is a great similarity between the main strips of the two clubs as both are blue with white trimmings. When, a number of years ago, the *Sunday Observer* featured 'The Life of Brian, a diary of violent [Loyalist] youth in Belfast', the tattoos, football jerseys, and posters of the FC formed a significant part of the photographic record (Bradley 1995).

As is the case with Celtic, Rangers FC has been linked with paramilitaries on a variety of occasions. For example, in 1991 a newspaper reported that the *Red Hand*, a Scottish magazine with links to the welfare association for loyalist prisoners in Northern Ireland and the Independent Orange lodge, was selling between four and five thousand copies at Glasgow Rangers and other loyalist matches (Bradley 1995). In March 1996 Jason Campbell, a Rangers supporter, was convicted of the murder of Mark Scott, a 16-years-old Celtic supporter, outside a pub in Glasgow's Bridgeton Cross. A year later the fringe loyalist Progressive Unionist Party (PUP) requested his transfer to a jail in Northern Ireland. Apparently the prisoner had close connections with Northern Ireland and had resided there at one stage. Moreover, both his father, Colin, and uncle, William, had strong association with loyalist paramilitaries, and according to the *Irish News* (26 September 1997), both were jailed in 1979 in connection with bombings in Glasgow and conspiring to further the aims of the UVF.

Controversies surrounding Glasgow Rangers have not been confined to the supporters, and in 1998, the FC was at the centre of quarrel when two of its players were accused of making sectarian signals on the playing field (*Irish News*, 11 January 1998). Following the murder of the loyalist leader Billy Wright in the Maze prison, the Rangers goalkeeper Andy Goram wore a black armband while playing a match against Celtic. Paul Gascoigne made a hand gesture which was interpreted by some spectators as playing a loyalist flute. When queries were raised, Gascoigne apologised for his actions but Goram stated that his armband was a symbol of mourning for an aunt who had died the previous October. This did not deter some fans from interpreting the black band as an emblem of grief for the loss of Billy Wright.

In May 1999 Rangers scored an important physical and psychological victory over Celtic, when they beat that FC on its own grounds. At the conclusion of the match, the Rangers team mimicked Celtic, when it performed an imitation huddle in front of its own supporters. As this gesture is normally associated with the Celtic team, Celtic fans interpreted Rangers actions as an insulting gesture. Large-scale violence erupted and continued for some time. Subsequently Ranger's vice-chairman, Donald Findlay, was reported as singing anti-Catholic anthems at a private party (*Daily Record* 31 May 1999) and was forced to resign. The irony of the match was that two of the goals scored on behalf of Rangers were kicked by one of their recently appointed Catholic players. For many decades Rangers had refused to select any Catholics to play for them but had lately reversed this rule. Of course their supporters, who regularly sing songs about 'Fenian scum', were delighted to cheer these Catholic players.

A lowland linguistic tradition

Northern Ireland's continuing interaction with Scotland has been enhanced with the revival of Ulster-Scots whose speakers are keen to establish that it belonged to the Region from very early times. In order to reinforce this point the tongue is linked to the Cruthin myth of origin. Scots is a Germanic language and there are some suggestions that the original language of the Cruthin may also have had Teutonic elements. Furthermore, Ulster-Scots speakers tentatively assume that the Frisian settlements in Dumfries from the fourth to the fifth centuries were paralleled on the Down coast, thereby enhancing the Teutonic influences on the Region (Ulster-Scots Language Society and Ulster-Scots Academy 1996). An affirmation of the early presence of a form of Ulster-Scots would confer upon it the quality of an indigenous language that would not only place it on a par with Irish but would also enhance its value as a discourse of belonging.

Native speakers usually refer to this symbol as 'Scotch' or the 'hamely tongue' (Fenton 1995) but it is sometimes called 'Ullans' by some modern writers, which could be interpreted as the Ulster rendition of Lowland Scots, occasionally designated as 'Lallans'. It could also infer that Ullans is the speech of those who belong to Uliad (Ulster). As a question on Ulster-Scots has not yet been included in the census there are no official estimates of the extent of this linguistic community, but the Ulster-Scots society proposes that approximately 100,000 people commonly speak the tongue, representing about 7 percent of the total population. Contemporary speakers of Ulster-Scots are keen to acknowledge its close association with Scots. Despite attempts to curtail the impoverishment of these vernaculars they are both being eroded by English and their validity as symbols of identity is undermined by several factors that are difficult to reverse.

The actual status and integrity of Ulster-Scots is controversial, as many linguists believe that its syntax and vocabulary are no longer sufficiently distinctive to justify conferring the status of a language on its current usage (Nic Craith 2001). Reaction from nationalist groups to Ulster-Scots is particularly vigorous with some commentators arguing that it is hardly a language at all. They insist that it is merely a dialect of Ulster English and is being promoted purely for political, even separatist, purposes. Of course it is also perceived as a threat to the state financial resources being made available to Irish. 'If the Irish language lobby received funding for anything, then the Ulster Scots lobby would demand equal funding for a similar project' (McVeigh 2000: 24). Accusations such as these place Ulster-Scots in a similar position to the Gallo language in Brittany, which is commonly perceived by the Breton community as 'hardly a proper language'. Instead it is viewed as merely a dialect of French that is 'getting in the way of Breton' (McDonald 1989: 141). This disputed status of the language is a problem, which is recognised by the speakers of the language, although they react with hostility to any suggestion that Ulster-Scots is hardly a 'proper' language.

Dissension regarding the status of Ulster-Scots occurs primarily because many speakers of English understand Ulster-Scots with little difficulty and the gap between English and Irish is far greater than that between English and Ulster-Scots. Ulster-Scots therefore fails to act as a boundary marker or a vehicle of exclusion. It is interesting that this places it in a similar position to Cant or Gammon, the language of Travellers (Binchy 1994; Meyer 1909; Ó Baoill 1994). Cant's similarity with English has ensured that few outside of the travelling people know of its existence. Travellers can use it freely to communicate because the casual observer very often does not realise that another language is being used. Travellers regard Cant's proximity with English as an asset, but in the case of Ulster-Scots, its similarity with English is perceived as a problem.

Conflicts regarding the status of a dialect or language always occur in circumstances where there is little difficulty with comprehension and the question of whether a particular form of communication is a language or a dialect is not unique to Ulster-Scots. One might suggest, for example, that there are only two Scandinavian languages: the Continental (Danish, Swedish, and two standard varieties of Norwegian) and the Insular (Icelandic, Faroese). As the Danes, Norwegians, and Swedes find aspects of their languages mutually intelligible, one might argue that their tongues are merely dialects of a single continental language. But other factors such as the independent and national status of these states have generated the acceptability of their tongues as separate and distinct languages.

The reverse situation is also prevalent. Very often languages that are not mutually intelligible, are identified as the same speech form for historical reasons. The Sámi language, for example, has three main dialects, which are mutually incomprehensible. Several hundred dialects of spoken Chinese are usually classified into eight main subgroups. Although the spoken languages are mutually incomprehensible, the written tradition is similar and it is possible for those who have acquired the Chinese system of characters to communicate with one another. Despite the extensive linguistic differences between the spoken dialects they are all classified as one language. The Ulster-Scots tongue is, therefore, experiencing a problem that is common to some of the major languages in the world.

Many speakers of Ulster-Scots still lack a sense of respect and esteem for their native tongue. Minority tongue groups commonly experience this sentiment of shame in one's indigenous language. McClure (1997: 22) suggests that the process of stigmatising Scots began in the eighteenth century and still continues. Several forces, such as schooling and parental conditioning, have combined to instil a sense of humiliation and embarrassment in the native speaker of Scots. As a result speakers of Ulster-Scots 'are somewhat ashamed or embarrassed at it, some regard it with a nostalgic or antiquarian interest, many at best feel a *local* pride in their Buchan or Border tongue; but a clear feeling that Scots could or should be developed as part of our national identity is not widespread in Scotland' (original emphasis).

A lack of pride in one's indigenous tongue is a typical feature of many colonised nations and is described by Memmi (1965) as the classic colonial syndrome. One might assume that a sense of humiliation in their own language would have eluded the Ulster-Scots, as they are descendants of the 'planters' rather than the 'planted'. In this sense their tongue is a particularly potent symbol of the strange double bind in which they find themselves. Although placed in a position that was considerably more advantageous than the Irish, the Scots were still regarded with condescension by the English.

Supporters of Ulster-Scots are contained primarily within the loyalist, rather than the entire British, community. This is not to imply that the language belongs solely to loyalists or is confined to these groups, but they are the primary endorsers of its relevance as a separate and distinct tradition. Although the tongue has a strong symbolic relevance for some loyalists, it appears to have little appeal for many civic unionists. This is not surprising as they claim that a focus is on citizenship rather than nationality, and regard an appreciation of culture as an obsession of nationalists, which I explore in Chapter 8.

Furthermore, many civic unionists might value the use of English as a potent symbol of their British (really English) tradition. From this perspective, the emergence of Ulster-Scots could possibly be perceived as belittling Ulster English and could enhance the sense of isolation from Westminster. Symbolically, the language emphasises the connection with Scotland rather than Britain. It reinforces the double identity of speakers of the language, as is exemplified in a verse penned in the eighteenth century by Samuel Thomson (original emphasis in 1992: 62):

> I love my native land, no doubt,
> Attach'd to her thro' thick and thin;
> Yet tho' I'm *Irish* all *without*,
> I'm every item *Scotch within*.

Public awareness of the Ulster-Scots language has increased considerably in recent years. This achievement can possibly be attributed to the efforts of the Ulster-Scots Language Society, Academy and Heritage Council, all of which have been formed in the past decade. At the level of local government Belfast City Council has passed a motion in appreciation of the linguistic and cultural diversity of the city. In June 1996 Ards Borough Council determined to erect bilingual streetsigns in the village of Greyabbey, an act which symbolically defines the local territory. A sign in Ulster-Scots welcomes visitors to the Ards distinct.

The language was used in the voting procedure at the first meeting of the Northern Irish Assembly in Stormont. Furthermore, a new cross-border implementation body for language has been established to cater to the Irish and Ulster-Scots speaking groups, although there are some suggestions that this actually embarrasses individual members of the UUP:

> Does the 'intellectually serious' Trimble believe in the Cruthin and Ulster-Scots? Some of his UU colleagues are embarrassed at the idea. Others buy the package. Trimble wrote in his December article that the cross-border body to work 'on Irish and Ulster Scots was our offer, and hopefully the new government of Northern Ireland will be genuinely culturally pluralist'. In the negotiations, some winced when Ulster-Scots appeared. Others, fingers crossed, hoped that it was no more than a ploy to 'hoist the Shinners on their own damned exploitation of Irish'.
>
> (O'Connor 1999a: 15)

At an international level the European Bureau of Lesser-Used Languages recently conferred the status of a distinct language on the Scots tongue in Scotland and has formally recognised Ulster-Scots as the Scots language in Northern Ireland, although there are some differences between the two. 'In all instances where there is some continuity of culture, there have nonetheless been transformations of old forms and the creation of new ones; mosques in the cane fields of Fiji will not be quite the same as mosques in India' (Fenton 1999: 23).

Caledonian connections

The revival of Lowland Scottish traditions has served as a means of raising the spirits within the Ulster-Scots community and building solidarity among its members. The symbolic and political relevance of Ulster-Scots is paramount to loyalists who speak it and regard it as a emblem of difference in contemporary Northern Ireland. Buckley (1989: 9) stresses this aspect of symbolism when he suggests that 'it is not the symbol so much as the historical narrative that is relevant to present realities. The symbol evokes the narrative, and it is the narrative which has significance for the present'.

Celtic sagas, such as the Ulster Cycle of Tales, continually emphasise the interaction between the Irish and Highland Scots. For example, the unique basalt columns at the Giant's Causeway in Antrim and in caves on the island of Staffa, off Scotland, are explained as a consequence of the interaction between the Irish giant, Fionn Mac Cumhail, and his Scottish counterpart, Finn Gall. According to these legends, the hero Cú Chulainn received his specialist knowledge in the art of combat from the renowned female warrior Scáthach, in the Isle of Skye. When Deirdre, the Irish version of Helen of Troy, fled with her lover and his brothers from Ireland, they found sanctuary in Scotland. Since the Celtic era there has been constant intermarriage and intermingling between groups on both sides of the North Channel.

Connections with Scotland are reinforced in a variety of other ways in contemporary Northern Ireland. For a long time the main breed of cattle in Ulster were Ayrshires (brown and white). Architecturally, a variety of buildings built in the late nineteenth-century reflect the link and several 'gentleman's seats' – Stormont Castle and Belfast Castle – were built in the Scottish baronial style. The Presbyterian General Assembly Building in Belfast is decidedly Scottish in style. Strong links exist between the Orange Lodges in Northern Ireland and in Scotland and many Northern Irish Orangemen journey to Scotland on the weekend before the 12th July to participate in parades held in the Strathclyde region. As a reciprocal gesture, several of their Scottish brethren return with them to take part in the commemorations in Northern Ireland. Furthermore the Black Preceptory of the Orange Order begins its marches with 'Scotland the Brave', although this tune is also known as 'Join the Parade'.

Emblems, such as murals, have a strong visual impact and some displays in the Protestant housing estates of Londonderry feature the Lion Rampant of Scotland and the flag of St Andrew. The Scottish Saltire frequently appears on loyalist murals and the flag is depicted on a mural in Belfast's Highland Drive referring to Ulster freedom fighters in the context of the flags of St Andrew and of Ulster. As part of its month-long celebration of Ulster-Scottish culture in Belfast in May 1999, four new murals appeared emphasising the continuing link between Northern Ireland and

Scotland. Many new books have been published emphasising the Scots Irish Diaspora (for example Hanna 2000; Kennedy 1995; 1996; 1997; McClelland 1994).

In some sense we are currently witnessing the invention of a new Ulster-Scot tradition. Hobsbawm (1983: 1) defines these inventions as 'a set of practices, normally governed by overtly or tacitly accepted rules and of a ritual or symbolic nature, which seek to inculcate certain values and norms of behaviour by repetition, which automatically implies continuity with the past'. Generally speaking such customs attempt to affirm continuity with an appropriate historic past. Very often these versions of history are factitious and represent new and novel responses to old situations. They commonly occur when a society has changed dramatically and seek to consolidate or establish a territorial claim. Many social patterns have been eroded in recent years and it is not surprising that Ulster-Scots groups have responded with the creation of an ancient past that may contain elements of fact and fiction. Such a tradition may generate social cohesion among a community and inculcate a belief in a cultural supremacy.

Trevor-Roper (1983) speculates that there were three stages in the creation of a Scottish Highland tradition. The first involved a cultural revolt against Ireland and the redrafting of early Scottish history. This mythology claimed that Ireland was a cultural dependency on Celtic Scotland. At the second stage of the process, Highland traditions, which were presented as ancient, unique, and singular, were artificially generated. Finally, these newly invented traditions were offered to and moulded by the historic Lowland Scots. Many American communities of Lowland Scots, Highland Scots, and Ulster-Scots ancestry are currently reinterpreting this same Highland tradition (Ray 1998). A variety of tartans and flags at Scottish heritage events combine to reclaim identities that were formerly suppressed.

'Celebrating the past and wanting to be in the past are vastly different phenomena' (Ray 1998: 43). Celebrations of Scottish heritage in America call for a return to the 'values' of ancestral times. In Northern Ireland, we are currently witnessing the recreation of the Scottish Lowland tradition. It is possible that the Highland tradition fails to attract broad support as it might be deemed to be too similar to Gaelic Irish traditions. But the Lowland tradition also has profound similarities with that of the Gaelic Irish. In many instances it has simply reversed the characters.

A similar reversal occurred in the epic ballads of Serbs and Albanians. In a fictional account of Albert Lord's trip to Albania in the 1930s, Ismail Kadare (1997: 101–2) noted of these groups that 'a ballad in one of the two languages is like an upside-down version of the same ballad in the other language: a magic mirror, making the hero of the one the anti-hero of the other, the black of the one, the white of the other, with all the emotions – bitterness, joy, victory, defeat – inverted to the very end'.

Conclusion

Loyalists propose a Cruthin myth of origin that refers, like the Celts, to the Book of Conquests. In common with the Gaels they claim that Ulster is their original homeland. Just as the Irish in the past have used the character of Cú Chulainn to bolster certain traditions, contemporary loyalists avail of this myth to reinforce a political point. A revival of Ulster-Scots has occurred at the same time as increasing numbers are becoming familiar with Irish. As with Irish, Ulster-Scots is offered to the community at large as an indigenous language that has been shaped by natives.

'Historically and sociologically such myths have emerged during periods of profound culture clash and accelerated economic and social change (Smith A. 1999: 83). The fact that there are competing myths is an indication of the failure to achieve social unity in Northern Ireland and – despite the GFA – of the persistence of old culture clashes and the emergence of new ones. While the incidents of violence have been reduced, there are now greater clashes at the level of culture and in many senses the opposition of the Cruthin and Celts could be regarded as the projection backwards of the two traditions paradigm.

Yet the reinterpretation of these Lowland traditions has not yet gained popularity across the general unionist or Northern Irish population although Scottish devolution may still have a profound impact on the appreciation of this tradition in Northern Ireland. Perhaps these traditions will always be viewed as a minority cult or a thin veneer, with their origins in a reaction to republicans who are seen as having too many of the good tunes and a more general postmodern dalliance with 'roots'. On the other hand, they may yet gain widespread popularity as an element of a tradition that is enjoyed not just by loyalists, but across all groups.

CHAPTER 6

AN UNCLAIMED TRADITION

The foreigner is within me, hence we are all foreigners.
(Kristeva 1991: 192)

While Celtic and Ulster-Scots traditions in Northern Ireland are frequently the source of competition and distrust, there appears to be little interest in the concept of Englishness. This is the tradition that does not say its name and English influences in Northern Ireland are not easily determined. Because of the sheer size and power of England in relation to Ireland, Scotland, and Wales, Englishness in one sense could be regarded as what is left in the British Isles when that which is specifically Irish, Scottish, and Welsh is accounted for!

It appears to me that Englishness constitutes not only the forgotten tradition in Northern Ireland, but also the unclaimed one. It seems that Northern Irish Protestants are happy enough to identify Scotland as a cousin nation, but relatively few are so explicit about England. Instead they identify with Britishness – or rather have done, for this is itself a more comfortable commodity the further one gets away from 1945 – Britain's high point. While English influences on the Irish have been quite strong over the centuries, few of them are eager to claim a share of the English cultural pool. In the minds of many, Englishness is still associated with imperialism and despite the Hibernification of many aspects of Englishness, such as the English language, there is little claim to ownership of this symbolic capital (Farren 1994).

In the context of Northern Ireland, there is some sense in which the English, as opposed to the British, are deemed to be outsiders. For example when the UU assemblyman, Duncan Shipley Dalton, commented on the Patten policing report (Independent Commission on Policing 1999), his colleagues immediately cast aspersions on his remarks saying 'What does he know? He's English' (O'Connor 1999b: 26). Of course they were also aggrieved that this politician had held conversations with members of Sinn Féin at Stormont.

English-born people living in Northern Ireland have an ascribed identity and can only improvise at being Northern Irish. There are very clear and distinct boundaries between the two main ethnic groups. As I noted in Chapter 2, endogamy and education have constituted these boundaries, and English people have been excluded from both processes. The English cannot voluntarily become Northern Irish Protestants or Catholics, for one must be born into the relevant family. Even if they acquire the Irish language or play the Lambeg drum, they shall still be deemed to be English and therefore outsiders. Cultural quirks are irrelevant here. Descent is the only factor of consequence. Children of English-born people may become skilful enough so they can pass as Catholics or Protestants, and if they marry into a local family group, they may get away with it more effectively. But only their grandchildren will be properly in a position to claim a Northern Irish ethnicity.

While terms such as 'English' and 'British' are often used interchangeably and the concept of a specifically English identity is notoriously difficult to determine, Irish culture is commonly understood to have been Anglicised rather than 'British-ised'. This primarily refers to the process of language shift, from Irish to English (Crowley 2000; De Fréine 1978; Hindley 1990; Ó Huallacháin 1994; Purdon 1999). But the Gaelic culture also exerted a powerful influence on incomers to the Region and several elements of British culture have been Hibernified over the centuries. In many senses the history of Northern Ireland is one of a series of transitions – from Old English to Irish, from New English to Anglo-Irish, from Gael to Gall (which in English literally means foreigner), from Gaelic to Irish, and from Irish to English.

The narrative of Englishness

There are few proprietary contests for cultural symbols of Englishness. This applies not only in Ireland but also in England itself. Until recently the phenomenon of English nationalism was denied and it is only in the wake of Scottish devolution and the setting up of Welsh and Northern Irish Assemblies that there is any appreciation of a distinctly English, as opposed to British, heritage. This awakening of interest in English culture, identity, and tradition has served as the catalyst for the recent publication of a plethora of books on Englishness (e.g. Haseler 1996; Heffer 1999; Paxman 1998; Vansittart 1998; Wood 1999).

Easthope (1998) suggests that the indeterminate nature of Englishness is a consequence of its imperial history, as when one nation subdues another, it must claim that it is acting in accordance with the common good. An expanded English Empire was justified in terms of enlightenment rather than Anglicisation. England could not afford to vindicate its actions in terms of self-interest, and emblems of English identity were redefined as general markers of civilisation rather than particularly English traits. Moreover, the input of Scotland into the process of empire building ensured that the process of homogenisation was construed as the promotion of British rather than English interests.

While England's imperial history partly explains the problem with defining Englishness, I believe that Anthony Smith's contention is more relevant. He argues that 'the lack of a "significant other" to serve as a traditional enemy coupled with an island location, and the continuing prevalence of alternative class images of Englishness, has muted this consciousness' (Smith A. 1999: 73). Of course it is also possible that the concept has been blurred by the sheer variety of peoples who have contributed to the composition of the population, although the concept of any 'pure' nation is itself a myth. Daniel Defoe captured this diversity in verse in 1701 when he wrote that 'A True Born Englishman's a contradiction!' (in Paxman 1998: 58). Matters have been further complicated by the fact that no 'English' king or queen has ruled the nation since the early eleventh century. Anderson (1991: 83) speaks of the 'motley parade of Normans (Plantagenets), Welsh (Tudors), Scots (Stuarts), Dutch (House of Orange) and Germans (Hannoverians)' who have sat on the English throne over the centuries. It appears that the concept of a pure-bred Englishman is a contradiction in terms and that every 'empirical Englishman' contains a foreign element. According to Žižek (1991: 110), this results in the concept of 'Englishness' becoming an internal limit or an unattainable point which prevents English people from achieving 'full identity-with-themselves'.

Proponents of the Irish cultural revival late in the nineteenth century were keen to emphasise the genetic diversity of Englishness. In an effort to counter the Anglicisation process, they indulged in valuation contests, which endeavoured to enhance the prestige of Irish cultural symbols and devalue those of the English. They advocated that a pure Irish identity was infinitely preferable to that of a 'mongrel, colourless, nondescript racial monstrosity' (O'Hickey, undated). In these terms, to allow oneself to become Anglicised ensured miscegenation resulting in the pollution of the linguistic and national 'purity' of the Irish people and its reduction to that of a mongrel breed (Crowley 1996). As I noted in Chapter 4, the Irish had worked hard to paint a picture of Celtic homogeneity but it is increasingly accepted that the notion of any people is relational and it is particularly pertinent in the case of the English. They are often defined in terms of the Other on the Celtic fringe. Their rigorous Anglo-Saxon qualities are contrasted with the dreaminess of the Celts.

While Celts contrast themselves with Anglo-Saxons, some English view the latter in opposition to the Normans who were later arrivals in England. In 1995 the Conservative MP Richard Body defined Englishness in terms of this Anglo-Saxon myth and suggested in the *New Statesman and Society* (24 February 1995: 39) that 'Englishness is grounded on Anglo-Saxon values' (in McCrone 1998: 57). From his perspective England was 'democratic and plain-speaking' prior to the arrival of corrupt Normans. He suggested that the 'Anglo-Saxons were libertarian, and believed in vigorous freedom of speech, which led to truth by jury'. Any snobbishness or conformist tendencies in the English were qualities derived from the Normans intruders who 'gave England two distinct streams that have mingled uneasily' (in McCrone 1998: 58). (This English sense of pride in the Anglo-Saxon tradition has doubtless been enhanced with the award of the 1999 Booker prize to the Northern Irish poet Séamus Heaney for his adaptation of the Anglo-Saxon myth *Beowulf*.)

England's lack of a national anthem is in some sense symbolic of the uncertainty accompanying English identity. Of course, the British national anthem usually concludes all official occasions, and the recent cessation of this practice at graduation ceremonies in Queen's University, Belfast, has grieved many members of the unionist community. In non-official English situations, Blake's 'Jerusalem' is often sung. In Chapter 3 I examined myths of ethnic election and this hymn reflects the once popular opinion that the English are a chosen people. It refers to a myth that Jesus visited the country as a child. Moreover, legend suggests that Joseph of Arimathea, who had acquired the body of Jesus from Pontius Pilate, brought part of the crown of thorns to the country (Paxman 1998: 93). Paxman identifies this tendency to regard oneself as a member of a chosen race as a peculiarly English trait that has now declined and refers to the fact that when the country was engaged in civil war in the seventeenth century, the rebels identified themselves as Hebrews. Cromwell compared their successful revolution with the delivery of the Israelites from Egypt. But this is hardly the case and in Chapter 2 I set this myth of election in a broad geographical context, indicating that it is not confined to the English, but is shared by a variety of groups.

A chosen people would hardly lack self-confidence, yet it is increasingly suggested that the English are currently suffering a crisis of identity. As a consequence of the Scottish Parliament and the regional assemblies in Wales and Northern Ireland, the question of whether the English are losing their self-assurance is raised. Whether or not this is actually the case is the subject of another book but I find it interesting to note that unionists in Northern Ireland are frequently portrayed as suffering a similar fate. This situation is often explained in terms of the increasing prominence of nationalist symbols, which has, of necessity, placed some restrictions on emblems of Britishness. Hesitancy regarding identity is a feature of unionism in Northern Ireland that is currently shared by the English but England's influence has pervaded the entire Region. Its influence in Ireland has been felt for centuries.

From English to Irish

The Norman Conquest of England occurred in 1066 and Ireland was subsequently, though unevenly, colonised in the twelfth and thirteenth centuries (Martin 1967). Ironically, the arrival of the Anglo-Normans, many of whom were Welsh rather than English, was at the request of an Irishman, the deposed king of Leinster. Their initial influence was immense and ruins of a Norman castle built in Belfast in 1177 testify to the temporary control of these 'English' over the Lagan valley. In fact, there are several such examples dotted throughout the landscape. Car-rickfergus Castle, for example, was built in the late twelfth century by the Anglo-Norman invader John de Courcey, and remained in use until 1928.

Although the arrival of the Normans ensured the establishment of a central administration in Dublin, their colony was in decline from the beginning of the fourteenth century. Anglo-Normans within the Pale region in Leinster remained loyal to the Crown, while those in other areas intermingled with the native population and rapidly became Hibernified. In fact they became what is popularly known as 'more Irish than the Irish themselves'. Such was the integration of these 'English' that the Crown issued a range of statutes aimed primarily at preventing the total assimi-lation of this community. The Statutes of Kilkenny, which were issued in French in 1366, 'had attempted to proscribe the use of the Irish language, laws and customs' (Cosgrove 1967: 168). They stated that

> [i]t is ordained to be established, that every Englishman do use the English language, and be named by an English name, leaving off entirely the manner of naming used by the Irish; and that every Englishman use the English cus-tom, fashion, mode of riding and apparel, according to his estate; and if any English, or Irish living amongst the English, use the Irish language amongst themselves, contrary to this ordinance, and thereof be attainted, his lands and tenements, if he have any, shall be seized into the hands of his immedi-ate lord until he come to one of the places of our lord the king, and find suf-ficient surety to adopt and use the English language, then he shall have restitution of his said lands, by writ issued out of said places.
>
> (in Crowley 1996: 101)

These laws are sometimes regarded as the first example of anti-Irish legislation, but it is my contention that this is less than accurate as the laws were aimed primarily at the 'English', rather than the Irish, in Ireland. Their intention was to halt the Hibernification of the Anglo-Normans. In fact they could be construed as an admission of failure. If the Norman administration had failed to conquer Ireland completely, it had to ensure that, at a minimum, its own people remained loyal to English traditions. This reassertion of English control was a response to an obvious weaken-ing in authority. Moreover, the Statutes of Kilkenny were issued a mere four years after a parliamentary statute in England displaced French as the official language. Henceforth all suits in England were to be conducted in English, rather than in French.

Despite the re-affirmation of the Englishness of the Anglo-Normans, Ulster remained almost entirely Gaelic for a number of centuries. At the beginning of the seventeenth century, the English renewed their conquest of the Region. The process of mapmaking was to prove an essential component of the Elizabethan conquest, and the Norfolk cartographer, Richard Bartlett, was employed to survey the Region. Ultimately Bartlett was a victim of English success in Ulster, as he was captured and murdered by the native Irish who regarded his work as contrary to their cause. The Crown gained considerable control of Ulster at this time and I have already referred to various aspects of the process of Plantation. Many grants of land were made to English undertakers at this time. Further gifts were made to English army officers.

Derry City is particularly symbolic of the changes that occurred in the early seventeenth century. In 1604 *Doire* became anglicised as Derry and was formally incorporated as a city. Some four years later, when an Irish chief, Sir Cahir O'Doherty, rebelled against the Crown, the city was burned to the ground, affording King James I with an opportunity for change. In 1610, some 130 workmen arrived from London and three years later the city was granted a landing charter and formally renamed Londonderry, in honour of the Twelve Companies of the Corporation of London that had provided assistance with its reconstruction. Orphan apprentice boys also arrived from London, and their contribution to the Siege that occurred later is commemorated annually by unionists. In 1616 various London companies were requested to send over families and craftsmen to the city, and within two years some 102 families were accommodated.

The arrival of the English did not necessarily result in the total expulsion of the Irish. These Londoners were particularly keen to retain certain Irish tenants on their newly-acquired estates, as 'the quickest and highest profits could be made by allowing the Irish to stay on their own land, which they were willing to work and for which they were willing to pay a high rent' (De Paor 1970: 7). The Londoners sent a formal petition to Lord Chichester, requesting that 'such natives as will be comfortable in religion, take the oath of supremacy and fashion themselves to the custom and habit of the English may be distinguished from the rest' and be permitted to remain as tenants on the lands (Russell and Prendergast 1880: 2). English and Irish settled in the city.

In consequence of the arrival of newcomers at the beginning of the seventeenth century, there were now two opposing English traditions in Ulster. A clear differentiation emerged between recent arrivals, commonly called the 'new' English and the Anglo-Normans, who were referred to as the 'old' English, although by this time most had become thoroughly Irish! Moreover, this dichotomy generated a new distinction between Gaelic and Irish identities (Mac Póilin 1994a: 5). Newcomers identified the original

Irish as Gaelic and the Normans as Irish. Anglo-Normans were largely viewed with contempt by the new English and were in the uncomfortable position of being regarded as Irish by the English newcomers but as English by the 'indigenous' Irish. Many contemporary unionists might appreciate the difficulties posed by such a dilemma! In part, the distinction between these groups raised some interesting questions regarding identity and nationality, particularly in relation to the question of origin. Although the Anglo-Normans claimed to be English, the new English disregarded this claim as the Anglo-Normans had been born in Ireland. A distinction was drawn between those who were 'English of Irish birth' and those who were 'English of English birth' (Alcock 1994: 82).

Catholicism was the great distinguishing factor between the Normans and the new English. Whereas the intention of the Ulster Plantation was the segregation of the Irish from the English and Scottish, it had failed to make any distinction between the 'mere' or 'native' Irish and the Old English as both were Catholic communities (Clarke 1967). Religious conformity was assumed to be the mark of loyalty. It was believed that any Catholic community would be unable to reconcile dual loyalties to both pope and monarch. Despite the fact that ' "English" Irish Catholics that had supported the Crown protested, affirming their Englishness and their loyalty . . . the government continued to distrust them, and took the line that more "English" English were required to balance the "English" Irish' (Alcock 1994: 82). This erroneous view of the Catholic Old English was to unite them with the 'indigenous' Irish against the Protestant English. It also ensured that Catholicism came to be viewed as an emblem of Irishness.

In an account of Ireland compiled by Moryson in the early seventeenth century, he suggests that the Old English had become so 'infected with the barbarous customs of the mere Irish and with the Roman religion' that they had grown as 'adverse to the reformation of civil policy and religion as the mere Irish'. They 'combined with them and showed such malice to the English nation as if they were ashamed to have any community with it, of country, blood, religion, language, apparel, or any such general bond of amity' (Litton Falkiner 1904: 250). Apparently this alliance had encouraged the use of the Irish language between the two communities. 'The mere Irish disdained to learn or speak the English tongue, yea, the English-Irish . . . though they could speak English as well as we, yet commonly speak Irish among themselves, and were hardly induced by our familiar conversation to speak English with us' (Litton Falkiner 1904: 262).

An ignorance of English was discernible at the assizes in the North: 'at like sessions in Ulster, all the gentlemen and common people (excepting only the judges' train) and the very jurymen put upon life and death and all trials in law, commonly speak Irish, many Spanish, and few or none could or would speak English' (Litton Falkiner 1904: 262). It is perhaps ironic that the use of Irish as a symbol of protest was regarded as a trait pertaining to the Old English rather than the Irish at this time. Dineley (1870: 23) confirmed this use of Irish by Anglo-Normans as an expression of rebellion. He reported that they had 'degenerated into such mere Irish that they have not onely suffred themselves and their posterity, by the neglect & scorn of the use of their own propper language, English, to for-gett it, but to be ashamed of the names of their ancestours, because English, though noble and of great antiquity, and converted them into Irish sir-names.'

Despite the tendency on behalf of the Crown to perceive Ulster people as belonging to either of two traditions, it is clear that the population was, in fact, much more diverse. According to Edward Wakefield (1812: 728) who toured the country at the beginning of the nineteenth century, there were at least four classes of people in the Region: '1st. The old native Irish, who, as already mentioned, speak their primitive language; 2nd. The Scotch Hibernians, whose ancestors settled in Ulster in the time of James 1.; 3rd. A mixed race between the old Irish and Scotch highlander; 4th. A class sprung from English progenitors, whose descent may be traced in their features, language and names'. This description indicates a variety of customs and expressions among the native Irish, and is particularly inter-esting with regard to what Wakefield terms the 'mixed race of half Irish and half Scotch' but it fails to give any indication of the process of Angli-cisation that was occurring. This process was not always fully appreciated as many indigenous Irish did not actively engage with visitors and for-eigners. This was possibly due to a variety of factors, including the remote-ness of their dwellings.

From Irish to English

At the time of the Plantation, there had been a deliberate attempt to iso-late the Irish in order to preserve the purity of the English language and customs as practised by the incomers. In a letter to the Treasurer concern-ing the Plantation Chichester noted that:

> It is worthy of consideration how the English language and customs may be preserved, pure and neat, unto posterity, without which he [James I] accounts it no good plantation nor any great honour and security to them to induce people thither.
> The way to perform that is to separate the Irish by themselves, to forbear marrying and fostering, and if possible to exceed them in multitude; for all other effectual courses are either too severe or too difficult to attempt.
> (Russell and Prendergast 1874: 358)

This point is articulated in the introduction to the state papers of 1603–24:

> It was therefore deemed advisable to lessen this intercourse between the two people, and to plant them separately in different quarters; the Irish in some

one place of the plainest ground of their own country; and the British by themselves in places of the best strength and command, as well for their greater security as to preserve the purity of the English language, which was likewise one of the reasons they were forbid to marry or foster with the Irish.

(Brewer and Bullen 1873: xlviii)

The process of assimilation of the native Irish was accompanied by a variety of measures that aimed at the Anglicisation of the indigenous population. In 1611 an 'Act to restrain the Irish habits and language, especially in cities and corporate towns' was passed (Russell and Prendergast, 1877: 192). A subsequent law endeavoured to prohibit the practice of keening – a word derived from the Irish term *caoineadh* (weeping). Later acts abolished the Brehon law and the custom of gavelkind and declared that 'all persons of the mere Irish septs and nations to be natural subjects and denizens' of the kingdom (Russell and Prendergast 1877: 250).

A diversity of languages was spoken in Ulster at this time. In previous chapters I drew attention to Scots and Scots-Gaelic that were the languages of migrants and planters from Scotland. A variety of English dialects were also spoken. For example, it is probable that Yola, an old form of English, survived in various pockets in the Region (Todd 1999: 46). Southern English planters spoke Elizabethan and Jacobean English. The native population communicated primarily in Irish but bilingual members also spoke Hiberno-English – a form of the language that reflected Irish influence at every linguistic level (Ó Muirithe 1996; Todd 1999). This acquisition of English by such individuals was a gradual process.

Following an insurrection in the mid-seventeenth century and the reconquest of land by the English parliamentarian Oliver Cromwell, a civil survey was taken between the years 1654 and 1656. This set out to map the territory and establish its ownership. A comprehensive redistribution ensured that all principal landowners were English-speakers. In a study of this civil survey, Adams (1965: 24) has established that 61.2 percent of the population of Ulster were speakers of Irish at that time. This was considerably lower than the overall figure for Ireland (82.5 percent). Not unexpectedly, the predominantly English-speaking areas in Ulster were located primarily in urban areas such as the town of Carrickfergus, the barony of Belfast, and the barony of Coleraine in Londonderry together with the city of Londonderry.

Despite an apparent resistance to Anglicisation, officers of the Crown were convinced that the native Irish lamented their lack of English. According to Sir John Davies, the Irish were particularly aware of the disadvantages caused by their lack of knowledge of English when dealing with matters of civil administration. 'Because they find a great inconvenience in moving their suits by an interpreter, they do for the most part send their children to schools especially to learn the English language; so as we may conceive a hope that the next generation will in tongue and heart and every way else become English' (in Ó Cuív 1951: 16).

As time progressed, the Irish gradually acquired knowledge of English. In 1787, for example, a landowner in Forkhill in South Armagh left 3,000 acres in his will for the benefit of Protestants. Free education was also to be provided for the improvement of the children on the estate, and one Alexander Barcley was appointed to give instruction in the locality. The school, which operated through the medium of English, intruded into a principally Irish-speaking area. A pamphleteer at that time had observed that 'the English language in many families is scarcely known' (Smyth 1992: 31). A month later, the schoolmaster was attacked, his tongue was torn out and his fingers removed. Other members of his family were also mutilated. This incident was immediately perceived as a sectarian act and although the circumstances surrounding it are far more complex than is immediately apparent, this outrage helped to polarise community relations in Armagh (Madden 1998).

Despite such incidents, Catholics increased their knowledge of English. In 1744 Harris had made the following observations regarding the languages spoken in County Down:

> The *English* Habit, Manners, and Language may be said almost universally to prevail here; but a *Shiboleth* of the *Scottish* and North Country *English* Dialects appears on many Tongues, and Multitudes of Words are adopted into the Language from *Cumberland* and *Westmoreland* . . .
>
> The *Irish* Tongue is in a manner banished from among the common People, and what little of it is spoken can be heard only among the inferior Rank of *Irish* Papists; and even that little diminishes every Day by the great Desire the poor Natives have that their Children should be taught to read and write the *English* Tongue in the Charter or other *English* Protestant Schools, to which they willingly send them.
>
> The Inhabitants are warm and well clad at Church, Fairs and Markets, their Trade and Commerce are carried on in the *English* language.
>
> (Harris 1744: 109, original emphasis)

In Chapter 3 I referred to the establishment of a national system of education in 1831, which reinforced the dichotomy between Catholics and Protestants. As English was the language of instruction, education was synonymous with Anglicisation (Nic Craith 1988; 1994; 1996/7; 1999c). But the precise contribution of the national system of education to the decline of the Irish is a matter of debate and many feel that its role has been somewhat exaggerated in the past (Akenson 1969; Coolahan 1981; Lee 1973). While it is obvious that national education afforded children with the opportunity to acquire English, it is increasingly clear that the motivation to learn the language came primarily as much from their parents as from their teachers. Economic rather than cultural factors influenced this desire. Business was conducted primarily through English, and Irish came to be associated with poverty.

Of course the national system of education was extremely influential in another context that I feel is often ignored. English acquired a new status as a language of print. Moreover, when reading English texts, the Irish child was afforded the opportunity of belonging to an imagined English community. Children in Irish schools were participating in the English print-community. Indigenous Irish could come to view themselves as English 'nationals' although they were still excluded from the boardrooms (Anderson 1991: 140). In other words, by 'means of a series of literary devices, the reading public created by print-capitalism is enabled to "imagine" a sociological community "narrated" by an author within the boundaries of given "print-languages"'(Smith 1993a: 18). English hegemony was promoted in the schools and a single ideological state apparatus dominated the system of education (Balibar 1991). Ulster-Scots was also disregarded in this system.

A parallel process occurred in many other communities when, for example, literacy in English was promoted among Welsh, Scots-Gaelic, and Scots communities or when French literacy was encouraged among Breton and Occitan communities. Colley (1996: 43) points to the importance of print media in the promotion of British identity. 'For the minority who could afford them, or who had the chance to pore over free copies in coffee houses and taverns, newspapers must have made it easier to imagine Great Britain as a whole'. Demirdirek (1998: 21) points to a similar situation in the former Soviet Union, which, she suggests, 'used mass media – not only print – to make people interrelate under the same shared Soviet roof'. By 1911 a mere 6 percent of the population in Ulster had knowledge of Irish (Nic Craith 1999b). Although the knowledge of Irish in the Region has increased considerably since then, the use of English in Northern Ireland is almost universal.

Contemporary emblems of Englishness

There are many markers of English influence in contemporary Northern Ireland. An English tradition has been reinforced by the school curricula, particularly in relation to the teaching of literature. Most students, for example, are familiar with the writings of William Shakespeare. While Ulster-Scots is recognised as some sort of entity, Ulster-English is hardly recognised at all – such is its power as the norm.

Provincial connections with England are reinforced in locations such as Greencastle, Newcastle, Oxford, or English Street in Armagh town. (Several other towns in Northern Ireland have streets indicating where various groups of people lived. This applies, for example, to Irish Street in Omagh or to Scotch Street in Carrickfergus.) Tourists can enjoy the Brontë Homeland Drive, located south-west of Belfast. Although there is no evidence that the literary daughters ever visited Ulster, their father was born and reared there before obtaining a place to read theology in Cambridge.

In 1854 Charlotte strengthened the connections with Ulster by marrying a man from the Region.

An English tradition is reflected in the pursuit of Anglophile sports, and cricket is the most quintessentially English of all games. A cricket club was established in Lisburn as early as 1836 (Sugden and Bairner 1995: 48). It was not until the formation of the North of Ireland Cricket Club in 1859 under the patronage of the Lord Lieutenant of Ireland, and the subsequent visit of an All-Ireland team to Belfast two years later, that the game began to gain popularity. An Irish Cricket Union was established in 1923, and many categories of clubs are in operation. 'Old boys' clubs are primarily linked with certain schools, particularly in Belfast. Certain clubs are connected to government bodies such as the RUC and the civil service, and to institutions such as universities. There are also numerous clubs in existence in major urban areas and in smaller towns and villages.

As clubs are predominantly Protestant, they are located primarily in unionist areas. In many cases, they were originally sponsored by the local gentry, 'who were either English by birth or educated in England' (Sugden and Bairner, 1995: 51). As a consequence of its Anglophile connotations, the game is seldom played in Catholic schools or attended by members of the nationalist community. Its association with one section of the community can result in the occasional destruction of clubs. For example, at the time of its establishment in 1879, Cliftonville Cricket Club was located in a primarily neutral area in north Belfast. As the proportion of local nationalists increased, the existence of a cricket club in the neighbourhood became unacceptable. In 1972, the building was burned to the ground and the club was forced to relocate to Greenisland, a largely Protestant district on the outskirts of Belfast. Unfortunately, some loyalists assumed that a club from a nationalist district was predominantly Catholic and the new building was daubed with anti-Catholic slogans (Sugden and Bairner 1995: 52).

English influences are also evident in some of the architecture and buildings and this applies particularly to Anglican cathedrals. According to Paxman (1998), Englishmen have a home rather than a fatherland, and many English people are very protective of their own hearth, although Gannon (1994) identifies the traditional brick house as a suitable metaphor for Britishness. The connection between Englishmen and their home is borne out by the old Appalachian proverb exhibited at the Ulster American Folk Park in Omagh, Co. Tyrone, which confirms that English settlers arriving in America immediately erect a house. On the other hand, Germans build a barn and the Scotch-Irish construct a distillery! In that context it is interesting to note that when David Trimble accepted the Nobel Prize in Oslo in December 1998, he drew a strong comparison between the work of unionists in Northern Ireland and the process of building a house. Trimble suggested that in their fear of being abandoned by the British, unionists had built a solid house. Many Catholics felt cold in this building and although it provided a roof for them, it appeared to unionists that Catholics were endeavouring very hard to burn down the building.

Emblems of Englishness in Northern Ireland have been strongly influenced by Irish culture over the centuries. In some instances, such as the Church of Ireland, this Hibernification is keenly acknowledged. In other circumstances there appears to be no great desire to claim ownership of the hybrid symbol. This applies particularly to Hiberno-English. Both of these symbols have their roots in England, and yet it is questionable whether either is particularly English any longer.

The Church of Ireland

For many Irish people one of the most clear-cut vehicles of Englishness in Northern Ireland is the Anglican Church. According to the 1991 census this congregation has 279,280 members representing almost 18 percent of the population (Department of Health and Social Services 1993: xvi). With the Book of Common Prayer and the King James Bible at the core, the influence of its weekly repeated sonorities on Church of Ireland people for generations must have been vast. Add to that the Church Hymnal, a common treasury of phrase not, admittedly, exclusively Anglican, thanks to the Wesleys and G.H. Newman. But this was not simply a one-way process. Many of the best loved hymns in the English-speaking world, such as 'When I Survey the Wondrous Cross' and 'All Things Bright and Beautiful', were written by an Anglican Irishwoman, Mrs. C.F. Alexander, who was the wife of the Bishop of Derry and later Archbishop of Dublin.

As I have already remarked, Anglican churches serve as architectural reminders of English influence in the Northern Ireland. Part of the reason for this is that Anglicans had older, more mature sites than Presbyterians or Roman Catholics and built their churches to more traditional designs. Derry's magnificent cathedral was the first Anglican one built since the reformation in the British Isles, and the quotation on the foundation stone 1633 lauds the London connection: '[i]f stones could speak then London's prayse should sounde who built this church and cittie from the grounde'.

Although non-members might regard this denomination as essentially English, it is clear that members of this congregation take an entirely different perspective. Clarke (1999: 29) writes of the Anglican Church in Ireland as being 'somewhat tarnished by associations with the established national church in England'. As outlined in Chapter 3 the Anglican Reformation was prompted by a dispute between the English king Henry VIII and the Roman pope. In consequence of his failure to obtain permission to divorce, Henry established himself as head of the official church in England and later of that in Ireland. For this reason the origins of the Anglican Church in Ireland are often located in England.

However, Clarke (1999: 30) is keen to set this Anglican Reformation in a much broader situation. Were it not for the 'nexus of bewildering changes throughout Western Europe' which was in part advanced by the invention of the printing press, the Anglican Reformation might not have occurred. He suggests that 'it would be more than foolish to imagine that this Reformation would have happened without the wider context of the Reformation in Europe as a whole'. In this manner he disassociates the Anglican Church in Ireland from a purely simple link with the English king.

Clarke asserts that this Church is fully Irish, as is implied in its title the Church of Ireland. But the close alliance of Catholicism with Irish nationalism has resulted in the disassociation of other denominations with Irishness. Members of the Anglican Church continually wrestle with the implication that they are not Irish simply because they are not Roman Catholic. Yet Anglicans contend that they are Irish rather than English for a variety of reasons, not least of which is the fact that their roots lie in the early Celtic church in Ireland. Until the 1960s, the Anglican Church understood itself as the sole legitimate heir of this Celtic tradition. Nowadays it is more widely accepted that several denominations have roots in this early period.

At the time of its disestablishment in the nineteenth century, the Anglican Church in Ireland felt that its sister church in England had abandoned it. Since then there has been some distance between the two churches and the 'Irish sense of Anglicanism is far from being a sense of Englishness' (Clarke 1999: 31). Moreover, 'even among members of the Church of Ireland who would have a very strong perception of being British, the Church of England is emphatically not a mother church to the Church of Ireland'. But it should be remembered that the Church of England also has an official, although small, congregation in Northern Ireland. At the time of the 1991 census its membership numbered 4,869 or 0.3 percent of the population (Department of Health and Social Services 1993: xvi).

Partition had serious implications for the Anglican Church in Ireland. It was clearly a minority religion in the Republic of Ireland. It was also a minority in Northern Ireland. While there is a sense of unity between members of this denomination north and south of the Border, there are differences of opinion between them. In the Republic, the Anglican Church has become less insular and although it is not aligned in any sense with the Church of England, it sees itself in the context of the Anglican tradition generally. In contrast, members of this denomination in Northern Ireland regard themselves as primarily Protestants rather than Anglicans. This may in part derive from their rejection of the link with England and a determination to re-affirm their credentials in the first instance as Northern Irish.

A 'grafted tongue'

English is universally spoken in contemporary Northern Ireland but the use of Irish and Ulster-Scots is on the increase. According to Bragg (1999: 58), the English language is a potent symbol of the determination of the English. In its survival of the Battle of Hastings, it 'proved mightier than the sword' and some 300 years later the English king opened parliament speaking in English. In that same year, 1362, the Law courts in England began conducting their business in English. Some 25 years later Chaucer would pen the *Canterbury Tales* (see the 1830 edition) which served as the catalyst for the emergence of literature in English.

Yet despite its origins in England, the language is no longer regarded as a vital symbol of Englishness by many outside of the country. In fact, English no longer 'belongs' to the English people. One could not assert, for example, that the English spoken by Afro-Americans or by Australians of Japanese descent 'really' belongs only to the pure whites! The name of the language is often qualified as British-English, American-English, or Hiberno-English. Computers offer spell-checks in at least nine varieties of English! Yet the English language can serve as a reminder of its country of origin.

Perhaps some of the resistance to contemporary Ulster-Scots as a distinct language derives from a desire to categorise it as a dialect of Ulster-English. In the early seventeenth century, the Scots language was associated with anti-English sentiment by many English people (Aikin 1822, Vol.1: 98). Moreover, the use of Ulster-Scots, rather than English, by a variety of weaver poets has been regarded as 'a literary Declaration of Independence from English models' (Herbison 1992: 60). Contemporary speakers of Ulster-Scots are also keen to promote an identity which is distinctly British but not English. The recent revival of Irish may also be perceived as a threat to the 'Englishness' of the Region and the use of Irish by certain speakers may follow the pattern of the 'old English' who promoted it as a symbol of protest.

Although the widespread use of English by all communities might suggest that the language is no longer a symbol of difference, it appears that this is not the case. James Joyce, one of Ireland's most notable writers in English, has remarked that even when an Englishman and an Irishman speak the same words, their experience of the language is different. In his *Portrait of the Artist as a Young Man*, the principal character, Stephen Dedalus, senses the shadow of imperialism while having a conversation with an English priest. Dedalus feels that the language in which they are speaking belonged to the priest before it became his. He remarks the difference between 'the words *home, Christ, ale, master*' on the priest's lips and on his own. Dedalus 'cannot speak or write these words without unrest of spirit'. The priest's language, 'so familiar and so foreign', will always remain 'an acquired speech' for Dedalus because he has not made or accepted its words. His voice holds them at bay. He remarks that his 'soul frets in the shadow' of the priest's English (original emphasis in Joyce 1977 [1916]: 172).

Although these comments were written early in the twentieth century, contemporary writers have echoed similar sentiments in other instances. For example, Said (1999: 144) speaks of the rift between himself and the Anglican clergyman Padre Fadden. As a child Said had learned to love the Book of Common Prayer and parts of the Gospels. But he always 'felt the rift between white man and Arab as separating' them in the end. In part this was because Padre Fadden was in a position of authority but also because English 'was *his* language' and not Said's (emphasis original).

A feeling that the English language somehow belongs to the English may have played a part in the recent revival of Irish in Northern Ireland. But the Irish contribution to the shaping of the English language has gradually been acknowledged (e.g. Kirk 1997; Todd 1984; 1999). While some have begun to regard their use of English as an important aspect of a distinctly Irish heritage, I think it unfortunate that to date the Irish have failed to claim ownership of Hibernified English. It 'is a powerful linking vehicle, wait to be loaded by us with new discourse and vision' (Fennell 1986: 398). But at least there has been some recognition of the significant influence of Irish (Gaelic) on Ireland's English, resulting in a speech-form known as Anglo-Irish or Hiberno-English. 'Green English' is the term given by Todd to this 'grafted tongue' which she describes as being 'an English foliage on an Irish stem, still nourished by an Irish root' (1999: 23).

Differences in vocabulary between the English spoken in Ireland and in England are not necessarily immense, but some variations in vocabulary can create occasional difficulties for Irish migrants in England. When I first came to England I had great difficulty trying to purchase food items, such as a 'sliced pan' (sliced loaf of white bread), rashers (sliced bacon), or 'tay-tos' (potato crisps). My vocabulary differences also extend to hardware items such as 'press' (cupboard) or 'jar' (hot water bottle) or to articles of clothing, such as the word 'slip', which I commonly use for a petticoat. Apart from variations in vocabulary, Irish has also had a significant influence on the syntax of Hiberno-English and phrases such as 'I am after doing it', 'there are six of them in it', or 'she made little of him', are direct translations of Irish constructions (Nic Éinrí 1971).

In some instances, aspects of the language that are regarded as peculiarly Irish features are not necessarily so. There has, for example, been some debate about the phrase 'do be' which appears to be an overwhelmingly Catholic form in the English spoken in Northern Ireland. (Of course it also appears in the English of Black Americans.) While some regard this as a phrase that has been retained through Elizabethan English, others are of the opinion that it is a direct translation of an Irish phrase (see e.g. O'Leary 1970: 98). According to Kirk (1997), both accounts are correct. While the phrase was introduced to Ulster through Elizabethan English, contact with the Irish language precluded its loss and actually reinforced its use.

Hiberno-English is not universally spoken throughout the Region. Geographers such as Estyn Evans (1951) suggest that a variety of forms of Northern Hiberno-English is spoken. Some linguists, such as Adams (1977) and Todd (1999), propose that spoken English in the northern part of Ireland differs from that in more southerly regions. But they are keen to point out that the imaginary line from Dundalk to Bundoran, which divides Northern and Southern Hiberno-English, does not coincide directly with the Border between Northern Ireland and the Republic. Kirk (1997) proposes a two-dialect picture, reflecting the east-west divide within Northern Ireland. His conclusion is that the river Bann, which effectively divides the Region in two, is also a linguistic boundary.

Variations in the spoken English are partly due to the regional diversity of the English who settled in Ulster. For example, people from East Anglia and Northampton settled in north Armagh, east Donegal, and north Fermanagh. The origins of Londonderry communities are obvious. Those who settled around Belfast, in south Antrim, and in south east Tyrone were from Devonshire and west Somerset. Many came from Warwickshire, Staffordshire, and Shropshire to settle in south Antrim, north west Down and across north Armagh. East Anglians were concentrated in central and southern Tyrone and east Fermanagh, whereas those who established themselves in the Lagan valley were from Lancashire, Cheshire, and south west Yorkshire (Adams 1977: 63). In the following passage, Estyn Evans (1951: 251) gives some indication of the heterogeneity of Ulster-English. He (as does Kirk) includes Ulster-Scots as a form of English:

> Already in Belfast you will notice old-fashioned words and turns of speech: you will be given a friendly 'good-evening' as soon as mid-day is past; you must admire the 'delph' – the crockery – if you look onto the bright coloured kitchen of a worker's home. You may hear the full flavour of Elizabethan English in the speech of county Tyrone. A visiting Scotsman told me he had not heard since his childhood old Scots dialect words he found in current use on the coasts of Antrim and Down. But there is also an admixture of words and phrases borrowed or translated from the Gaelic tongue. 'That's a brave (i.e. fair) day!' is a greeting you cannot fail to hear.

Research has been conducted on whether there is any variation in the English spoken by different denominations. According to Milroy (1981), any differences are regional rather than denominational. Others (e.g. Kirk 1997; Todd 1984) have countered this research. I assume that Irish (Gaelic) has had a more significant influence on the English spoken by Catholics, although the ancestors of some Protestants spoke Scots-Gaelic. According to an account written by a medical doctor in the mid-1970s, most Catholics and Protestants recognise one another by their accent difference (Fraser 1974: 115–6). This view is confirmed by individuals, such as Polly Devlin

(1983: 383), who grew up in Northern Ireland and describes her early experience of being recognised as Catholic (papist) in the following manner:

> We went further along the lough shore and went on playing and paddling and one girl followed us, pursued us. She said: 'C'mere you two, are you two papishes?' I knew that there was something amiss, and so did you, but I tried to answer the question, I said, 'What are papishes? Papishes?' 'You're papishes,' she said, 'Come on over here.'
>
> We were scared, but her companions were with her, watching us, waiting, and we went over to her. She said 'Say the Lord's Prayer. Go on say it, at once.'
>
> 'Our Father Who art in Heaven,' I said. But you wouldn't say it. You wouldn't. You stood your ground. But I did, and when she heard 'Who art in Heaven' instead of 'which art' which is how they said it, she said, 'You dirty wee papishes, you wee bitches, get on home.' And we ran home crying, and said to Daddy, 'What are papishes Daddy? They called us papishes'.

Although this piece refers to set prayers rather than colloquial parlance, it demonstrates that Protestants and Catholics are aware of clues in one another's speech which alert them to the denomination of the speakers. Devlin (1983: 384) suggests that the vocabulary of Catholics is antique and is more full of meaning than the 'pale nimble English' spoken by Protestants. She explains the constant use of violent imagery and exaggeration in terms of the 'damage done to Ireland' in the past.

Hybrid identities

The Anglicisation process or the 'patchwork quilt of cultures' (Kiberd 1986: 92) has generated a confusion of identities in many people. Northern Irish gentry are commonly assumed to have English ancestors and to feel thoroughly English. But a study by Shanks (1990) has concluded that this is far from the case. Although they speak English with an English accent and regularly discuss their orientation towards England, they usually regard themselves as Irish. Their homes are located in Ireland and their families have resided in the country for a number of centuries. However, they are not always regarded as fully Irish by those who perceive themselves as 'indigenous' Irish, although in fact it is highly unlikely that there is a single person in the country with a 'pure' genetic line of even 500 years! Yet the Irishness of the gentry is often represented as a hyphenated identity, which is often not Anglo-Irish but Scots-Irish.

Many Northern Irish who went to live in England have noted confused reactions to their identities. For example, Hewitt (1972: 123) writes of himself that his mother tongue is English, he admires English history and draws upon the English literature. As a consequence of his various degrees of empathy with English tradition, he feels that he is 'set apart' from the majority of people in the Northern Ireland. Yet when this poet came to live in England, it was automatically presumed by his new friends that as he had come from Ireland, he was Irish, and by implication, Catholic. Those who heard him speak assumed that he was Scottish or occasionally from Devon or the West Country. Others have similarly experienced this problem. Watson (1986: 226) writes of being an exile in his native Northern Ireland, 'who responded to versions of Englishness'. Yet when he went to live in England, he was 'driven back' on his Irishness. This is not an unusual phenomenon and has applied in many other countries. Tschernokoshewa (1997: 149) cites the example of migrants from Turkey to Germany who 'do not become "Turkish"' until they have actually arrived in Germany. Yet they are viewed as 'German' in Turkey. This writer maintains that they remain '"Turkish" for years after leaving Turkey even in the second or third generation'.

One might assume that at least Northern Irish Catholics, who have never lived away from home, feel thoroughly Irish and do not in any sense feel English. Yet perhaps this is not the case. Devlin (1983: 387-8) suggests that there is a great confusion of identities among the Catholic/nationalist community. She believes that the thoroughly English system of education has generated this experience of confusion:

> Northern Ireland for us is neither one thing nor the other; in it we are neither English nor Irish. We are taught English history as the record of our past, and whenever the history or culture of Ireland is mentioned it is presented as arcane, obscure, and unconnected with the country in which we live and the people to whom we belong. We read English literature and recite English poetry without anyone making the point that many of the writers and poets we study have come from our country. We study natural history, but it is all done from reference books dealing with the English countryside. No reference is ever made to the lough, just beyond the school-yard, and its unique shoal of fish. At school we sing English folk songs and warble Greensleeves, Barbara Allen and Scarborough Fair. At home my father sings My Lagan Love in his cracked and off-key voluptuous voice but I never hear his song as a distinct expression of a nation's voice and memory.

This is an interesting point as the denial of access to an Irish background is usually related to Northern Irish Protestants rather than Catholics.

The question of whether one is English or Irish, or indeed British or Irish, is a dilemma that I feel is imposed by an adherence to the two traditions model. It assumes two strong traditions in Northern Ireland and presupposes that the two are radically different. This is partially a legacy of the historical model of opposition between Anglo-Saxon and Celt that I explored in Chapter 4. This later evolved into an opposition between English and Irish, or between John Bull and Paddy. Although the character of John Bull was a Scottish, rather than an English invention, it came to portray a superior English culture – a hierarchical model that was resented and yet internalised by England's Celtic neighbours. John Bull represented industry and reliability whereas Paddy was lazy and stubborn. John Bull was a manly adult whereas Paddy was childish and a rather feminine character (Kiberd 1986).

This antithesis has been examined in literature from Ireland, now called Irish literature in English, rather than Anglo-Irish literature. A notable example is *John Bull's Other Island* by George Bernard Shaw (1924). This play explores English and Irish stereotypes and portrays the Englishman, Tom Broadbent, as the romantic idealist and the Irishman, Larry Doyle, as a ruthless cynic. Similarly, O' Casey's *The Plough and the Stars* (1966) implies a commonality of culture between the English and the Irish. Both sides in the conflict employ similes and clichés that are interchangeable; at the conclusion of the play, the British soldiers are sipping tea that has been brewed for the Irish. Oscar Wilde's *The Importance of Being Earnest* (1899) also explores the absurdity of such antitheses, although in this case it referred to male and female stereotypes, rather than oppositions between the English and Irish. The women are portrayed as being practical and businesslike whereas the men are essentially effeminate, impractical creatures.

In all of these plays there is an emphasis on the similarities between the two cultures and every time an Irishman meets an Englishman, he meets 'an alternative version of himself'. The 'Irish Question' is really the 'English Question', and vice-versa. The Irish are accused of never forgetting, but that is because the English never remember. The Irish are accused of endlessly repeating their past, but they are forced to do so precisely because the English have failed to learn from theirs (Kiberd 1986: 93).

The idea that there is a commonality of cultures between the Irish and the English is not new. In 1866, Luke Owen Pike published his book *The English and Their Origin: a Prologue to Authentic English History,* in which he advanced the theory that English were largely a Celtic people. This is perhaps less dramatic than the claim by Kiberd (1986: 83) that the difference between the two nations has largely been an English invention. He maintains that the 'English did not invade Ireland – rather, they seized a neighbouring island and invented the idea of Ireland. The notion "Ireland" is largely a fiction created by the rulers of England in response to specific needs at a precise moment in British history.'

Conclusion

Some difficulties engendered by a commonality of cultures have been explored in this chapter. Many writers refer to situations where different ethnic groups lay irreconcilable claims to similar identities (Blok 1998; Harrison 1999; Ignatieff 1999). In such circumstances it is the similarity of the other that often generates conflict and both groups strive to accentuate their differences and erect distinct boundaries. The paradox that I have explored in this chapter deals with the reverse. Here different ethnic groups enjoying some common cultural characteristics have no desire to claim a similar identity. History has determined that they view themselves in opposition to one another although Celts, Normans, and Vikings have similarly conquered both groups. Resentments generated by Ireland's colonisation have ensured that many Northern Irish define themselves in opposition to their former colonisers (Gray 1999: 67) and prefer to be viewed as culturally different from the English. This has translated into a nationalist versus unionist or Catholic versus Protestant paradigm in Northern Ireland.

I find the two traditions model paradoxical. At its best it aims to provide legitimacy for two distinct traditions each believed by the other to be still intent on marginalisation of the said other. But it can actually deny legitimacy to all those who don't identify wholly with either tradition. While many of these can articulate their non-conformance to either tradition, the model denies the existence of hybrid identities. It ignores the fact that people participate in a mixture of traditions and take or leave things much more eclectically than the model proposes. It also ignores foreign influences on cultural traditions, particularly those that have been generated in America, although not necessarily American in roots, such as Nicole Kidman, Coca Coca, and the infamous MacDonald's burger!

CHAPTER 7

ETHNIC NATIONALITY

Tradition is the forgetting of the origins.
(Husserl 1970 in Davis and Hersh 1990: 32)

Contemporary societies reinforce a sense of belonging to an 'imagined community' (Anderson 1991) with emblems of local, regional, and national unity. Culture is always contested and the process of culture production is ongoing. Traditions are invented, folktales portraying national heroes are generated, and mythologies consolidate the concept of nation. As the construction of meaning is a two-way process, Hall (1977) proposed the term 'cultural circularity' to emphasise the manner in which cultural meaning is both received and sent.

In this chapter I explore the concept of an Irish ethnic nation and examine symbols that reinforce the cultural link between nationalists in Northern Ireland and their counterparts in the Republic. From the perspective of Northern Irish nationalists, public recognition of Gaelic or Irish traditions is an essential element in the peace process and it is important that their cultural identity and 'webs of significance' are accommodated. Many nationalists assume that Ireland would have developed into a single unitary Gaelic state had it not been colonised, but this is not necessarily the case!

Because of the prevalence of the two traditions paradigm, symbols of Irish cultural nationalism are frequently viewed in an oppositional context. Emblems of Irish culture are interpreted as emphasising difference from the British. Unionists can construe them as indicators of a separatist agenda. Worsley suggests that cultural traits are not absolute categories. Instead, they are 'strategies or weapons in competitions over scarce resources' (1984: 249).

The concept of culture is bound indissolubly to politics and the relationship between the two has generated considerable academic debate (e.g. Chaney 1994; Mulhearn 1998; Spencer and Wollman 1999). Gibbons (1996:

8) argues that 'to engage in cultural activity in circumstances where one's culture was being effaced or obliterated, or even to assert the existence of a civilization prior to conquest, was to make a political statement'. Particularly pertinent to the links between culture, power, and representation in the context of the dichotomisation that has occurred in Northern Ireland are the concepts of ethnicity, nationality, and ethnic nationality.

Ethnies

Ethnicity is a socially constructed phenomenon (Jenkins, 1997). Fenton (1999: 3–4) argues that the term ' "ethnic" or "ethnic group" is used primarily in the context of *cultural* difference, where cultural difference is associated above all with an actual or common perceived shared ancestry, with language markers, and with national or regional origin'. This differs from the term 'race', which is primarily focused on biological factors although there is often inconsistency in the use of both terms.

Ethnies are not the same as nations and Connor (1978) suggests that the vital difference between an ethnie and a nation is that while others may construct an ethnie, a nation is always self-defined. But this, for me, raises the question of the self that defines the nation. Why do some decide that they speak for all and why do minorities fail to participate in the process of self-definition? Furthermore, I would argue that nations are sometimes exogenously defined or at least stereotyped. Former colonies were often characterised according to the interpretation of dominant powers, and in some instances the denotations remained unchallenged for centuries. Perhaps it could be countered that such groups only became nations when they sought to replace the coloniser's interpretation with a self-definition. However, very few nations are completely self-defined. Does this mean that they constitute incomplete nations or are, perhaps, on the way to nationhood?

Very often the process of definition is marked with the adoption of a proper name – a process that is liberating and power embracing. Benveniste (1969) notes that any assumption of an ethnic category is separatist and implies difference. He contends that the assertion of a distinct name, even in ancient times, implies separation from one's neighbours and serves as a means of affirming identity and superiority. In the Book of Genesis (2:19) Adam asserts control over animals by naming them. Throughout the Bible, the new naming of a person implies that they are invested with an additional significance and power (Israel, Immanuel, and Peter). Of course the proper names of many states often fail to include minorities, which generates an impression that somehow these are irrelevant.

There are no tangible attributes that can be regarded as essential to an ethnie except that members of the group share an awareness of identity as significantly different to that of others. Ethnicity 'involves a classification based on duality' (Lyon 1997: 187). In logical terms it 'expresses relationships of both inclusion and exclusion. It is a classification involving a set and its subset. An ethnic group, then, is an acknowledged subset of an acknowledged set; all members of A are also members of B; some members of B are also members of A' (Lyon 1997: 187).

The process of differentiation between groups cannot occur without a minimum of two characters. An ethnie is actually defined through its relationship to other groups and the boundary is itself a social product. Ethnicity occurs at the boundary between us and them (Wallman 1979). Barth (1969) proposes that ethnicities are the social organisation of cultural difference and the essence of an ethnic identity is to emphasise the boundary between insiders and outsiders. As the focus of his attention is the boundary, Barth proposes a processual and relational approach to ethnicity. This is a major difference between ethnies and nations. Although nations in theory strive to include the culturally different, ethnies still operate on an exclusive basis.

But very often the characteristics that are common to members of distinct groups are unclear (Cohen 1986). Ethnicity links the members of 'we' not because we are all essentially the same but because somehow we are different from 'them' (Hobsbawm 1992: 4). Externally and symbolically, the group frontier is symbolically very simple. Internally matters are complex and often fragmented. Diverse groups do not have an ethnic relationship unless there is some form of contact between them and unless they have a sense of their cultural difference.

As the essence of ethnicity is to emphasise cultural difference, it is obvious that the social process generating this differentiation is often tense. Variations in culture can be regarded as an asset or a difficulty. Barth (1969) maintains that relationships between various ethnies are of far greater significance than the cultural characteristics actually shared by members of the groups. Diverse approaches can express themselves through dichotomisation, an us-them relationship, or complementarisation, a we-you alliance (Eriksen 1993). Vying for power between groups often results in social disorientation and an emergence of xenophobia and paranoia. According to Renfrew (1996), tensions caused by conflicts between territorial groups frequently result in a heightened awareness of one's own identity.

This is certainly the case in the context of Northern Ireland where a more pronounced ethnicity is a product, rather than a cause, of dissent. It also pertains to the relationship between Serbs and Croats which was largely harmonious prior to the outbreak of civil war in former Yugoslavia in 1991 (Eriksen 1993). Before the war, both communities spoke 'two closely related languages among which almost total interintelligibility exists' (Nekvaplu and Neustupný 1998: 117), although they used different scripts. Both practised variants of Christianity. Following the war, cultural differences that had previously seemed irrelevant were suddenly invoked as evidence of incompatibility, and cultural variation became a consequence rather that the catalyst of ethnic boundaries. Since the war the Serb and Croat languages and other markers of their respective cultures have become increasingly different.

Nations

Serbs and Croats view themselves not only as belonging to different ethnies, but to different nations. As with ethnicity, the concept of 'nation' has generated a plethora of definitions (e.g. Renan 1882; Gellner 1983; Smith 1986). Weber (1968) defined the nation in strongly cultural terms when he stated that its significance 'is usually anchored in the superiority, or at least irreplaceability, of the cultural values that can only be preserved and developed through the cultivation of the individuality (Eigenart) of the community' (in Smith A. 1999: 34).

However the interpretation that has received the greatest attention in recent years is that of Anderson (1991: 5–6) who defines nation as an 'an imagined political community – and imagined as both inherently limited and sovereign'. He suggests that such a community is of necessity imagined, as members will never meet all or even most of their counterparts. Yet each person knows of the existence of the others and feels an affinity with the total group. Members are conscious that their nation, however large, is finite and no nation regards itself as encompassing the entire human race. Despite a variety of inequalities operating within nations, Anderson believes that a concept of horizontal camaraderie among its members promotes a sense of identity, fraternity, and community. History has demonstrated that individuals are often willing to sacrifice their lives for such communities.

Anderson has been greatly lauded for his definition of a nation. However, this definition assumes a dichotomy between a 'real' and an 'imagined' community and, as Balibar (1991: 93 original emphasis) has countered, this juxtaposition is probably false:

> *Every social community reproduced by the functioning of institutions is imaginary,* that is to say, it is based on the projection of individual existence into the weft of a collective narrative, on the recognition of a common name and on traditions lived as the trace of an immemorial past (even when they have been fabricated and inculcated in the recent past). But this comes down to accepting that, under certain conditions, *only* imaginary communities are real.

Furthermore, Balibar suggests that as nations rarely extinguish class conflicts, the challenge to them is to stimulate their members continually to conceive of themselves as the national community. It is necessary to generate a sense of national identity and unity to ensure that people perceive themselves to be the basis of political power.

Nationalists in Northern Ireland clearly define themselves as members of the Irish ethnic nation. Their citizenship of the UK does not detract from their sense of Irish nationality. Instead, it allows them to define themselves in a dual context; as Irish nationals in a British state. While some may wish to withdraw from the UK, I noted in Chapter 1 that others are less dissatisfied with the concept of the Union. All are conscious of their political separation from their counterparts in the Republic – a fact that has enhanced rather than diminished their sense of ethnic nationality. The imagined community of nationalists extends throughout the 32 counties and the sense of identity reflected in the public sector in Northern Ireland has failed to satisfy many nationalists.

Civic and ethnic nationalism

In general terms, the successful generation of a national identity has largely depended on the force of nationalism – a term that has given rise to a multiplicity of definitions (e.g. Anderson 1991; Hobsbawm 1992; Kohn 1945; O'Brien 1988). Nationalist sentiments often rely on artificial constructs, such as newly devised flags and revived languages. Yet, as Gellner (1983) points out, the force itself is neither an artificial nor an ideological invention. According to Wallerstein (1991), nationalism is frequently a consequence of inequalities between sovereign states.

Throughout this book I have examined various dichotomies in Northern Ireland. Nationalism has also served to reinforce a sense of polarity. Bauman (1992: 678) speaks of nationalism in terms of 'we-talks' that 'tend to promote ego-centred binary divisions, divide the world into *friends* and *enemies* – sharply separated from each other by mutually exclusive sets of assigned rights and duties, moral significance and behavioural principles' (original emphasis). In this context, nationalism operates as a force of division. An essential element of the self-assertion of political leaders is the reinforcement of cultural difference and the drawing of boundaries between 'indigenous' and 'foreigners', between insiders and outsiders. It is in this context that Bauman conceives of nationalism as the racism of intellectuals. Conversely, he also suggests that 'racism is the nationalism of the masses' (Bauman 1992: 686).

When discussing the force of nationalism in the context of this chapter, it is important to differentiate between its civic and ethnic forms – between an understanding of nationhood that is state-centred and assimilationist and one that is *Volk*-centered and differentialist (e.g. Brubaker 1992; Ignatieff 1994). It is commonly accepted that civic nationalism promotes a concept of citizenship rather than nationality. This type is perceived as both civilised and inclusive. In these circumstances the state takes the role of nation building – shaping and defining the population on the national territory.

As the French Revolution generated the concept of civic nationalism, France is usually cited as a prime example of a civic nation. Here people choose to belong to the nation, regardless of their language, race, or creed. They become citizens (as Tom Paine did). But there are problems with this example. When the state set out to create a French nation within its territorial boundaries, unity was often equated with uniformity. The 'voluntaristic' notion of nationhood shaded into the 'ethnic' or 'cultural', which is usually regarded as more typical of Germany. Inclusion in the nation entailed cultural assimilation and regional and minority languages and cultures were demoted (Ager 1999). Even in contemporary times, France does not cope well with expressions of ethnic identity. For example, Muslims who wish to wear the *Hijeb* (veil) generate 'symbolic problems' for the state (McCrone 1998: 39). But this should not be perceived as a lack of appreciation of culture. As Smith (1981) quite rightly points out, the original Jacobin Revolutionaries were not unconcerned with culture. In fact they were so enamoured with the French language and civilisation that they wished to enhance it at the expense of other regional identities!

As an example of civic nationalism, France might be described as a state-nation rather than a nation-state. The functions of such a state include the assimilation of youth by education and the unification of adults through the homogenisation of their traditions and the subordination of their religious or political conflicts to sentiments of nationalism. A unified French identity is dependent on a capacity to assimilate migrants and the culturally different (Balibar 1991; Loughlin 1998).

Germany is the case study usually proffered as an example of the contrasting form of ethnic or cultural nationalism. The original sense of 'German-ness' was built on a relatively homogenous linguistic base, that is, the *Kulturnation* of the German Romantics, and this variety accords priority to the concept of blood relationships rather than that of citizenship. Generally speaking regional cultures are not inhibited in Germany and the 'cultural sovereignty' of the German Länder is a constitutionally enshrined privilege. However, as noted by Llobera (1998b) the term 'ethnic' is possibly inappropriate for this type of nationhood, as in linking it with nationalism one assumes it to embrace racial characteristics solely. Such patriotism would place no value on culture.

Furthermore, as noted by Ignatieff (1994), the country that is presented as the paradigm of ethnic nationalism has occasionally resorted to civic and state nationalism. This is illustrated by the Frankfurt Parliament convened after the 1848 revolution, which accorded German citizenship to all residents of the state regardless of their language or country of origin. Moreover, the intolerance of the German race towards minorities during the Hitler era is a well-known example of a drive towards hegemony, which is commonly regarded as a facet of civic nationalism.

Some academics have proposed that the collective force of nationalism in the West is more usually state-centred whereas in the East it is more orientated towards emblems of culture and history (Kohn 1945). But these classifications are rather general and cannot be regarded as applying to all situations. Furthermore, they may unconsciously reflect a view that Western society is civilised whereas that of the East is, as yet, unrefined. Northern Ireland is often considered a region where ethnic and civic nationalists are in conflict with one another – a fact that may reflect the nature of Irish nationalism.

Irish nationalism

In Ireland, the distinction between civic and ethnic nationalism is useful for disentangling the complex strands of Irish nationalism. This borrows, simultaneously, from the republican traditions of the French Revolution, but also, and contradictorily, from the ethnic traditions of Irishness, some of which I have already set in a Celtic context in Chapter 4. The constitution of the Irish Republic, drafted in 1937, expressed great certainty with regard to the nature and extent of the Irish ethnic nation. Article 1 established the inalienable right of the nation to political sovereignty and identified the 'national territory' as Éire with the tricolour as its national flag and Irish as its national language.

More contentiously, the second Article affirmed that the territory of this ethnic nation consisted 'of the whole island of Ireland, its islands and the territorial seas'. In a subsequent article, the parliament and government affirmed the application of their laws to the entire 32 counties (Ó Tuathaigh 1988: 47). In this manner, the constitution of the Republic of Ireland claimed to apply to the entire nation whose cultural symbols were clearly defined.

Irish nationalism has changed considerably since 1937 and during the peace process the Republic of Ireland reviewed its constitutional claim to the six counties of Northern Ireland. But while the official national territory was resized to a mere 26 counties, the concept of the nation was amended and is now considerably more extensive than previously. The GFA (1998: 4–5) proposed that 'It is the entitlement and birthright of every person born in the island of Ireland, which includes its islands and seas, to be part of the Irish nation. That is also the entitlement of all persons otherwise qualified in accordance with law to be citizens of Ireland.'

An enhanced awareness of the Irish Diaspora has led to an appreciation of the Irish community worldwide, and the revised Articles propose that 'the Irish nation cherishes its special affinity with people of Irish ancestry living abroad who share its cultural identity and heritage' (GFA 1998: 5). The new Article defines the Irish Nation in terms of an 'extended family' or 'migrant nation' (Kearney 1997). While the latest definition of the nation remains partly ethnic, as in the case of the Jewish nation, it also includes all the exiles and emigrants who live abroad. But even this definition is problematic. As pointed out by Sinha (1999: 23), the revised Article 2 still 'reinforces the notion of a single culture of the Irish nation, and thus maintains the exclusion of other ethnicities'.

All nationalist members of the Northern Irish Assembly assented to the revision of Articles 2 and 3 although their interpretation of the original reason for partition varies. While constitutional nationalists conclude that the Northern Irish State was created in an attempt to pacify unionists, republicans believe that partition was a consequence of British imperial policy. Britain had a colonial interest in the country and was determined to retain control for as long as possible. Both views imply that the British government is primarily responsible for the 'artificial' division of the Irish nation (Bean 1994; Roche 1994).

These different interpretations of partition reflect their diverse nationalist traditions. Republicans regard themselves as following in the footsteps of the rebels of 1916 and the Irish Parliament of 1919, whereas constitutional nationalists avail of the discourse of rights first advanced in America by Martin Luther King. Republicans endorse the concept of ethnic nationalism while constitutional nationalists lay greater emphasis on the question of citizenship. These differing perspectives reflect Eriksen's (1993) diverse approach to the process of dichotomisation. Whereas republican nationalists think of the unionists in an oppositional context, civic nationalists regard the two traditions as potential partners.

Regardless of their contrasting interpretations of partition, all nationalist groups aspire to the reunification of Ireland. In common with their constitutional colleagues, most republicans now endorse the political process as the best method of achieving this aim. But while they accept the current partition of Ireland, many of them view it as being of a temporary nature. Their political ideology holds that the boundaries of the nation-state should be co-terminous with the ethnic group. For them the Irish ethnic nation has always extended to the entire 32 counties. Characteristics such as language and religion already operate as important cultural affirmations of this Irish ethnicity. By promoting these emblems in Northern Ireland, they strengthen their affiliation with the Republic. Here I focus on three such emblems of which the most significant is that of Roman Catholicism.

Irish Catholicism

Catholicism is regarded by many Northern nationalists as the primary focal point of their identity. Unionists constantly point to the strong association of Catholicism with authentic Irishness south of the Border. Such restrictive perceptions of Irishness preclude many of them from asserting their Irish cultural identity. But as I noted in Chapter 3, it was the new English in the seventeenth century who initially linked the Catholic Church and the Irish people by assuming that all Catholics, including the Anglo-Normans, were Irish. As the Penal Laws persecuted Catholics simply because of their religious affiliation, the priest acquired a special status among the afflicted community. While the Catholic community closely associated Protestantism with British domination, many Protestants continued to view themselves as Irish. At an official level the 'Irish nation' referred to politically active Protestants, who primarily belonged to the Church of Ireland. Catholics were deprived of any active part in the political process during the eighteenth and part of the nineteenth century (Ruane and Todd 1996: 23). In Chapter 2 I argued that O'Connell, one of the most prestigious Catholic leaders in the nineteenth century, was anxious to include all denominations in the Irish Nation, yet the link between Catholic and Irishness became more firmly entrenched.

Several factors led to the close association of these entities (Ó Tuathaigh 1986). In Chapter 2 I reviewed the consolidation of separate Catholic and Protestant communities, particularly during the latter half of the nineteenth century. As the great majority of people in Ireland were Catholic, they tended to regard themselves as the 'real Irish' (Walker B. 1997). At this time the Irish language was in rapid decline and Catholicism replaced the Irish language as the indisputable emblem of Irishness (Hastings 1997). Paul Cullen, a Catholic archbishop, founded the National Association in 1864. For him the identification of Irish and Catholic was 'axiomatic' (Corish 1985: 195). Just over 20 years later Ireland's four Catholic archbishops stipulated that independence was necessary for the Irish people. Irish nationalism and Catholicism were perceived as immensely compatible although there were some occasions on which these ideologies clashed (Wright 1973). A similar phenomenon occurred in Poland about the same time. At the end of the nineteenth century the 'modern' nationalism as proclaimed by Roman Dmowski and his National Democrats asserted that the authentic Pole was a 'Polish-speaking Catholic Slav' (Ascherson 1996: 162). Other citizens of the former Royal Commonwealth, such as the Jews, were now perceived as preventing the achievement of the national goal.

Although Douglas Hyde, Ireland's first President, was Protestant (Dunleavy and Dunleavy 1991), partition afforded the Catholic clergy with an opportunity to dominate the political scene in the new Republic. As the vast majority of the population was Catholic, church teaching and principles were reflected in state legislation and in the Irish Constitution of 1937. An Eucharistic Congress in 1932 celebrated the Catholicism of the Irish people at political, moral, and emotional levels. Clerics had a special, largely undisputed, status in political life and met with little resistance from the primarily rural population. The social dominance of the clergy was only seriously challenged on one occasion when the Minister for Health, Noel Brown TD, attempted to introduce what became known as the 'mother and child scheme'. The Irish Medical Association, which opposed the introduction of this program for pregnant mothers, gradually gained the support of the Catholic clergy. As a consequence, the initiative was abandoned (Ruane and Todd 1996; Whyte 1971).

Protestants in the Republic were in a very vulnerable position during these decades. Not only were they a small community, but they were also internally fragmented. In general they felt abandoned by their counterparts in Northern Ireland and this particularly applied to Protestants in the three Ulster counties that were now part of the Republic. Bowen (1983) explores the further differentiation between rural and urban Protestants in the Republic, and between lower and middle classes in urban districts. Many Protestants moved to Northern Ireland or Britain as soon as the new state was established. Emigration was a contributory factor to the decrease in numbers. Low marriage rates among Protestants compounded the situation. Any Protestants marrying Catholics were bound by the *Ne Temere* decree to raise their children in the Catholic faith, and increasing rates of marriage between these communities contributed to an overall decline of the Protestant population. While Protestants in the Republic were not politically oppressed, their sense of British identity was neither recognised nor accommodated. Only one tradition was recognised in the new state that had embarked on a vigorous process of re-Gaelicisation. There was little concept of cultural pluralism.

As time passed changes have occurred in the Republic and the relationship between the Catholic Church and the Irish State has become less entrenched. In 1972 the special position of the Catholic Church in the Irish Constitution was removed. A falling attendance at weekly mass has diminished the local influence of the priest. Fewer vocations have resulted in the closure of certain religious institutions and clerical control of education has weakened although it still remains influential. Lay people are less apprehensive of criticism of the church and the state has become increasingly liberal and radical.

While the public arena is still Catholic in ethos, and public processions and rituals still take place, these are on a far lesser scale than previously. Even the status of the 'Angelus bells', a regular marker of ritual Catholic prayer on the mass media, is regarded by some as inappropriate for a plural state and possibly offensive to Protestants. In fact, McVeigh (1999: 19) argues that one should not ask whether 'it is possible to have a society which doesn't have the Angelus on TV and radio but rather to ask how is it possible to have a society which insists that we have the Angelus'. (He is equally opposed to the annual celebration of 'sectarian triumphalism' on the 12th July.)

Catholicism in the Republic has become more liberal and less essential to the general definition of Irishness. Yet many Northern Protestants regard the Irish Republic as the physical embodiment of an Irish, Catholic-nationalist tradition. From their perspective a comfortable alliance with

this state is impossible, as it has continually laid claim to their British territory. It has also proved a breeding-ground for terrorist activities. Some of
them are keen to emphasise the lack of pluralism in society south of the
Border. But a monocultural perspective was similarly promoted in Northern Ireland: 'In the Irish Free State it was against Protestants or the unionist minority, and in Northern Ireland it was against the Catholic Irish
minority (Hutchinson 1987: 62). Not all Northern Protestants are equally
hostile towards the Republic, and some have a more open attitude towards
it than others. But even those who feel themselves to be Irish or to have an
Irish cultural identity are keen to stress that this form of Irishness is very
different from that espoused by narrow-minded Catholic nationalists.

Catholics south of the Border would argue that this biased perception of
the Irish Republic is no longer accurate. They believe that their state has
gradually become accommodating and pluralist and no longer strives
towards a hegemonic Gaelic Catholic ideal. Southern Catholics believe
that a variety of changes have helped neutralise Ireland's image as a
Catholic, Gaelic state for a Catholic, Gaelic people. For example, many of
the regulations regarding compulsory knowledge of Irish for various posts
have been removed. Following a second referendum in 1995, divorce is
permissible.

But Northern Catholics also have a problem with their southern counterparts (Ruane and Todd 1996: 260). While these Catholic groups originally had a great deal in common, their experiences have gradually
diverged and the distance between them increased. For working-class
Catholics in Northern Ireland, there is a strong association between their
religious commitment and the ideals of nationalism and Gaelicism. These
elements have become less significant and less closely linked in the Republic. And as I noted in my initial chapter, class differences also influence attitudes. Middle-class Catholics in Northern Ireland sometimes regard the
Republic in the same manner as their Protestant counterparts. For some
the Republic is different, and even perhaps foreign, and does not reflect
their own experiences.

The Gaelic Athletic Association

While Catholicism is a significant element of Irishness for nationalists in
Northern Ireland, many of them view their participation in the Gaelic Ath-
letic Association (GAA) as equally significant. In any context sport 'provides a focus for class and communal identification and becomes central in
sustaining a way of life' (Chaney 1994: 77). The charter of the GAA was
drafted in Thurles, County Tipperary in 1884 – a period of great fervour
for the revival of Gaelic culture. This organisation linked sport with
nationality and set out in an oppositional manner to enhance a sense of
Gaelic identity that was clearly distinct from Britain. 'Nationalists of all

shades of opinion were attracted to the new association . . . and as a result, their ethnic consciousness was widened and heightened' (Ó Huallacháin 1994: 46). Ironically, in pursuing this separatist aim the GAA adopted a policy originally devised by the British who had recognised the usefulness of sport in the advancement of nationalist fervour (Sugden and Bairner 1995: 26).

Throughout the Empire, the British government used sporting rituals in order to strengthen cultural domination. Structurally the GAA reflects English influence in that its competition is based on the county unit, which is a feature of English administration. But it also uses the four traditional provinces of Gaelic Ireland in its championship structure. Moreover, to suggest that the organisation could have opted to focus on traditional Irish territorial divisions such as baronies or tuaths is hardly practical as these territorial divisions were no longer used in the late nineteenth century.

In modern times the organisation remains committed to its founding principles and the GAA aspires to an enhanced Gaelic identity throughout the island of Ireland. Its rulebook states that the

> Association is a National Organisation that has as its basic aims, the strengthening of the National Identity in a 32 county Ireland through the preservation and promotion of Gaelic Games and pastimes. The Association further seeks to achieve its objectives through the active support of Irish culture, with a constant emphasis on the importance of the preservation of the Irish language and its greater use in the life of the Nation; and in the development of a community spirit, to foster an awareness and love of the national ideals in the people of Ireland.
>
> (in Sugden and Bairner 1995: 28)

While the GAA, strictly speaking, has never officially recognised partition, this also applies to all other sports in Ireland except soccer. But the GAA places particular emphasis on the display of national symbols during matches. It stipulates that the Irish national anthem should precede all matches and the Irish flag should be displayed, although the Association has not always insisted that the tricolour be flown in areas in Northern Ireland where it might provoke confrontation (Bryson and McCartney 1994).

Operationally the GAA differs north and south of the Border. All formal aspects of provincial council meetings in Connaught, Leinster, and Munster are conducted in English. This contrasts sharply with the Ulster board, which uses Irish in its formal proceedings (Corry 1985; Cronin 1999). This practice is possibly due to the fact that the GAA maintains a controversial political profile in Northern Ireland and still regards itself in a context that is oppositional to British culture. Here, the use of the Irish flag, anthem, and language 'confirms for Ulster Protestants that the activities of the GAA are no less than the thin end of the wedge of a campaign to bring about the unification of Ireland under Dublin rule' (Sugden and Bairner 1995: 37).

As an organisation, the GAA believes that it maintains an officially neutral position but its stance on a 32 county Ireland could hardly be regarded as impartial. Individual members are not prohibited from lending support to organisations advocating the use of violence. Tóibín (1987) records how the Tyrone players competing against Kerry at the all-Ireland final dedicated their game to republican prisoners in Long Kesh. During the late 1970s and early 1980s specific Gaelic clubs openly supported the republican hunger strikes.

Obviously the GAA's constitutional reference to a 32 county Ireland does not appeal to unionists. Of particular offence to them are the exclusion rules originally designed to prevent the influence of foreign games and pastimes in Ireland. A police rule prohibits security forces from membership of the GAA while a boycott rule formerly censured any sporting events organised by English people. Members of the GAA who participated in or even watched games not considered ethnically Irish or organised by any other institution could be expelled under the foreign games rule.

This dictum was designed to imply that all Gaelic games were indigenous to the country – a fact that is not necessarily borne out by a closer examination of the facts. Although bearing some resemblance to shinty in Scotland, hurling is clearly different from many other games and has developed solely in an Irish context. As such it differs from football which was played in a similar fashion not only in Ireland and in the British Isles, but also in continental Europe throughout the Middle Ages. There are very few references to football in the annals of Irish history prior to the nineteenth century, which indicates that Gaelic football did not play a significant part in traditional Irish cultural activities. 'Nevertheless, today Gaelic football is played and defined in opposition to non-indigenous forms of football (rugby and soccer) as if it were the chosen sport of ancient Hibernia' (Sugden and Bairner 1995: 25).

As time has passed some of the rules regarding foreign influence have been modified or revoked. In 1971 a special congress in Belfast abolished the ban on participation in foreign games but the prohibition on membership of the British security forces remains and the spirit of exclusion prevails and can prevent potential events of an inclusive nature. For example, in October 1991 it was proposed that a special Gaelic football match in the showgrounds of the Royal Dublin Society would mark the centenary of the Clanna Gael-Fontenoys GAA Club. Invitations were issued to the Dublin and Down County Boards who duly accepted and it was decided that a League of Ireland soccer fixture would precede this game. Within a month the Games Committee of the GAA determined that the Gaelic football match would not proceed, as the venue did not belong to the organisation. In fact, the location was traditionally used for horse-riding and showjumping and insistence on formal dress suits at some of its events ensures that this place is more often associated with a British rather than an Irish culture.

In its current format, rule 21 of the GAA states that 'members of the British armed forces and police shall not be eligible for membership of the Association'. Moreover, 'a member of the Association participating in dances, or similar entertainment, promoted by or under the patronage of such bodies, shall incur suspension of at least three months' (O'Brien 1998: 5). This effectively implies that the two traditions in Northern Ireland are mutually exclusive. It prevents significant numbers of Northern unionists from participating in the games because their families are associated at some level with security forces. Their exclusion at an official level by the governing body of the GAA inhibits unionists from taking an active interest in this aspect of Gaelic culture although some follow the matches on television with enthusiasm.

Following on the GFA in April 1998, a special GAA congress was called to debate the exclusion rule. A two-thirds majority was required to remove the ban from the official constitution but it quickly became clear that the Ulster council would oppose any such move. Their argument proposed that the peace process had not yet resolved all difficulties for nationalists. Ulster boards argued that exclusion of the RUC and the British Army was necessary as these bodies had engaged in the abuse of nationalists. Members of the GAA were not free to express their national identity through Gaelic sports in an unmolested fashion. They experienced harassment on journeys to and from sporting occasions and matches were often disrupted. For these reasons the Ulster boards proposed that the ban be maintained until the operations of RUC were officially reviewed (Cronin 1999). A motion from the Cork board advised suspension rather than deletion of the rule, until policing reforms took place. As this motion preserved the unity of the organisation it was carried, though not without some reservations.

As defender of a 32 county national identity, the GAA is in a difficult position in the context of the quest for peace. Citizens of the Irish Republic have opted to drop their constitutional claim to the six counties; yet the GAA has given no indication that it will consider removing nationalist aspirations from its constitution. Since its foundation the organisation has promoted an all-Ireland ethos and has advocated a dual sporting and political mission. If it now withdraws from this position will it be regarded as deserting its members in Northern Ireland? Could such moves be portrayed as destroying 'their self-constructed version of Irish nationalism?' (Cronin 1999).

The Patten report on policing in Northern Ireland (1999) calls on the GAA to delete Rule 21. While the exclusion rule may seem archaic and reprehensible in any context, it is important to remember that exclusion is a shared narrative among Northern nationalists and unionists. Just as the GAA prohibits members of the security forces from joining its association, the Orange Order has a similar proscription on Catholics. Members of the Order are also prevented from marrying Catholics. But I would argue that there are great differences between the operation of these forces of exclusion. In the case of the Orange Order, the ban is explicitly sectarian and could not be lifted without changing the nature of the organisation. In contrast, the GAA's ban reinforces a political rather than a sectarian division. Many of the diverse denominations that I explored in Chapter 3 are quite welcome to the GAA. The ban applies to those espousing political rather than religious loyalties. It is simply a means of political protest. This is not to imply any justification for the exclusion ban in the GAA but rather to reinforce the fact that exclusion is a common fact of life in Northern Ireland and boundaries are often impermeable.

Overall, the vast majority of unionists have been very hostile to the GAA 'and regard its political position as an aggressive one' (Corry 1985: 5). For many of them, the activities of the GAA represent a threat not merely to their political affiliations but also to their religious beliefs and in particular to the sabbatarian ethos of the Protestant community. In this context Protestant and Catholic traditions were in direct conflict with one another and up to the 1960s, restrictions were placed on Sunday games. This generated a great deal of bitterness, resulting in a number of court actions. An example cited by Sugden and Bairner (1995: 38) refers to the refusal of Craigavon Borough Council to grant a lease for land to St Peter's GAA Club in order to develop a structure for Gaelic sports. This site was located adjacent to the headquarters of the Royal Black Preceptory, a prestigious organisation within the Protestant community. Councillors here pointed out that the practice of Sunday games was seriously offensive to traditional sabbatarians, particularly where the games occurred in Protestant localities. In this instance, St Peter's GAA Club appealed the decision in the High Court and won its case. Similarly, there was serious discontent among the unionist community when the city council in Derry granted planning permission for two Gaelic football pitches in the Protestant district of the Waterside.

Unionists also object to the financial support given by the British government to the maintenance of the organisation. Knox (1989: 149) argued that the GAA received £819,000 in grant aid in the 20 years from 1962 to 1982 while still maintaining its prohibition on members of security forces. Members of the GAA would counter that they are entitled to this money because, in common with everybody else in the state, they pay their full share of taxes and are entitled to government support for expressions of their cultural tradition.

Despite financial support from the British government, nationalists complain that the security forces constantly disrupt games and have deliberately built army and police barracks next to Gaelic pitches. Of particular concern in the past has been the construction of a security forces installation on playing fields in Crossmaglen, South Armagh. According to the security forces, this location is the best vantage point for such military installations but the local population regards it as a violation of their game.

As a gesture towards the nationalist community the British government has announced the return of this land to the Crossmaglen Rangers GAA Club and indicated that the departure will occur 'as soon as practicable' (Moloney and Collins 1999: 4).

The Irish (Gaelic) language

While the GAA probably remains the most exclusive aspect of nationalist culture in Northern Ireland, there have been serious efforts in the last decade to ensure that the Irish language becomes less prohibitive. Two decades ago, many unionists regarded the use of the language as a tangible expression of separatism, as an emblem of a conflicting tradition. Nowadays it is more commonly accepted that speaking Irish is simply emblematic of an Irish ethnic identity. While it can have separatist overtones, it is not necessarily viewed in an oppositional context.

The association of Irish language with the separatist cause is not recent (Nic Craith 1995). Nor is it particularly unusual. 'The Polish and Czech languages, like Roman Catholicism in Ireland, became hallmarkers of nineteenth-century nationalisms because at some time or other deliberate efforts had been made to eradicate them' (Wright 1987: 1). When Northern republicans adopted a discourse of de-colonisation (O'Reilly 1999), they merely followed a tradition that had been established by many cultural nationalists a century earlier. In his famous speech on 'The Necessity for De-Anglicising Ireland' (1892), the Protestant leader, Douglas Hyde, argued that Ireland could never achieve real independence as long as it continued its slavish imitation of English language and traditions (see Hyde 1986). Arthur Griffith, the founder of SF and a journalist, D.P. Moran, popularised the cultivation of the language as a symbol of difference and independence. Members of the Irish Republican Brotherhood (IRB) infiltrated the Gaelic League, which is a prominent Irish language organisation. 'Although it claimed to be non-political the league had provided the best argument yet for the recognition of Ireland as a separate national entity' (McCartney 1967: 297). Many of those involved in the 1916 separatist rising were ardent promoters of the language (Garvin 1987a, b). With independence, the narrative of de-colonisation fell into disuse. Instead it was replaced by a national language discourse associated with several cultural and ideological elements which 'had to be swallowed whole: Irish music, dance, republicanism, particularistic versions of history, conservative Catholicism and general anti-Britishness' (Tovey et al 1989: 20).

In the late 1970s and early 1980s the Irish language became linked with the armed struggle in Northern Ireland. Other indigenous languages, such as the Basque, Catalan, or Breton have also become associated with political movements (e.g. Conversi 1997, McDonald 1989). In Northern Ireland, the Irish language became highly significant for a proportion of the nationalist community. It is possible that they felt that this politicisation of Irish was necessary to guarantee the success of revival efforts (McGimpsey 1994). It is also probable that they wished to link any achievements with the republican tradition.

But the association of Irish language with separatism enhanced the concept of two traditions and reinforced the sense of Irishness in an oppositional context. Many unionists resented the association of the language with separatist and sectarian agendas. During a debate at the Forum for Peace and Reconciliation in Dublin, the Alliance councillor, Séamus Close, suggested that Irish had been used almost as a territorial weapon: 'it was seen as being negative. It was seen as being anti-Protestant. It was seen as being anti-British. It was seen as being anti-anyone who was not republican. In a way, Irish language and Irish culture has suffered from this stigma of violence of this past twenty-five years' (Department of Foreign Affairs 1995: 48–9).

Some Orange journals have condemned this political use of Irish. For example an unacknowledged writer in the *Orange Standard* (December 1986, January 1987: 3) suggested that s/he 'will not disarm Sinn Fein (sic.) or their armed masters because they have already made Gaelic language and culture weapons as important to them as the bomb and the armalite. Every street name in Gaelic, every broadcast in Gaelic, every Gaelic lesson rammed down the reluctant throat of an Ulster Protestant child is a victory for them.'

Loyalists have reacted to this association of Irish with the arms struggle by claiming that the language belongs as much to the British as to the Irish tradition. Some of them have adopted a discourse of culture and asserted a close emotional bond with the language. In common with many of the republican H-Block prisoners, they affirm that the Irish language represents their native, rather than their cradle, tongue. A former prisoner (in Smith, W. 1994: 17) describes the sensation as follows:

> Now it was strange for loyalists at that time to hear the Gaelic language actually being spoken, but after a while it became just a feature of camp life. It had an even stranger effect on me, because I was listening to a language that I couldn't understand, that I had never heard before, but it was not a foreign language. It was my own native tongue.

In this context, Irish still remains a marker of the separate traditions as many loyalists regard the acquisition of the language as a reclamation of a distinctly Ulster-Scottish rather than their Irish heritage. As examined in Chapter 4, many Gaelic-speaking Highland soldiers had engaged in Ulster warfare from the twelfth to the fourteenth centuries and a proportion of the Scottish settlers at the time of the Plantation was Gaelic speaking. From that perspective the Gaelic tongue is a common heritage and the acquisition of Irish enhances rather than diminishes a sense of Britishness. Billy Hutchinson (1997: 56) of the PUP captured this sentiment when he said: 'I suppose the Irish language somehow belongs to my cultural heritage, as I believe my ancestors, at least on my mother's side, at one time would have spoken the Gaelic language, as was, and to some degree still is, the practice among the people living in the Scottish Highlands'.

Loyalists also locate Irish in an Ulster tradition, describing it on occasions as 'Ulster Gaelic'. This terminology associates it with both Scottish-Gaelic and Ulster-Scots. It acknowledges the sea as a facilitator of, rather than a prohibition on, movement between Northern Ireland and Scotland. This position roots the language in a provincial tradition and emphasises the difference between Northern Irish and that of the Republic. It may also indicate a desire to develop a 'new' Irish that will evolve independently of Irish in the Republic. In this way loyalists hope to disengage the connection between Irish speakers north and south of the Border and to depreciate the language as an emblem of de-colonisation.

But in recent years the de-colonising discourse of Northern Irish nationalists has become more moderate and there have been numerous attempts to disengage the language from a narrow sectarian agenda. Much of the success of this work can be attributed to the efforts of the ULTACH Trust, an organisation in operation since 1989 (Mac Póilin 1994b). One of the primary aims of this institution has been to enhance the general awareness of the Protestant contribution to the survival of the language (Mac Póilin 1990a–d). At the same time nationalists have increasingly adopted a discourse of culture, separating the language from politics. There is some recognition that having an Irish identity does not necessarily imply separatist aspirations.

For this reason certain unionists have begun to attend Irish language lessons (McCoy 1997a, b) and some have justified their learning experiences on the basis of their Irish rather than their British cultural identity. They wish to have access to another cultural tradition, which is not viewed in an oppositional context. Knowledge of the language enhances their sense of Irishness without diminishing their British identity. Fluency in Irish does not necessarily imply any republican tendencies nor can it be ascribed to any desire for unity with the Republic. The language is a shared experience and does not belong exclusively to the nationalist tradition. One learner describes the experience in the following manner:

> At first it was a bit scary because I didn't want to admit I was Irish. I didn't want anything to do with being Irish, I was British. But then I learned that I am Irish and I can reclaim all my Irishness, the Irish dancing, the Irish language, everything. That's as much part of me as it is to anybody in the nationalist community. I'm very proud to be a Protestant and very proud to be British, but I'm also very proud to be able to sit here and say, 'I'm Irish too' and have as much right to be as anyone.
>
> (in Cochrane 1997: 58)

But many unionist learners of Irish remain in a linguistic closet. Nationalist reaction to them ranges from delight to suspicion while those of a different persuasion can sometimes prove extremely hostile. Consequently learners often feel compelled to defend their commitment to the UK in British circles. At the same time when moving in Irish language environments they are required to conceal their loyalties to the language. In recent times nationalist parties have responded to the unionist interest in Irish. The SDLP has reiterated on numerous occasions that the language is a shared cultural and historical experience and belongs to both nationalists and unionists. SF's discourse has altered radically and this party no longer speaks of the language in terms of a cultural conquest.

Nationalists are increasingly adopting a discourse of rights with regard to the language and demanding equal status for the language in many sectors. In this context the signs debate at Queen's university provoked particular controversy. When the student's union removed bilingual (Irish-English) signs from the corridors of the university, some nationalists were quick to intimate that this situation was paralleled in other countries. An article by Eoghan Ó Néill, the editor of *Lá*, in the *Irish News* (24 August 1997) suggested that

> Even though the population of this state is, and always has been both British and Irish in character, no expression of Irishness has ever been reflected in the institutions of state. Just as some of the whites of the United States viewed equality for black citizens as a nightmare, a threat to their culture and ethos, just as some men viewed equality for women as a nightmare, so there are those in the north of Ireland who view equality for Irish speakers as offensive, insulting and a threat to their culture.

Ó Néill compared the British government's treatment of the Irish language community with that of the old Soviet Union's manipulation of minorities in the pre-Gorbachev era. His defence of the signs lay in the fact that they were bilingual rather than solely in Irish. For this reason 'no-one was excluded'. These signs gave recognition to two communities thereby acknowledging those who felt that they were either Irish and/or British. This, he suggests, contrasts sharply with Orange parades in Catholic locations or 'the portrait of the Queen in businesses employing both Catholics and Protestants' which only bolster the loyalties of one sector. While Ó Néill has a point in contrasting the inclusive nature of such signage with the exclusive dimension of the Orange Order, Protestants could easily counter with the example of the GAA, although, as I have argued, there are significant differences in the two processes of exclusion.

The discourse of rights with regard to Irish is not confined to the nationalist community and many unionists use it to justify their own interest in the language. This view expresses their entitlement to the resources of Irish while affirming their commitment to the union. Aughey (1995b: 14–15) has stated that although Irish 'has become a nationalist fetish there is nothing to prevent Protestants subverting the cultural enclosure of the language issue in a positive way'. Moreover, he argues that 'no cultured person in Northern Ireland ought to be ignorant of the linguistic influences – in place-names, in figures of speech – of their own land. This will mean some familiarity with the Irish language, not as a badge of separatism, but as a means to cultural enrichment. Why should Protestants be deprived of that cultural resource?'

Conclusion

Cultural differences, such as language and religion, are not definitional characteristics in themselves and while Gaelic cultural identity is enjoyed in both states, its implications for the community at large are not necessarily similar. Citizens in the Republic of Ireland achieved independence at the beginning of the twentieth century and they no longer view themselves simply in opposition to the British. In consequence, the significance of Catholicism and the Irish language has declined, while the GAA is largely enjoyed as a cultural activity. I am not implying here that the Republic of Ireland has lost its national culture with the acquisition of independence, but that it is no longer viewed in an oppositional context. This discourse represents Irishness 'as a progressive European identity that is taking its place amongst the identities of developed Western countries' (Gray 1999: 67). Gray has also identified other discourses of immigration and diaspora that are emerging in the Republic.

Northern Ireland still remains part of the UK. For this reason the post-colonial discourse is highly significant and emblems of ethnic nationhood have far-reaching political implications. That is not to suggest that there is a one-to-one relationship between Irish ethnic nationhood and emblems, such as language. But as citizens of the UK, many Northern nationalists deem cultural markers, such as the GAA, to be particularly relevant. (Some republicans in the 26 counties hold a similar perspective). These markers set the boundaries to a Gaelic cultural tradition. 'The boundaries themselves are "policed" by symbolic guards such as language, religion and culture that help to perpetuate the community internally. This implies a degree of fixity about the boundaries (and hence of bounded ethnic identity) and possibly underplays variations in types and conditions of ethnic allegiances' (McCrone 1998: 29).

But I noted in my initial chapter that definitions of Irishness vary not only according to one's location in relation to the Border, but also according to one's class. Middle-class Protestants and Catholics possibly share similar views on a range of Irish cultural activities and the definition of Irishness itself. Although they would probably reject such a viewpoint it is quite possible that their interpretation of Irishness does not differ substantially from that of many middle-class Catholics and Protestants in the Republic. Unlike their counterparts in Northern Ireland, citizens in the Republic of Ireland have benefited from a very positive relationship with

Europe and are no longer concerned solely with their relationship with Britain. In Northern Ireland the connection with Britain is still of primary importance, not just to Protestants, but to Catholics as well. Their sense of Irishness is still defined in opposition to their Britishness.

CHAPTER 8

THE 'FUZZY FRONTIER'

*The shape and edges of British identity are thus historically changing,
often vague and to a degree, malleable — an aspect of the British identity I have called 'a fuzzy frontier'.*

(Cohen 1994: 35)

Although the term 'British' is frequently perceived in an oppositional
context to 'Irish', its meaning is not always clearly defined. Robin Cohen
uses the phrase 'fuzzy frontier' to describe the conundrum of Britishness.
Here he is making an analogy with the concept of 'fuzzy logic' in mathe-
matics where a solution is attained by eliminating the uncertain edges to a
problem. Similarly, the term 'British' is ambiguous and can refer to a range
of political identities and relationships. Usually it alludes to the link
between Scotland, England, and Wales, which was formally enacted by an
Act of Union in 1707. This ensured that Scots, in common with England
and Wales, were represented at Westminster. Yet relations between Scots
and English were not necessarily harmonious and reactions to the new
arrangements depended on individual circumstances.

For poorer and less ambitious Scots and English, the Act of Union was
largely irrelevant. Prosperous Scots were alarmed at their loss of independence but were pleased at the opportunities offered by a wider home territory. Although some Scots resented the English, they were determined to
achieve full parity with them. Many English then as now were not entirely
happy with the promotion of the term 'British' at the expense of 'English'
(Colley 1996: 12). They were concerned that Scots would gain access to
English jobs while refusing to pay a fair share of taxes and were also wary
of former levels of hostility between the two countries. Such fears were
further exaggerated by the Scottish rebellions in 1715 and 1745. 'At one
level, then, Great Britain at the beginning of the eighteenth century was
like the Christian doctrine of the Trinity, both three and one, and altogether
something of a mystery' (Colley 1996: 13).

But the term 'British' cannot be confined to the relationship between the English, Scottish, and Welsh. It also refers to that between English and other Celtic groups such as the Cornish and Irish. Ironically, the term 'British' is itself closely related to 'Briton', referring to peoples of Celtic lineage who were driven west by the Angles and Saxons. The term also denotes those jurisdictions that are politically independent of Britain but linked to it for a variety of historical and often colonial reasons. Today the British Commonwealth is a voluntary association of 53 countries and their dependencies.

A meta-identity?

The concept of Britishness, both in a historical and contemporary context, varies in meaning throughout the regions of the UK. While the term 'British' offers a sense of common meta-identity, it does not negate internal differences or homogenise divergent cultures. Moreover, it does not dissolve strong regional attachments or dissipate loyalties to local communities or municipalities. National identities are not monolithic and no single attribute determines the significance of the word 'British' or 'Irish', or 'German'. Normally a range of characteristics, such as language, religion, territory, or myth of origin contributes to a sense of national unity and similarity. Any society exhibiting some of these characteristics can claim to participate in the national community. It does not necessarily have to demonstrate all the relevant attributes (Miller 1995).

'British' as a term poses a particular difficulty in that it is often confused with 'English'. In his examination of *The English Tribe*, Haseler (1996: 30) asserts that the very title of Great Britain, which was coined by a Francophone aristocracy, was inaccurate. Instead, ' "Greater England" would have been better'. There are several reasons for the confusion of these terms. Perhaps the most pertinent is the fact that the unity of the crowns in the early seventeenth century was accompanied by a drive towards Anglicisation both in Ireland and in the Highlands of Scotland. As I have already noted in Chapter 5, the Statutes of Icolmkill issued in Scotland in 1609 banned the patronage of Gaelic bards and intimated that *Inglis*, the language of the Lowlands, should become the sole language of Scotland. 'This Act was significant for its attitude towards Scots-Gaelic and was the first of many to be explicitly concerned with the status of the language' (Withers 1984: 29). Moreover these statutes 'attempted to break the linguistic link between clansmen and their chiefs by requiring clan chiefs to send their children to the Lowlands for an English education' (Durkacz 1983: 5). As a consequence of Anglicisation, the professional literary circuit of poets was broken and British rule was associated with the dominance of English or Lowland Scottish culture.

For some contemporary unionists and nationalists, the terms 'British' and 'English' are equivalent. While historically the identification of the Anglicisation process with the British legacy is in part responsible for this confusion of terms, the location of both the UK parliament and the British Crown in London has further generated the misnomer. Walker (1999: 156) suggests that 'for Republicans, and indeed for most constitutional Irish nationalists, "Britishness" means "Englishness" and the Union is equated with the English connection specifically'.

Buruma (1998) intimates that such a strategy was entirely necessary. While independent states require progressive political institutions, they also benefit from a predominant culture or language. Prevalence in cultural terms does not necessarily imply a dominant ethnic group. He points to Britain as the classic example of such a case. This state is composed of a variety of nations and accommodates members of different religious denominations. Yet the culture of the English prevails to such an extent that many English citizens fail to distinguish any difference between England and Britain. Buruma suggests that Britain could not function as a state until its members had adapted themselves to the English culture or at least to the English language.

Yet there are differences between the two terms and the notion of Britishness in Scotland differs from that in England. Whereas there is not necessarily a conflict between the two terms in England, there has always been a fear that the English would dominate and assimilate Scottish culture north of the border. Britishness in Scotland incorporates a strong sense of Scottishness. Moreover, 'in the working-class west-central belt it involves an affinity with Ulster Protestants' (Bradley 1995: 188). A Gallup poll conducted early in 1999 confirmed strong differences between the perception of Britishness in Scotland and England. Scottish respondents were asked to define their identity in terms of their Scottishness or Britishness. English respondents were given the options of 'English' or 'British'.

According to the results more than half of the English questioned were happy to identify themselves as primarily British, but 62 percent of the Scottish recorded themselves as Scottish in the first instance (King 1999). Obviously such replies do not imply that Scots reject a sense of Britishness. It merely indicates that they are less likely to merge their national identity with the larger concept of state. Further queries by this survey established that the Scots are clearly more aware than the English of symbols of nationhood. While more than 40 percent of Scots knew that St Andrew's day occurs in November, only 30 percent of the English were aware of any details regarding St. George's day.

Many unionists in Northern Ireland strongly cherish their Scottish inheritance. It is possible that the sense of Britishness in Northern Ireland is closer to that in Scotland rather than in England. Interestingly, even though some Northern Irish Protestants might confuse the terms 'English' and 'British', very few actually claim to be English, preferring instead to emphasise their Scottish connections. 'Their culture and identity is British and, for a great many Ulster people, a specifically Scottish expression of Britishness, whether it be the music of the pipes, the poetry of Burns or Scottish country dancing, let alone a religio-political or intellectual *mentalité'* (original emphasis in Thomson 1996: 77).

British identity in Northern Ireland

A commitment to the UK constitutes the dominant ideology in Northern Ireland. In Chapter 1, I noted that according to the NISAS of 1994, 71 percent of the Protestant community identified itself as British. A further 10 percent of Catholics opted for a similar classification. Trimble (1989: 47) suggests that the significance of the term 'British' lies in its emphasis on membership of the larger group. Unionists in Northern Ireland do not see themselves in the context of 'this little bit of narrow ground'. They are part of the British state and their own sense of Britishness has increased rather than decreased in the last decade.

Yet there are significant differences between a sense of Britishness among Scottish and Northern Irish communities, not least of which is the fact that Northern Irish Protestants accord the highest priority to their British identity. This may be a direct consequence of the fact that Northern Ireland is not officially part of Britain. To define themselves as British is to reinforce the links between Northern Ireland and Britain. Moreover, the question of whether an Irish identity was ever placed on a par with that of Scotland or Wales is highly contentious. Colley (1992: 327) argues that Ireland was never treated 'as an integral part of a truly united kingdom. Ireland was in many respects the laboratory of the British Empire'. For that reason, some Protestants might feel that a claim to be Irish devalues their sense of Britishness.

Walker (1995) suggests that there are further differences between Britishness in Northern Ireland and in Scotland in that the majority of Scots who are not separatists tend to identify with the concept of a British state rather than a British nation. This, he suggests, contrasts with Northern Irish Protestants who have a stronger concept of the British nation, although that is not to deny their constant emphasis on the significance of the British state. In my view this is due to the fact that Northern Irish Protestants are generally very keen to distance themselves from the Irish nation, unlike the Scots, who clearly identify with the Scottish nation. But this would not have been the case in the nineteenth century when unionism (north and south) often presented itself as a form of Irish patriotism, which was chiefly a concern for the good of the nation. In that context the concept of unionist Irish patriots is conceivable.

But Northern Irish unionists are often regarded as 'not quite British' or 'un-British' by people in Britain. This places them in a similar position to nationalists who are sometimes construed in the Republic as being British or British and Irish, rather than purely Irish. I believe that there are several reasons for this perspective. For some English, Welsh, or Scottish, the fact that these people are born in Ireland, albeit Northern Ireland, defines them as Irish rather than British. This community has not officially resided in Britain for centuries. Others reject the Britishness of these unionists with an assertion that they do not subscribe to British principles of impartiality, magnanimity, or tolerance (Ruane and Todd 1996). My own view is that their Britishness is rejected because it has been associated with conflict. Failure to achieve genuine lasting peace on home territories disturbs many British citizens. The British state has successfully sent emissaries to Bosnia, Serbia, and other situations of conflict. Yet peace in Northern Ireland is in a very fragile state. Therefore British citizens distance themselves both from the people and the distressing circumstances of Northern Ireland (Guelke 1988: 196).

Moreover, the Britishness of the Northern Irish is frequently censured. Sometimes unionists are criticised for failing to construct a specific national identity! Nairn (1981) argues that their tendency towards crude imperialistic 'Britishism' is a consequence of the primitive nature of their nationality. But as I noted in Chapter 6, indecisiveness regarding one's identity is an attribute that is exhibited on a variety of levels of the British society and is particularly associated with the English. Viewed in that context, 'unionism appears less exceptional than has been conventionally assumed' (Coulter 1994: 10). Unless there is a standard, universally-accepted definition of Britishness, and as far as I'm aware there is not, it is not feasible to accuse unionists in Northern Ireland as being un-British. In reality, this concept generates a variety of meanings in disparate contexts (Walker 1999). Diversity is the essence of Britishness and 'national identity is a deeply ambiguous and sometimes multi-layered phenomenon' (Walker 1992: 71).

There is a view that Northern Irish unionism is perhaps 'replete with un-British-like qualities, and an unwelcome reminder of some of the elements that contributed to building the British state – Protestantism, ethnic dominance, settler mentalities and violence' (O'Dowd 1998: 84). Cochrane (1997: 70) asserts that these unionists relate to a mythical, rather than a real, British community, which owes more to 'Kipling's Britishness' than to a modern, multicultural UK. (Perhaps Kipling was a deliberate choice on the part of Cochrane as some of his writings reflect strong anti-Irish sentiments.)

If it is true that Northern Irish unionists display a more extreme form of Britishness, then they are not unlike nationalists, who often place greater emphasis on symbols of Irishness than their counterparts in the Republic. There is a variety of reasons for such a view. In the first instance, while Northern Ireland is officially part of the UK, it is not part of Great Britain. 'In a sense then, Northern Ireland is a less integral part of Britain than Algeria was as a *département* of France' (Miller 1998: 6). Unionists in

Northern Ireland are physically separated from Britain by the Irish Sea and are therefore defending a tradition from a distance. Outpost people whom Ascherson (1996: 100) defines as 'faithful defenders of some tradition whose centre is far away and which, often, is already decaying into oblivion' are usually more excessive in their adherence to any tradition. He compares them to the Krajina Serbs living on the border between Croatia and Bosnia-Herzegovina who believe that 'they are the truest and purest Serbs, uncorrupted by whatever may happen in Belgrade, standing guard against the "Germanised" Croats and the imaginary onslaught of fundamentalist Islam'. Unionists in Northern Ireland are more commonly compared with Afrikaners who have regarded themselves as the guardians of the Christian principles of the West among barbaric peoples (Akenson 1992).

Perhaps this kind of atavistic tendency reflects insecurity on the part of these unionists whose double minority status I have explored in earlier chapters. Unionists are aware of the attraction of Britain for the most talented members of their community (Foster, J. 1988). Numerous writers, such as C. S. Lewis, Helen Waddell, and Louis MacNeice, left the Region in order to reside in Britain. In consequence, society in Northern Ireland has contributed enormously to the artistic diversity of Britain – a process that has not been reciprocated, thereby generating a certain sense of mediocrity. 'We grew up in Lilliput, save we were aware from the start of the country of the giant Gulliver, as the Lilliputians were not' (Foster, J. 1988: 19). Of course, many noted writers in the Republic of Ireland also left. Wilde, Shaw, and Joyce all benefited from international experience. Memmi (1965) complains of a similar syndrome in Tunisia where only the less talented remained at home while those with greater skills journeyed to Britain.

In exhibiting what is regarded as an extreme form of Britishness, Unionists in Northern Ireland are, in my opinion, merely demonstrating their own interpretation of this identity. Such renditions of Britishness are perhaps more emotional and more obvious than those of other constituent nations such as Scotland, but this is a natural consequence of their physical separation from Great Britain and the pressure of constantly feeling under siege. Identity generally is constructed in oppositional terms and these unionists define themselves in terms of two, rather than one 'other'. Relationships with both the UK and the nationalist community are a constant source of concern. According to Alcock, (1994: 145) unionists are

> children of the British family. Many, especially Irish nationalists, will consider them illegitimate children. Now the family wants to be rid of them. But in the meantime the children have grown up. They have been pushed in upon themselves, hardened – even brutalised – by rejection by their kin on the one hand and Irish Republican terrorism on the other. Cold-shouldering by their kin has made them as different as the English have always wanted to believe them different. But Irish terrorism has ensured the rejection of their Britishness will not mean they will open themselves to the Irish.

In this sense they are not unlike the Afrikaner community in the apartheid era, who regarded themselves as distinct from the Black African majority but also defined themselves in terms of their relationship with the empire (Johnson 1990).

Although they constitute the majority in Northern Ireland, unionists are aware that the principal British parties do not run candidates in the Northern Irish elections. In this sense unionists represent a marginal interest within the UK. Their perception of belonging to the Union is constantly under threat. As I outlined in my initial chapter, these unionists are aware that, under certain circumstances, the British government might relinquish its dominion over Northern Ireland, thereby extending the authority of the Dublin parliament to the 32 counties (Guelke 1988: 4). Furthermore, the new Assembly may result in a gradual diminution of symbols of British identity or in some restrictions on the cultural activities of unionists.

Civic and ethnic unionism

In common with Irish nationalism, British ideology has its civic and ethnic components (McGarry and O'Leary 1995). A commitment to the concept of citizenship within the UK is the essence of its civic form. Prior to 1948, inhabitants of the British Isles and the British Empire were regarded as subjects of the Crown but in that year, subjects of the Crown acquired citizenship under the 1948 Nationality Act. All citizens are considered equal, regardless of their religious or cultural commitments.

The ethnic version of Britishness celebrates the Union as an expression of British Protestant accomplishment and lays particular emphasis on various discourses of belonging. It was a form of Britishness that was reinforced ideologically through the influence of Margaret Thatcher and was given vocal expression in 1968 by the conservative MP Enoch Powell, who spoke disparagingly about the influx of immigrants to the country. Powell was an 'ethnic essentialist' (Ignatieff 1998: 18) who assumed that all human beings were members of primary racial groups. From his perspective, the British constituted an ethnically homogenous group whose political traditions were threatened, rather than enhanced, by the arrival of non-white immigrants who would find it impossible to endorse British values. He believed that the legitimacy of one's civic beliefs arose from one's ethnic tradition. A British individual was born with an appreciation of democracy and fair play. Non-indigenous immigrants would be incapable of appreciating these 'British' values.

Powell stated that this arrival of foreigners filled him 'with foreboding'. He believed that an influx of large numbers of members of an alien culture was a mistake and compared himself to a Roman viewing the river Tiber foaming with blood. In this Powell misused the metaphor as when the river Nile turns to blood in the Book of Exodus, it is because the Jewish migrants are trying to leave, rather than enter Egypt! Powell's address, which subsequently became known as the 'rivers of blood' speech, was greeted with public outrage and revulsion and his discourse was subsequently officially ostracised. Yet it is possible that a considerable proportion of the population secretly endorsed his perspective (Paxman 1998: 72).

Civic and ethnic versions of Britishness are present in Northern Ireland. Todd (1987) has distinguished between the two groups of unionists using the terms 'British Unionists' and 'Ulster Loyalists' – between those with British or Ulster identities. According to Todd (1987), British unionists primarily identify with Great Britain rather than Northern Ireland. But this implies that these unionists are exile-minded (perhaps like some Irish in Britain). Instead I feel that their primary imagined community lies in the UK and that they are completely committed to the maintenance of Northern Ireland, Scotland and Wales within this framework. Some of them have a particularly strong relationship with England and Longley (1990: 23) states that 'Anglo-Unionism often imports Englishness to stand in for Britishness (and fend off "Irishness"), just as the English themselves confuse "British" with "English"'. Because its concerns are with the UK rather than solely with Northern Ireland, this group considers itself more international than parochial. Its advocates are proud of the antiquity and diversity of the British tradition and regard it as the epitome of civilisation. However its actual relationship with Britain is often fraught and tense.

Citizenship is the central tenet of British unionism, although the British never developed the concept of citizenship as the French did. Instead, British citizenship developed from the pre-modern definition of people as subjects of the Crown. Citizenship is usually perceived in contrast with, rather than as a form of, nationalism – a dichotomy that is reinforced in part by a common insistence on 'two' communities whose aspirations are perceived as being in opposition to one another. British unionists regard their Britishness as a reflection of their citizenship rather than their nationality. 'There are only British citizens who happen to be English, Scottish, Welsh, Irish and some who would be none of these' (Aughey 1995b: 12). Issues of equality, rights, and the calibre of citizenship within the Union motivate them and they believe that a nationalist obsession with concepts of loyalty, identity, and nationhood is confusing and detrimental.

This perspective reinforces a dichotomy between citizenship and nationalism. But recent events in Europe may yet alter that duality. According to the Amsterdam Treaty passed in 1998 'every national of a Member State is a citizen of the Union' (European Commission 1999: 29). This statement equates the two concepts. Thus any British national is automatically a citizen of the EU. But the term 'British' commonly denotes citizenship, not nationality, which in this context is usually Welsh, Scottish, or English (Kockel 1999c). According to Ascherson (1996), the concept of citizenship as a unifying force may derive from history when the Ottoman Empire, the old Polish-Lithuanian Commonwealth, and other former powers did not require their citizens to conform ethnically, religiously, or linguistically. Instead, great emphasis was placed on military allegiance and obedience to the civil code.

'Liberal Unionism' is the term given by Porter (1996) to the ideology of civic unionists; the author proposes that the concept is equally attractive for Catholics and Protestants. Perhaps it includes those Catholics that I mentioned in my first chapter as identifying themselves as British in the 1994 NISAS. As this form of unionism is a civic concept, it is reputed to include all traditions. This is reflected in the following statement issued by the Ulster Democratic Party (UDP) in 1997:

> The UDP believes that remaining part of the United Kingdom offers people of both traditions room for expressing their identity. Britishness – unlike a single Irish identity which is fully exercised by the issue of ethnic community – is a civic concept which is pluralist, overarching and inclusive. The Union embodies equal rights and respect of values of its different national components: Scotland, Wales, England and Northern Ireland.
>
> The United Kingdom is multi-national, multi-ethnic and multi-religious. With the emphasis being on citizenship rather than ethnicity, Britishness is able to accommodate people regardless of ethnic identity or religion. It is a modern political doctrine based on rights and citizenship which transcends the limited concepts of nationalism. Therefore, the UDP believes that the best future for all the people of Northern Ireland lies firmly within the United Kingdom and within a form of unionism which is democratic, responsible, accountable and inclusive.

This statement places citizenship in opposition to nationality. Furthermore, it assumes a single Irish identity together with a variety of British identities, which are perceived as being of Scotland, Wales, England, and Northern Ireland. Despite the contrast between civic and ethnic forms of unionism there is no reference to the diversity of identities within the British tradition in Northern Ireland.

In contrast to British unionists, the primary imagined community of loyalists lies in the six counties of Northern Ireland, which they commonly call Ulster although this term, strictly speaking, refers to nine rather than six counties. Proponents of an ethnic form of Britishness are often of Scottish rather than of English descent, and are keen to emphasise the unique association between Northern Ireland and Scotland. These Scotch-Irish have endeavoured to heighten awareness of the link between Northern Ireland and Scotland and many unrelated activities in recent years have begun to focus on the relationship between the two countries. A Research Institute of Irish and Scottish Studies in Aberdeen has already set up symposia to explore the collaboration between the two countries. Sabhal Mór Ostaig in the Isle of Skye has run conferences on the Gaelic and Scots linguistic links. Loyalists are also keen to raise the awareness of the Diaspora in places such as Pennsylvania, Appalachia, and many regions in the American South (Kay 1997).

Ulster loyalist culture is profoundly religious and covenantal and, as is the case with British unionists, its relationship with Britain is suspicious and distrustful. But as I have already argued in Chapter 5, no modern democracy maintains an attitude of unquestioning obedience to its government and British history provides many examples of political upheaval. Far from being different to other members of the UK, unionists in Northern Ireland display a trait that is quite typical of other parts of British society, except that in the case of Northern Ireland it is displayed in a more extreme form (Coulter 1994).

Walker (1995) suggests that the emergence of nationalist fervour in Scotland is a direct consequence of the contractarian nature of Scottish allegiance. In pre-Parliament days, many Scots felt that British policy was failing to accommodate the separate and distinct identities of the Scottish and English. In the case of both Northern Ireland and Scotland, 'there are important questions raised about what Britishness means politically, questions which indicate that the British state, although a unitary one, is underpinned by different, and perhaps conflicting, interpretations' (Walker 1995: 171–2). As a consequence of differing interpretations, 'Britain and Britishness take on the nature of something negotiated, bargained for, covenanted, or contracted'.

The Northern Irish Protestant

One essential attribute in the forging of a sense of Britishness was the Protestant religion or at least a particular exclusionist, sectarian version of it. In the previous chapter I explored the link between Irish nationalism and Catholicism. In a similar fashion, British ideology was closely linked with Protestantism. But the alliance between nationalism and Catholicism in Ireland was, comparatively speaking, a rather late development and did not really occur until the late nineteenth and early twentieth centuries. In contrast, the forging of a sense of Britishness was clearly linked with a sense of shared Protestantism from the eighteenth century forwards.

Protestants in England, Scotland, and Wales defined themselves primarily in opposition to Catholics of continental Europe (Colley 1992). While Catholics in Britain were usually able to attend mass and socialise with their neighbours, they were conscious of their representation as a threat in public consciousness. Until 1859 Protestant congregations commemorated the infamous gunpowder plot in which a Catholic, Guy Fawke, endeavoured to blow up the British king and Parliament. Today children commemorate this event on the 5th November by seeking 'a penny for the Guy' and firework displays are common on the anniversary.

Throughout the first half of the eighteenth century there was a constant fear that a Catholic monarchy would be restored by forceful means in Britain. Popular mythology reinforced the misfortune that befell Charles I when he married the French Catholic queen, Henrietta Maria. Apparently James II, the last Catholic Stuart king, would have done untold damage but for William of Orange, who championed the Protestant cause in Europe. Catholics were held responsible for a variety of disasters such as the Irish brutalities in Ulster in 1641 or the Great Fire of London more than 20 years later. Moreover, a variety of wars with Catholic states in Europe ensured that the Protestant experience became essentially associated with Britishness. 'This mythic interpretation of history, a characteristic of all nation building, was emphatically *British*, not just English in its scope' (original emphasis in Colley 1992: 317).

While Catholics lived in Britain, they did not really belong to the British state. They were commonly hypothesised as 'outlandish', inferring that conceptually they were beyond the boundaries, on the outside (Colley 1992: 320). Similarly, Ulster Protestants viewed themselves as uncompromisingly British in opposition to the large numbers of Catholics surrounding them. Just as Protestants in Britain were wary of a continental Catholic threat to their liberties and privileges, Ulster Protestants constantly feared for their own security. From their perspective, the threat of the other tradition was immediate and overwhelming due to the close proximity and sheer numbers of Irish Catholics.

Divisions between Catholics and the established Church were given legal status during the era of the Penal Laws. Many of these also applied to the Presbyterian community but restrictions on that group were relaxed early in the eighteenth century. A variety of factors including the decline of support for the Stuart dynasty persuaded the established Church gradually to reduce discriminatory laws against British and Irish Catholics. Yet there were reservations against such moves and they provoked a nation-wide petitioning campaign from Welsh Protestant groups. Despite such resistance a Catholic Emancipation Act was passed in 1829 and some rights were restored to Catholics in Britain and in Ireland. Until then 'in law – if not always in fact – they were treated as potential traitors as un-British' (Colley 1996: 20).

Contemporary society in Britain is far more tolerant with regard to religious diversity. Miller (1995: 160) speculates that this is a 'specifically Protestant form of tolerance' respecting persuasions that emphasise individual conscience and belief, but disapproving of denominations with hierarchical authority. While Catholics have probably crossed the 'borderline of respectability', there is a great opposition to Muslims 'probably because of images of Ayatollahs apparently controlling masses of adoring believers', an experience that is totally unrelated to any aspect of Protestant culture. In part this is a reflection of the shift in paradigm that I alluded to in Chapter 3. Christian traditions are realigning themselves as separated members of a single tradition, preferring to view non-Christian denominations in an oppositional context.

Yet there is one aspect of official anti-Catholic discrimination that still survives. In Britain the throne is clearly a Protestant institution and no Catholic is permitted to accede to it or to marry its heir. Any member of the royal family who converts to Catholicism must forfeit his or her succession rights. On accession the incoming heir takes an oath as 'Defender of the Faith'. I find this incredibly ironic as this title (which is still engraved on British coinage) was originally conferred by the pope in Rome on the then Catholic king Henry VIII. This title was in recognition of Henry's treatise in favour of the sacraments against the assertions of Luther and is of particular significance for Orangemen who define their duty as serving the Protestant monarch. In consequence, if the monarch is not Protestant, Orangemen are no longer bound to serve him or her (Wright 1973).

But Prince Charles, the incumbent heir, has strongly indicated that he may revise this title to 'Defender of Faith', thereby loosening the bonds between the throne and the Church of England. Moreover, he has explicitly indicated that his Catholic partner is a non-negotiable aspect of his personal life. Protestants in Northern Ireland have reacted strongly against any intimations of change in the religious oath:

> Firstly, I feel a certain amount of confusion. The British throne to which Ulster Protestants claim allegiance is rapidly becoming non-Protestant. The heir to the throne is an enthusiast for multi-faith services and the New Age movement, he is most unlikely to be willing to take a solemn oath to maintain and defend the Protestant religion. Should we claim allegiance to a throne that is rapidly departing from the Protestant faith?
>
> (Thomson 1996: 34–5)

Although there is no other example of official anti-Catholic discrimination in Britain, some controversy has emerged regarding an anti-Catholic ethos in Scotland. At the opening of the Edinburgh Festival in 1999, a playwright, James Macmillan, claimed that his country is rife with anti-Catholic bigotry. While it is generally accepted that the supporters of Glasgow Rangers frequently express anti-Catholic sentiments, many Scottish Catholics have denied that they have experienced any form of discrimination on the basis of their religion. Their situation contrasts with that of Catholics in Northern Ireland, many of whom still feel stigmatised because of their religious affiliation. It is certainly the case that in this instance Northern Ireland compares unfavourably with Scotland.

Belfast's first Catholic Lord Mayor was elected in 1995 whereas Glasgow's first Catholic Lord Provost was chosen in 1938. Despite advances made since 1972 it is still the case that Catholics in Northern Ireland are more economically disadvantaged than their Protestant counterparts whereas all the evidence in Scotland suggests that there is no perceivable variance in the socio-economic status of the two groups. A Scottish Social

Mobility Survey conducted in 1972 demonstrated minor variations between the social class profiles of Protestants and Catholic in the older age groups, but this difference did not pertain to younger groups (Bruce 1999a).

In the initial chapter I referred to the extent of residential and social segregation of Catholics and Protestants, particularly in urban districts in Northern Ireland. This contrasts sharply with Scotland where few urban areas could be defined as distinctly Catholic or Protestant, but of course Catholic Scots tend to be Highlanders or Irish. In Chapter 3 I noted that interfaith marriages were still relatively rare in Northern Ireland whereas they feature commonly in Scotland. Such marriages are still strongly resented in Northern Ireland and the partners endure a great deal of social discomfort. In Scotland 'were it not for Catholic schools little or nothing would now distinguish the descendants of the Irish from native Scots' (Bruce 1999a: 3).

While anti-Catholicism may have featured prominently in British society in previous centuries, it does not appear to prevail to any great extent today. But in Northern Ireland, there is a feeling that 'under the surface of everyday life there is a common bond of fundamental Protestant values that unite Ulster Protestants and people on the mainland' (Loughlin 1995: 251), although even here it is in decline. Where it arises, hostility towards Catholics on the part of Northern Irish Protestants usually derives from a sense of Britishness or loyalism, rather than from actual religious differences (Walker 1995). Catholics in Northern Ireland regard Orange banners as one of the more visible expressions of antagonism. Many emblems display a strong sense of division between the different religious traditions, along with a tangible sense of superiority:

> What carried the Orange monarch to victory? His wholehearted submission to God's will was reflected in his belief that the faith which had battled its way out of the papist tomb in the reformation years was the only faith by which to live. He held that the doctrines, statutes and precepts of the reformed faith should be the dominant forces in the lives of men, politically morally, socially and religiously. How wise he was!
>
> (Banner 1990: 32)

Not all Protestants regard these hermeneutics as relevant or appropriate. McMaster (1997: 112) claims that such interpretations of Bible stories suggest 'a religious and cultural superiority, they legitimise exclusiveness, dominance and a political arrangement of power that I cannot connect with the mind of Christ. The image of God that emerges is an image of God on our "Protestant" side'. Perhaps the real message of these depictions is not so much that God supports Protestants as much as that S/He favours the British tradition in Northern Ireland.

Civilisation or culture

Whereas nationalists are frequently criticised as being overly attached to cultural symbols and traditions, British culture has somehow been regarded as almost 'voiceless' in Northern Ireland. Proponents of a 32-county Ireland are associated with an obsessive love of national history, the Irish language, and the GAA. On the other hand, the image of the Northern Irish Protestant is that of an industrious, assertive, self-reliant but 'culture-less' individual in a bowler hat. Culture 'imparts subtle signals to outsiders as to who are the good guys, and who are the anal types, best avoided. Somehow, republicans have always won on this front, while unionists refuse to play or repudiate the value of any culture other than hard graft and gerrymandering' (Lynch 1998: 17).

For me, the lack of culture associated with Northern Irish Protestants is in part a reflection of a general difficulty with the concept of British culture. This is probably due to the fact that the concept of Britishness does not entirely encapsulate the ideology of any single nation – although, as I noted in Chapter 6, Anglican forces have heavily influenced it. There is tension between British and national cultures in all member states of the UK. This applies even in England itself where there is an increasing demand for symbols that are distinctly English, rather than British.

But unionists' apparent lack of interest in culture also reflects their adherence to a civic tradition. The polarity between civilisation and culture is merely an endorsement of differing emphases between civic and ethnic nationalism although, as examined in the previous chapter, there are increasing difficulties with these categories. Irish nationalism is located on the ethnic end of the spectrum whereas British nationalism is deemed to be civic in nature. Yet in my view any examination of history suggests a variety of instances contradicting this clear-cut distinction. For example, the Plantation of Ulster was 'an explicit attempt to control Ireland strategically by introducing ethnic and religious elements loyal to the British interest in Ireland' (O'Dowd 1999: 177). At this time the intention was to civilise the indigenous population, but markers of civilisation were ethnic and included the English language and loyalty to the Anglican Church.

Civic unionists, in particular, profess to have little concern for cultural matters or at least to make no connection between cultural and political issues. As I have already noted, citizenship is the central component of this ideology and its proponents believe that they are unaffected, and indeed unencumbered, by any form of cultural nationalism. Their ideology is reputedly 'culture-blind' (Porter 1996: 66). Many sociologists would dispute this apparent lack of interest in cultural affairs (Cochrane 1997) as in recent times all unionists have demonstrated various levels of anxiety concerning aspects of the British culture of Northern Ireland, such as Orange parades, which have been accorded great priority. Social cohesion has been generated among unionists who perceive a threat to this expression of

British Orange culture. Despite a claim to 'culture-blindness', civic union-ists regard certain official emblems and rituals, such as the Union Jack and the British anthem, as highly significant. These symbols reinforce their sense of belonging to the UK. Moreover, the UU party opted to take the Ministry for Culture, Arts and Leisure in the Northern Ireland Assembly.

Overall, loyalists appear to have a greater concern for culture than civic unionists do, and profess an ethnic rather than a civic form of Britishness. Its proponents especially value the unique symbols of a British Ulster cul-ture. Such emblems include, for example, Orange marches, the Star of David, King Billy on his white horse, and Red Hand. Many of these emblems are arcane and often inspired by a Masonic tradition (Buckley 1989). Some have little relevance outside of the Region (Gallagher 1995) and reinforce the loyalist sense of belonging in Northern Ireland. Pro-ponents of loyalism also cherish strongly the links with Scotland. Symbols of culture that reinforce the connection between the two regions are gain-ing greater relevance. These symbols include the Cruthin myth of origin and the Ulster-Scots Tongue, which I have examined in Chapter 5. 'Cul-tural Unionism' is the term given by Porter (1996) to the loyalist stream of thought.

The Orange tradition

Orange marches are a particularly strong contemporary expression of Protestant culture in Northern Ireland (Bryan 1998: Bryan et al. 1995; Jar-man 1997; Jarman et al. 1998). In fact, the Order was a minority movement among Protestants until the final decades of the nineteenth century. Gener-ally speaking loyalists and unionists begin their association with the Orange Order as adults and usually progress to membership of the Royal Arch Purple Chapter – a body that is virtually indistinguishable from the Order (Malcomson 1999). Members are then entitled to join the Imperial Grand Black Chapter of the British Commonwealth, although this is not necessarily pursued, as it is regarded as representing more conservative, conventional, middle-class individuals. Some Orangemen also join the smaller, 12,000-strong, Apprentice Boys of Derry.

The format of Orange parades is an old tradition inherited from the Irish Volunteer Movement originally established to obstruct any French invasion of Ireland in the 1780s. Lambeg Drums are beaten loudly at these occasions and are commonly linked with the Dutch regiments that accompanied King Billy *en route* to the Boyne (Montgomery and Whitten 1995; Scullion 1981). All these groups have a common purpose in asserting the Britishness of the Region, each Orange lodge has its own identity and retains a limited auton-omy from the county lodges or the Grand Lodge. Each lodge selects pic-tures to be printed on their silk banners, which are largely dominated by images of King Billy and 'display subjects relating to the Protestant faith and British nationality' (Jarman 1999: viii). Sometimes they choose historical themes of British significance and they also display great historical British leaders or religious features. Local scenes can also feature.

Relations between different groups, and in particular between working- and middle-class unionists and loyalists are not entirely free from stress. Dissatisfaction with the British State is reflected within the Orange organisation and the lodges are gradually proving unpopular with young working-class Protestants. This may prove ominous in the future for the UUP as its electors tend to be drawn from these institutions. Moreover, the structure of the parades has changed, with a rapid increase in the number of 'blood and thunder' bands in poorer urban locations, such as Belfast, Portadown, and Lisburn (Bryan et al 1995). These band players, often DUP supporters, can add a competitive, hostile, and almost militant element to the occasion. On the other hand, rituals in wealthier and rural venues can appear less aggressive and more refined as country parades tend to feature a greater proportion of pipe and silver bands. Of course there is no clear-cut distinction between the two groups and both elements are usually present in the most marches.

Despite inherent tensions, Orange commemorations reflect an affiliation between divergent peoples who are connected in a common affirmation of Britishness. Many are also united in an expression of hostility towards the British government, which, from their perspective, is not fully committed to its own people in Northern Ireland. This sense of alienation pervades the entire community but is particularly prevalent among Protestant working classes that have recently suffered increased rates of unemployment. Parades are more than a device of historical commemoration and representation. They have become a symbol of protest against the status quo and their numbers have increased as anxieties have grown.

Orangemen regard their marches as a unique expression of their Britishness 'and every year "the Twelfth of July" is a gigantic exercise in catharsis which serves to give a kind of identity to what would otherwise be a variegated and much fragmented Protestantism' (Lyons 1971: 720). Because Orangemen represent a territorial claim to Northern Ireland regardless of unionist or nationalist occupancy, parades constitute a discourse of belonging that is sometimes reliant on antagonism and opposition. Should attitudes change in nationalist areas and Catholics welcome Orange marches in their localities, the discourse of belonging would lose some meaning. Orangemen would march with the permission of Catholics thereby denying the Orange claim to ownership of the territory!

Although Orangemen regard marches as an expression of their Britishness, some observers view them as symptomatic of a hybrid, rather than a British, identity. When speaking of the Orange parades that he viewed as a child in Northern Ireland Glendinning (1997: 57), a founder member of the Alliance Party, reported that they served as a reminder of how Irish the occasions seemed:

Each banner carried the name of a townland derived from the Irish language. The whole event was born out of Irish history and its nature and significance had altered down the years with the historical changes that had taken place. The peculiar mixture of religion and politics, of the local and the national, of gaiety and solemnity, the respectable and the outrageous, seemed to me to be very Irish indeed. Indeed, the way in which the flags, bunting, banners, the painted kerbstones, the marchers and their supporters, the young men throwing the maces in the air and wilder bands expressed loyalty to Britain and Britishness was done in a quintessential Irish way.

It is his opinion that this expression of British identity is unrecognisable in Britain. 'No one on the mainland of Great Britain, outside Liverpool or Glasgow, would have thought any of it had anything to do with being British. It demonstrated, I felt, that the word British, as seen in Northern Ireland, must refer to a loyalty to the Crown and the UK and not to an ethnic group called British'. The primary impression that Glendinning (1997: 57) derived from these occasions was that the 'brethren were in fact loyal Irishmen'.

These comments raise the question as to whether this expression of British identity is recognised in Britain. As Glendinning correctly observes, the Orange community has networks in various parts of the UK and the Republic of Ireland. For example, a parade is traditionally held in County Donegal on the Saturday before the Twelfth. Considerable numbers of Orangemen from Northern Ireland partake in this event, signalling solidarity with their comrades in the South. Members also participate in the Orange parades held at this time in Strathclyde. As a reciprocal gesture, many of their Scottish brethren return with them to take part in the commemorations in Northern Ireland. Similarly, several Orangemen from England prefer to participate in the Northern Irish, rather than the English, commemorations. This unity may be a response to a perceived threat to British identity in Northern Ireland.

Scottish Orangeism derives its roots in Northern Ireland and was first brought to the country by soldiers returning to south Ayrshire, having completed their duty as British soldiers in the North. Some of the early Orangemen were also Protestant migrants from Northern Ireland. Currently there are some one thousand lodges in the Loyal Orange Institution of Scotland but many other Protestants play in the traditional bands who take part in the parades. As is the case in Northern Ireland, an independent Orange Order exists in Scotland, representing the more militant dimension of the movement.

A survey conducted by Bradley (1995) on a sample group of Scottish Orangemen demonstrated that a mere 6 percent of the community claimed an Irish background although a further 13 percent invoked both an Irish and Scottish heritage. Interestingly, while 14 percent of the group classed themselves as British, the dominant classification was Scottish. While nothing prevented individuals from identifying themselves as both

Scottish and British, half of the respondents indicated that they had solely a Scottish identity. These conclusions support the results of the 1999 Gallup survey, which revealed that Scottishness is more important than Britishness in Scotland. But Bradley argues that for these Orangemen their Protestant identity is even more significant that their sense of Scottishness. As Colley (1992) asserts that Protestantism was once the essence of Britishness, perhaps the Scottish Orangemen are espousing a form of Britishness that has already been abandoned in England.

Mural painting

Mural painting is another expression of British culture in Northern Ireland (Jarman 1992; 1998; McVeigh 2000; Rolston 1992; 1995; Vannais 1999). From the beginning of the century until the time of the nationalist hunger strikes in the early 1980s, this form of political statement was solely the prerogative of unionists. The origins of this tradition lie in the elaborate exhibitions of flowers for the annual July commemorations in the nineteenth century (Jarman 1998). These floral tributes identified the loyal Protestant territories of a British Ulster but blossoms are of a very temporary nature and when the first loyalist mural was painted in Belfast in 1908 a more permanent expression of Britishness was established. This picture illustrated the defeat of the Catholic king James II by the Protestant king William III, thereby emphasising the centrality of Protestantism to British identity in Northern Ireland. This theme that was to dominate murals for many decades.

When the Northern Irish State was established, loyalist murals provided a more constant affirmation of a Protestant state for a Protestant people. These paintings, renewed during the marching season, were present throughout the remainder of the year. Streets could be more permanently identified as belonging to Protestant or British people. Such markings served not merely as discourse of belonging but also as affirmations of ownership. Murals operate as pictorial boundaries, and were further supported by loyalist graffiti and the painting of the kerbstones in the colours of the Union Jack.

In this context, paint identifies commitment and images of loyalty are especially prevalent in working-class areas (Woods 1995), reflecting the class divide referred to in earlier chapters. Residents in working-class neighbourhoods approve of murals, particularly on walls they rent rather than actually own, such as houses that are the property of the Northern Ireland Housing Executive. There are no murals in middle-class localities and perhaps this social class is less concerned with affirmations of belonging to the Region. It is also possible that a middle-class sense of identity operates at an individual rather than a communal level. Of course, many in these localities are proponents of a civic rather than an ethnic form of unionism. But it is most likely that middle-class neighbourhoods are conscious that murals or graffiti can lessen the monetary value of local property.

While the public at large is already aware of the political tendencies of various vicinities, murals operate as a more conspicuous display of residential ethnic segregation (Jarman 1998). They also constitute an effective tool of propaganda and the changing images over the years reflect the prevailing anxieties of loyalist and unionist communities. For example, when Britain's commitment to Northern Ireland was under scrutiny after the signing of the Anglo-Irish Agreement in 1985, new murals reflected the concerns of loyalists and contained strong combative images. Prior to this, militaristic representations had been relatively rare (Rolston 1992). Murals also delivered new conspicuous anti-nationalist messages. This response may have been provoked in part by the adoption of the mural tradition by nationalist groups.

The first nationalist mural was erected in the Bogside, Derry, in 1969 and signalled the initial domination of a public location by republicans with a slogan that proclaimed 'You Are Now Entering Free Derry'. This was a perceptible indication to unionists that they were not welcome in that neighbourhood – an assertion that clearly disrupted their sense of belonging to the entire Region. However, this remained an isolated example until the early 1980s when 'the brush joined the armalite and the ballot box as a facet of political strategy' among those who sought unity with Ireland (Jarman 1998: 97). Hundreds of republican murals were drawn in the early months of 1981. Although these gave considerable attention to the hunger strike in H-Block prisons they also presented military images of the armed struggle of the IRA. As soon as they had adopted a unionist tradition, nationalist murals took on a combative tone (Rolston 1992).

In recent years further changes are apparent in the tone of unionist murals. Although King Billy featured as a central image for many decades he has proved less popular as a theme since the early 1990s. Occasional new images of him appear but many older ones have been allowed to decay (Rolston 1995). Of particular note was his depiction in the Fountain area in Derry where his image had been constantly renewed for some 70 years. When the locality was redeveloped the mural was taken down but subsequently reassembled by the Northern Ireland Housing authority. Prior to the wall's decay and collapse in 1994, a revised image of King Billy appeared in the locality. In this depiction the king featured the face of the loyalist hero, Michael Stone, who had shot three individuals at a republican funeral. The new illustration was symbolic of changes taking place among loyalists while the failure to renew older versions may symbolise a crisis in unionist identity. I think it also represents the beginning of a shift of focus from emblems of Britishness to representations of belonging to Northern Ireland.

The fact that republican murals have developed in parallel with loyalist counterparts particularly in the last decade may have lessened the value of this art form as an expression of British identity but it is certainly an activity that is not recognised as particularly British elsewhere in Britain. Jarman (1992) explains that it can be compared with Mexican and Latin American mural traditions but in the latter instances, the murals are funded by the state. But this has also applied to some recent murals in Northern Ireland.

British sport

Just as Irish nationalists regard their participation in the GAA as crucial to their cultural identity, British culture in Northern Ireland is reflected in the enjoyment of sport such as rugby. The first rugby club in Northern Ireland was established in 1865, and soon after another club was set up at the Queen's University of Belfast. Some 20 years later, the Irish Rugby Football Union (IRFU), which is a 32-county organisation, was established.

Although rugby is also associated with Britishness, it appears to be quite acceptable to the nationalists. Its acceptability may derive from a belief among Gaelic circles that rugby originally evolved from Cad, a form of football that was played in ancient times in Ireland. It is possible, although improbable, that William Webb Ellis, the youth that introduced rugby to English public schools, had played Cad while on holidays in Tipperary, where his father served as an officer in the British Army. Sugden and Bairner (1995: 54) have discounted this theory. Nationalists are aware that even if they themselves do not play rugby, it is quite a popular game in the Republic. A crucial factor is the fact that it is probably the only genuinely all-Ireland game played by Protestants and Catholics alike on a large scale. Rugby, north and south of the Border, is a game for the middle classes. For example, it is played in Bangor in County Down and in Blackrock in Dublin. But it does not feature in poorer Catholic districts such as the Falls or among impoverished Protestant groups on the Shankill in Belfast.

Despite the fact that rugby is more acceptable than other games (such as cricket) to the nationalist community, it has not been entirely free from controversy. When the UVF was established, it received support from North of Ireland, Ulster's leading rugby club at the time. In the decade prior to partition, some of the rugby seasons were cancelled in order to allow Protestants to focus their energies on defence of the union with Britain. Apparently the rugby grounds on Ormeau Road were used for the training and drilling of Protestant paramilitaries (Williams 1989).

As the Irish Rugby Union is an all-Ireland organisation, the partition of the country at the beginning of the 1920s led to numerous controversies regarding its use of flags and anthems at international matches. Initially the Irish tricolour flew in place of the Union Jack at international matches in Dublin, but after three years it was decided to replace the tricolour with a new rugby union flag. This decision was altered seven years later when it was decided to fly both flags at international matches in Dublin and only the rugby union flag at matches in Belfast. Further controversy was generated in 1954 when it was agreed that the tricolour would be flown at all international rugby matches in Dublin and that these games would be preceded by the national anthem of the Republic of Ireland. In 1987 the Londonderry Air, a tune that is highly esteemed by all groups, replaced the anthem. Four years later this decision was again reversed and Irish rugby matches in the 1991 World Cup were preceded by the national anthem of the Republic.

Controversies generated by the use of emblems at these matches may lead one to speculate why Northern Protestants are happy to play in an Irish team that is selected in Dublin. In my view this is due to a variety of factors. Protestants are perfectly happy to play for Ireland as they are conscious of the British connotations of the game. Rugby matches constitute a reminder of British influence throughout the entire country. Moreover, apart from the cases that I have just cited, there have in fact been remarkably few instances of the association of politics and sectarianism with rugby, and although rugby players have differing allegiances and sympathies, this does not affect the game (Van Esbeck 1974). Whether players are nationalist or unionist, Protestant or Catholic is irrelevant. 'They eschew all sectional labels when it comes to pulling on a rugby jersey' (Diffley 1973: 14).

Conclusion

The combination of these markers of culture defines unionists in Northern Ireland as British. But their sense of British identity differs to that of Britain itself. Similarly, as I explored in the previous chapter, Northern Irish nationalists espouse a sense of Irishness differing from that in the Republic. This is not unusual. Variation in loyalty to specific cultural traits is the norm in any group 'and the forms are frequently contested and constantly being defined and redefined' (Fenton 1999: 9). In the case of nationalist and unionists in Northern Ireland, identity is concerned with security and there is a constant feeling of threat. Nationalists are concerned that since the foundation of the state, a sense of Britishness has pervaded the public sector. There has been little acknowledgement of Irish culture. Those advocating a sense of British identity are equally aggrieved at any proposed dilution of emblems of Britishness. In particular they are anxious to maintain the links between Northern Ireland and the UK.

Of the three countries in Britain, Scotland has had the greatest input into Northern Ireland and yet, as already illustrated, the sense of Britishness there differs from elsewhere in Britain. Whereas British identity in

Northern Ireland is concerned with maintaining the status quo, in Scotland it endeavours to preserve its national distinctiveness and to prevent 'the kind of English nationalist trampling over Scottish institutions and sensitivities which was held to have occurred in the Thatcher years' (Walker 1995: 172). Yet Scots appreciate loyalist concerns in Northern Ireland. Just as they have endeavoured to ensure that Englishness does not dominate their Scottishness, loyalists in Northern Ireland wish to maintain their Britishness against the increasing influence of the Dublin parliament.

Scottish devolution and the establishment of the Assembly for Wales have intensified the debate regarding the current interpretation of the term 'British'. The decline of the Empire and the decreasing significance of Protestantism are but two of the factors attributed to the de-construction of the term 'British state'. In some instances it is clear that the designation has fallen into disfavour. In April 1999 the *Sunday Times* reported that the BBC had decided that the term 'British' has offensive connotations even though it is part of the company title. At a series of discussions, staff were instructed that the term should no longer be used 'to describe the generality of people living in the British Isles because it might cause offence among the Scots and Welsh' (Brooks 1999: 9). These seminars established that the word 'nation' was also insulting. A number of years ago, British Airways spent 60 million pounds changing the design on the tails of the company aeroplanes from the Union Jack to more inclusive emblems but they subsequently reversed this decision.

Perhaps this reversal is an indication of the fact that a sense of Britishness is not so much in decline as it is in a state of change and possibly renewal. New Assemblies in Wales and Northern Ireland and a new Parliament in Scotland will have an impact on the concept of the UK, but they may help ensure that the UK is increasingly perceived as plural and diverse. The immigration of a variety of new groups into post-war Britain is also having an impact on the term 'British' and there is a new focus on whether these ethnic minority groups will be assimilated, accommodated, or merely tolerated (Modood et al. 1997). But in Northern Ireland the term 'British' is still held to represent a group of people belonging to a particular tradition. In time this may change but whether or not such revised definitions of Britishness could alleviate tensions remains to be seen.

CHAPTER 9

THE 'COMMON GROUND'

Essential to the task of creating a new collective identity is the need to find less common ground in the extremes of the two traditions than in achieving common-ground between the moderate sides.

(Delanty 1996a: 30)

Throughout my book I have examined various strands of tradition in Northern Ireland. While such an exercise risks essentialising these concepts, my aim has been to demonstrate the fluidity of cultural narratives and to suggest that boundaries between traditions are primarily products of historical and contemporary political manipulation designed to portray distinct Irish and British traditions at odds with one another. Yet it is abundantly obvious that the separation of these traditions is often quite ambiguous.

To speak of contemporary Northern Ireland in terms of opposing traditions is to justify the manoeuvres of various historical political leaders and to deny the full variety of cultures. But the recognition of its diverse aspects poses several questions, some of which I address in this final chapter. Of primary importance is whether the two traditions model can be adapted to promote reconciliation between groups espousing varying British or Irish identities. Multicultural societies usually encounter difficulties when attempting to balance tensions generated by rival cultural traditions. In the case of Northern Ireland the question of equality or due recognition for the two traditions is particularly pertinent.

The two traditions model

I have explored sets of rival traditions in this book, such as settler and native, Anglo-Saxon and Celt, British and Irish. In an atmosphere of insecurity, many cultural symbols are deemed to belong to particular traditions and are perceived primarily as assertions of power for specific cultural identities. From the nationalist perspective, speaking Irish asserts the Irish presence. But, many Irish south of the Border are not necessarily convinced of the value of the language as a modern means of communication (Ó Riagáin 1997). Orange parades affirm the Britishness of Northern Ireland – at least to Orangemen. To the (Great) British public they simply confirm the otherness of Northern Ireland. When the European anthem replaced that of the British at graduation ceremonies at Queen's university, the action was construed as depreciating the Britishness of the institution. Similarly, the removal of bilingual signage was perceived as an insult to students espousing an Irish identity.

Promoters of particular cultural traditions often portray the curtailment of customs as an affront on the entire community and 'protecting one's cultural membership has costs for other people and other interests' (Kymlicka 1995: 107). In Chapter 7 I noted that Sunday restrictions on GAA games in certain Protestant localities are viewed as an insult to the whole nationalist community. Subsequently, I reviewed the affront experienced by unionists when constraints are placed on an Orange march. In both instances the concept of cultural traditions is used to emphasise internal group homogeneity and to sustain the idea of two endogamous groups in conflict. 'But the definition of these does not arise from the facticity of cultural variation. Instead it arises out of the use to which these variations are put' (Buckley and Kenney 1995: 200).

As I outlined at the beginning of this book, political declarations at the end of the last millennium have endorsed the two traditions model but have also determined to end the power struggle between them by endorsing a concept of parity of esteem for both. The model proposed in Anglo-Irish Agreement (1985), the Framework Document (1995), and the GFA (1998) could be classed as the 'identity model' that Fraser (2000: 109) pinpoints as starting from the 'Hegelian idea that identity is constructed diagonically, through a process of due recognition'. In this instance, 'recognition designates an ideal reciprocal relation between subjects, in which each sees the other both as equal and also as separate from it'.

Implicit in such propositions is that Northern Ireland in the future would reflect a sense of Irishness and Britishness. Protestants and Catholics would be represented in public life. Symbols of Irish and British cultural traditions would receive similar recognition. Proponents of this model point out that it prevents the misrecognition of minority groups, which is important, as to claim an identity that is ignored or devalued by the dominant group is 'to suffer a distortion in one's relation to one's self' (Fraser 2000: 109).

In the context of Northern Ireland parity of esteem is generally assumed to imply the unquestionable existence of two separate traditions, which should be recognised and respected in equal terms. For this reason alone – although 'it contains genuine insights', the identity model is rejected by

Fraser. 'It encourages both the reification of group identities and the displacement of redistribution' (2000: 110). The need to affirm the existence of two communities pressurises individuals to conform to a particular group culture. Dissidence or difference is equated with disloyalty and is actively disencouraged. 'The overall effect is to impose a singly drastically simplified group-identity which denies the complexity of people's lives, the multiplicity of their identifications and the cross-pull of their various affiliations' (Fraser 2000: 112).

In the context of Northern Ireland, parity of esteem could lead to a fossilising of cultural traditions into two distinct groups that do not necessarily reflect reality. To a certain extent this has already occurred and the concept of two traditions is widely accepted without questioning. While some of those who subscribe to this model genuinely appreciate the ambiguities relating to the boundaries of these traditions, others accept the paradigm in an unquestioning fashion generating essential interpretations of what it means to be British or Irish in Northern Ireland.

But there are other problems with this model – not least of which is the great difficulty in determining the precise meaning of the term 'equality'– particularly as there has been a shift in an understanding of the term at a more abstract level. Does it mean that each tradition should be equally valued or simply respected? Does it simply imply that the major traditions should receive equal representation in all aspects of the public sphere? Alternatively, the term 'equality' might be understood as simply the right to assimilate to the dominant cultural tradition in the public sphere and the acceptance of difference in private (Modood 1997: 20).

In the past this was the unionist understanding of the term. All peoples in Northern Ireland were British citizens. In public this principle of citizenship should reflect itself in terms of loyalty to the state. Privately, individuals were free to espouse their own cultural traditions. But nationalists have sought a different type of equality. For them the term implies recognition and support of their Irishness in both public and private spheres. Obviously these differing perspectives reflect contrasting mindsets of ethnic nationalism and citizenship.

But these contrasting perceptions of equality may also reflect a differing sense of morality among Catholics and Protestants as identified by Elliott (1997). While Protestants place great emphasis on individual freedom of conscience, Catholics are concerned with their communal role. Public recognition of their emblems of culture is an endorsement of a communal perspective. Does this mean that British and Irish traditions should be represented on an absolutely equal basis in all spheres of public life? From a nationalist perspective, even this might not suffice. Some believe that Irish cultural traditions should be afforded special recognition in order to ensure a significant presence.

While the precise definition of equality of esteem remains undefined, unionists have objected to it in principle for a number of reasons. In the first instance, unionists argue that if the necessary infrastructure is in place, minorities do not need any 'extra rights' (Williams 1998). Many liberals, particularly since the Second World War, believe that the common right of citizenship protects membership of cultural traditions. If a universal system of individual rights is in place, then cultural differences are accommodated. Instead of granting special protection to vulnerable groups, basic civil rights are guaranteed to all individuals regardless of group membership. The implication of this is that as all individuals enjoy equality of treatment, minority groups cannot legitimately demand special protection (Claude 1955; Kymlicka 1995).

From a unionist perspective, the concept of parity of esteem affords the nationalist minority with rights and privileges that are equal to those of the majority. To them it is simply not fair that a minority should be treated in this manner. Some unionists also argue that equality for Irish cultural traditions is a dividend of the peace process rather than an entitlement of a substantial minority group. Equal status is merited rather than granted. 'In Northern Ireland we are now being subject to the latest propaganda "in" phrase – "parity of esteem for the two traditions". Esteem is not a "right" which can be granted. It must be earned and it is only by their deeds and words that republicans will be so rewarded' (Finney 1995: 57).

Orangemen insist that the concept of parity of esteem already applies throughout their community worldwide. Groups that traditionally opposed one another, such as Presbyterians and Anglicans, have overcome their hostilities and happily treat one another on an equal basis. In circumstances where they are regarded as equals, Orangemen will reach out the hand of friendship to others. Unfortunately, many of them feel that the minority nationalist community undervalues their cultural traditions.

Nationalists reject such arguments on the basis that the terms 'minority' and 'majority' are inappropriate as their group constitutes more than 40 percent of the population and this number is expected to rise. From their point of view, nationalists make up such a large proportion of the population that they can hardly be considered a minority. Moreover, the fact that they are an indigenous rather than an immigrant group further necessitates full government recognition of Irish cultural traditions. Kymlicka (1995) has argued that the rights of indigenous minorities are far more robust than those of migrants – although many, myself included, disagree with this contention. Nationalists demand equal recognition for their cultural traditions not merely because they are an indigenous minority, but also because they are the original inhabitants.

If both communities were placed on an equal footing, the nationalist minority in Northern Ireland would operate in a manner similar to those espousing a German identity in the region of Trentino-Alto Adige, Italy. In these regions the cultural traditions of German language speakers are given equal status with those of Italians and a variety of safeguards serves to ensure that the German ethnic and cultural character is preserved. But there is one vital difference between the circumstances of nationalists in Northern Ireland and those of German speakers in South Tyrol. Austria has completely renounced its claim to the territory of South Tyrol and these German speakers view their future solely in an Italian context (McNamee 1986). Although the Irish Republic has renounced its constitutional claim to the six counties, this will not deter many republicans from aspiring to the reunification of the 32 counties – a factor that disturbs many unionists.

Some of them had suggested that equity rather than equality of treatment would provide the best solution to tensions between the traditions. Porter (1996) proposes that the concept of parity of esteem has severe limitations, not least of which is that one is being asked to affirm the intrinsic value of another's identity and way of life. He suggests that it is inappropriate to expect Catholics to esteem an Orange culture that they view as inherently triumphalist. It is equally absurd to assume that Protestants will admire the expression of an Irish identity that they perceive as threatening. It is also the case that there are extreme elements in all traditions in Northern Ireland that liberals cannot or should not esteem. For these reasons Porter argues that 'due recognition' is a more appropriate phrase as it implies an absence of hierarchy and affirms relations of reciprocity.

Unionists are keen to establish that minorities in other countries appear happy when proportional public recognition is given to their ethnic identity. Alcock (1975) cites the example of the Croat and Slovene minorities in Austria. While designated secondary schools in the provinces of Carinthia, Burgenland, and Styria cater on a proportional basis to these ethnic groups, they do not receive full equality in all aspects of the public sphere. Alcock also refers to the German minority in the province of North Schleswig, which has its own separate educational institutions and is represented proportionally in the political sphere.

Of course, however, there are major differences between the circumstances of some of these minorities and those of the Irish in Northern Ireland. In the first instance those espousing an Irish identity in Northern Ireland might emphasise the magnitude of their community. Proportionally they represent a far greater minority than the respective German group. In fact, the size of the German ethnic minority is no longer easily established as census forms in Denmark do not query the ethnic identity of respondents. Moreover, as in the case of South Tyrol, there is no uncertainty regarding the border between these two countries. In the post-war period, Denmark and Germany negotiated a political solution for their problems (Kockel 1999a; Pedersen 1991). Their respective minorities are aware that the border is a permanent fixture and there is no attempt to alter its location. In the case of Northern Ireland, some republicans are determined to reverse the Border drawn in the early 1920s. But unionists are not solely concerned with nationalist aspirations for reunification as they also fear nationalist demographics.

Overall, it appears that unionists are less happy than nationalists with any proposal of change but this is hardly surprising. As historically their cultural traditions have dominated the public sphere, any alteration in procedure automatically implies a reduction in emphasis on Britishness in the Region. This situation is not peculiar to Northern Ireland and applies in any context where a dominant ethos is learning to accommodate other minority cultural traditions. 'If, however, different cultural, ethnic and religious subcultures are to co-exist and interact on equal terms within the same political community, the majority culture must give up its historical prerogative to define the official terms of the *generalized* political culture, which is to be shared by all citizens, regardless of where they come from and how they live' (original emphasis in Habermas 1996: 289).

From the unionist viewpoint, changes in the past have always weakened their prospects (Bruce 1999b) and changes in recent decades have further enhanced the nationalist ethos in Northern Ireland. From a unionist position, nationalists flaunt emblems of their own cultural traditions such as the Irish language and the tricolour but fail to respect those of the British tradition such as Orange parades or the Union Jack. Although expressions of an Irish cultural tradition remain limited, unionists are increasingly insecure. Of particular irritation is the government monetary support afforded to the reclamation of Irish cultural traditions.

While unionists propose a variety of reasons opposing the concept of parity of esteem for nationalists, their greatest fear is that recognition of Irish cultural traditions will eventually induce an even greater input from the Republic of Ireland into the affairs of Northern Ireland. Concession of further rights of cultural expression may be followed by increased interference from Dublin. There is genuine apprehension that parity of esteem will reduce the influence of the British government in Northern Ireland and will gradually introduce joint sovereignty. In time, this could facilitate the withdrawal of British interest from Northern Ireland and the rule of Protestants by a Gaelic unitary state.

Many extreme nationalists are similarly disillusioned with debates concerning parity of esteem. Groups such as the INLA and the 32-County Sovereignty Council will never accept that it is possible for Catholics to gain parity of esteem in a devolved Northern Ireland. For them the very existence of the state is a reminder of the partial failure of the thrust for separatism and is perceived as an affirmation of the dominance of the cultural status of unionists. Catholic communal identity has traditionally derived its solidarity from its difficulty with British rule. The challenge will be to transform this perception of alienation into a spirit of co-operation and progress (Ruane and Todd 1996).

From an extremist nationalist perspective this will not be easily achieved in a cultural landscape that has been created by the unionist community. For many of them the walls of Derry are a reminder of the rout of Catholics in 1689. Anglicised placenames reinforce the loss of the Irish language. The cranes of Harland and Wolfe serve as intimations of past unionist prosperity. Protestant churches dominate the landscape. Emblems of British culture are unavoidable. The Crown is engraved on multiple items in the environment such as the postage stamp and the telephone box and is worn by many of those in uniform. The British flag is flown in the city centre and on public buildings. OBEs and other honours are awarded annually and the royal family remains a central symbol of importance. Cox (1988: 43) speaks of the 'ubiquity of references to the Crown' in the cities of Northern Ireland. He notes that 14 thoroughfares commemorate Queen Victoria. Belfast's university is officially designated as the Queen's university and five of the most distinguished grammar schools in the six counties are 'royal'.

Some efforts have been made to decrease the Catholic perception of alienation. Even the extremists cannot fail to notice the recent changes that have served as Irish imprints on the environment. Many murals have Irish language slogans. Londonderry has been reversed by the city council to Derry. Selected districts throughout Northern Ireland have bilingual placenames. The Irish flag is permitted in nationalist districts and Irish language organisations receive government funding. In time it is likely that further changes will be introduced which will increase nationalist support for the concept of a devolved state. This should change the perception of most Catholics that 'structures of the Northern state and public sphere constitute "chill factors"' (Ruane and Todd 1996: 196).

But these changes have angered unionists who argue that the concept of parity of esteem could ultimately damage the traditions that it is designed to protect. It is suggested, for example, that an insistence on equality of respect could actually result in a dilution of cultural traditions, as any assessment of the value of cultural customs implies that they are measured against pre-determined standards. But the application of similar measures to differing traditions can itself have a homogenising effect. 'By implicitly invoking our standards to judge all civilisation and cultures, the politics of difference can end up making everyone the same' (Taylor 1992: 61). Democratising esteem can actually devalue traditions as it implies that all groups automatically deserve equal esteem. There are no value judgements involved and there is no requirement to evaluate any culture. This discourse of recognition is actually a disservice to differing cultural situations and in a Northern Irish context could ultimately impoverish rather than enrich society:

> There are two distinct traditions in the island of Ireland. Two cultures, each of which (rightly or wrongly) finds the other alien. But is that really so wrong? People are different and they should be allowed their differences as long as they don't impinge adversely on others. . . . If people of one culture don't wish to mix with peoples of other cultures – fine.
>
> (Finney 1995: 57)

Unionists also argue that the promotion of parity of esteem could desta-
bilise society and ultimately split it in two. As greater recognition is given
to Irish cultural traditions those espousing this identity will become more
demanding and may ultimately be even less happy to live in a British
state. In this context, parity of esteem for two cultural traditions might
impede rather than harmonise relations between various groups.

A common tradition

While it is clear that there are two major self-defined ethnic groups in
Northern Ireland, it has not been proven that they enjoy separate cultural
traditions. For this reason I believe that it is time to review the two traditions model. It is important to question whether politicians should concentrate on this well-established concept or consider an alternative
paradigm.

As noted in the previous chapter, Buruma (1998) suggested that the successful operation of any state requires a dominant culture, language, or
religion. He provides many examples to support his case. For example, the
state of India contains a variety of peoples espousing different identities.
Although it is not a Hindu state 'it is impossible to imagine India without
Hinduism' (Buruma 1998: 38–40). Similarly the USA portrays a political
ideal of liberty for all its citizens. But even here the English language prevails. Christianity is the predominant religion and the political culture is
rooted in British traditions. While one is not required to convert to Christianity or to acquire English in order to migrate to the USA, individuals
inevitably adopt such practices in the pursuit of success in this environment.

Buruma's analysis of cultural expressions in Britain leads to a similar
conclusion. While the country is ethnically very diverse and is composed
of several nations and religions, the dominant culture is English. 'But for
Britain to function as a state, its various national and ethnic components
have had to adapt themselves to English culture – or at least to speak English' (Buruma 1998: 38–40). Such examples might indicate that while a
modern state requires liberal political institutions, it also needs a dominant
cultural ethos.

In a sense what is at issue here is the distinction between the public and
private spheres. If Westminster parliament were to consider the promotion
of a single cultural tradition in the public sphere, what elements, if any, of
the present cultural traditions should be reflected in such an ethos? Perhaps this should mirror merely civic principles. According to Habermas
(1994: 139), a democratic state will 'preserve the identity of the political
community, which nothing, including immigration, can be permitted to
encroach upon, since that identity is founded on the constitutional principles anchored in the political culture and not on basic ethical orientations

of the cultural form of life predominant in that country'. This implies that in the case of Northern Ireland, the public sphere should reflect a civic entity, which is unalterable even in circumstances of rapidly changing demographics. It also assumes that public and private spheres are two completely separate domains. But of course, as pointed out by Modood (1997: 17), 'no state stands outside culture, ethnicity or nationality, and changes in these will need to be reflected in the arrangements of the state'.

If politicians wish to promote the concept of a common tradition they will have to overcome the problems encountered by perceptions of commonality among rival groups in the past. In the introduction, I referred to the fact that many groups seek to enhance their differences because they conceive of themselves as having irreconcilable aspirations to similar identities (Blok 1998; Ignatieff 1999: 34–71). 'In these situations, it is the perceived similarities of the ethnic Other that are experienced as threatening, rather than the differences' (Harrison 1999: 239).

In the case of Northern Ireland perhaps it would be possible to forge a new sense of Irishness or Britishness that would incorporate elements of other traditions, including those of ethnic minorities such as the Jews, Chinese, or Pakistani. But as nationalist and unionist identities have always been defined in opposition to another, I think this process is unlikely to succeed and may generate a sense of resentment instead. Such a process could potentially be perceived as the appropriation of the cultural symbols of one group by another. In the context of a redefinition of Britishness, for example, it might be regarded as the domination of the subordinate by the superordinate.

When the Turkish government failed to suppress Kurdish nationalism, it endeavoured to appropriate certain key emblems of it and to reinterpret them as elements of Turkish rather than Kurdish culture (Yoruk 1997). The intention was not so much to eradicate Kurdish culture as to characterise it as part of the Turkish cultural pool. Not surprisingly, this attempted redefinition merely generated resentment rather than cordiality. Similarly, a more inclusive definition of Britishness would have to incorporate elements of other cultures in Northern Ireland while maintaining their distinctiveness. For this reason it might be more appropriate for a government to consider the generation of a new cultural pool and the promotion of a single public tradition unrelated to competing traditions of Britishness and Irishness.

A common European tradition

When speaking of the impact of the process of globalisation on culture and the nation-state, Hall (1992) noted that its effects can operate in a contradictory manner. In particular, he explored the way in which globalisation compresses our concept of time and space, which could, in principle, generate the development of a transnational identity, leading to greater similarities between national cultures. In the context of Northern Ireland, it is important to consider whether the reinforcement of a transnational rather than a national identity would serve to ease community tension.

Perhaps it is possible that the expression of an EU identity would resolve the conflict generated by the two traditions paradigm. When Jean Monnet and Robert Schuman originally designed the plan for Pan-Europeanism, their intention was to provide a model that would negate national rivalries, particularly those between Germany and France (Kearney 1988). If this archetype could succeed in neutralising such conflicts, perhaps it could also serve to dilute tensions in Northern Ireland. Moreover, one could argue that it is entirely appropriate for groups in Northern Ireland to regard themselves in a European context. Here I draw a distinction between the identity of the EU and a concept of Europe which is identified in Delanty's critique (1995) as a cultural construct and not as a self-evident identity. There has always been an international dimension to life in Northern Ireland. The Region has never operated as an isolated entity. Its people are cosmopolitan and they have made many significant international contributions.

The promotion of a sense of belonging to the EU would not imply that British and Irish traditions are no longer relevant but I feel it would lessen the significance of these national loyalties. It offers a supra-common tradition that might be acceptable to all spheres of the community. It may seem somewhat a contradiction in terms to suggest that an emphasis on the EU could lessen the tensions aroused by an apparent clash of cultural traditions. After all, the philosophy of the EU is to emphasise cultural divergence. Contemporary Europe is increasingly concerned with regionalism, multilingualism, and variety. Dialogue with other cultural traditions appears to be the essence of its ideology. Yet a common approach to Europe should, at least in theory, ease tensions in Northern Ireland. It should offer citizens a common ground or space where they could meet one another on an equal basis, although Chinese, Pakistani, and others may find it more difficult to identify with this concept. This shared sense of commonality should ensure that variations in perception can be managed and discussed rather than proving an ongoing source of tension. At a minimum it should reduce the zero-sum dimension of the conflict. If all were perceived to be Europeans, it matters a little less which specific territorial colonisation has occurred – at least for the more cosmopolitan citizens. This, however, would not apply in Portadown.

Unfortunately it appears to me that there are several reasons why unionists and nationalists could reject the concept of a supranational, common EU tradition. Some of these reasons are related to social rather than cultural issues. As outlined in the previous chapter, a state-centred model predominates in British politics, and moves towards European integration are still perceived in some quarters as detrimental to the role of the British state. Similarly, the nationalist concern is for the concept of nation rather than state and in the Republic of Ireland there is also some reluctance to embrace the concept of internal federalism. Unionists and nationalists in Northern Ireland are allied to two of the most centralised states in Europe. 'The UK with its tradition of parliamentary absolutism, and the Republic of Ireland, with its Jacobin nationalist tradition, have been of all European countries the most reluctant to embark on internal federalism' (Delanty 1996b: 127). This could constitute the primary reason for a potential lack of enthusiasm towards the concept of a common EU identity.

But in recent years there have been some variations in attitude towards a concept of a federal Europe. At the end of the twentieth century the Labour Parliament has introduced several changes that ensure the dispersal of power from the centre in Britain. Scotland has its own national parliament and Wales has its assembly, albeit with more limited powers. Although England does not yet enjoy its own parliament, the government has created eight regional development agencies. The Bank of England determines British monetary policies without interference from politicians. Reforms of the House of Lords are widely publicised and a great proportion of hereditary peers has been dismissed. A new scheme of proportional representation has been implemented in elections in Scotland and Wales, and this also applies to European elections. The citizens of London have nominated Ken Livingston MP as their elected Lord Mayor. All of these changes serve to lessen the significance of centralised power and therefore of Westminster itself. But the effects of such changes will take time and many unionists in particular are not entirely happy with the concept of a federal UK.

According to Alcock (1994), this concept is not viable economically. He maintains that disadvantaged communities, such as Northern Ireland, would be forced to rely on more successful regions for their survival. Apart from the fact that unionists would react with animosity to any suggestion that they should ally themselves to the Republic, the economic prosperity of Britain would imply that Northern Ireland should connect itself with the richer territory, which he identifies as Britain. Although this argument was written in 1994 prior to the emergence of the 'Celtic tiger', many unionists are convinced that affluence in the Republic of Ireland is merely a consequence of financial assistance from Brussels rather than any real inherent progress. 'Today a favourite comment of the nationalist politicians is that Northern Ireland is "a failed political entity", ignoring the corruption of the southern state as it grows rich on European handouts, largely subsidised by the United Kingdom' (Smyth 1996: 3).

There is no doubt that the Republic of Ireland has enjoyed considerable financial incentives since its entry into the EU. Ireland's economic viability is no longer largely dependent on its relations with Britain and the Republic has shed its inferiority complex. While Britain was also given grant aid from Brussels, it appears to have received fewer financial benefits than the Republic of Ireland from its membership of the EU. Unionists doubt the extent of EU financial aid for Northern Ireland and in any case, whatever financial assistance has been received, it appears to have bene-fited Catholics rather than Protestants. This is largely due to the fact that Catholics are more economically disadvantaged than Protestants in North-ern Ireland. But all groups are aware that EU funding for Northern Ireland is set to decrease and there may no longer be major financial incentives to align oneself closely with the EU.

Unionists identify the concept of Europe with nationalist ideologies and expectations. A federal Europe could be construed as being Celtic in char-acter in that its primary concern is to devolve, rather than centralise power. John Hume has been particularly active in the promotion of Europeanisa-tion and unionists are wary of some of his previous statements in support of this process. Hume argues that minority cultures get increasingly excited when they become involved in the European network. 'They find that they can come out from under the shadow of the dominant culture in their state' (1988: 49). This implies that by being allied with EU, national-ists will overcome the domination of British cultural traditions and gener-ate an Irish ethos in the Region. Those espousing an Irish identity will rediscover their cultural traditions when they interact with other minority groups.

Nationalists view Europe in a more positive manner than unionists. Some of them interpret the focus on regions rather than on nation-states as an opportunity to redefine the entire Ireland as a single region. 'A "Europe of the regions" is a subtle means towards realising the goal of national unity' (Delanty 1996b: 129). The promotion of the single European market has already generated new economic transactions across the Northern Irish Border and there is always the possibility that this economic co-operation will engender further political developments operating on the basis of the 32 counties.

For somewhat similar reasons, some Scottish nationalists are favourably disposed towards the EU although there is also a historical dimension to the pro-European stance of the Scots. Prior to its alliance with England in 1701 Scotland enjoyed close links with many European countries. Its alliance with France dated to the thirteenth century. Scotland had also well developed trade links with the Baltic, Low, and Scandinavian countries (Ichijo 1999). Contemporary Scottish National Party politicians have cam-paigned for full membership of the EU arguing that currently Scotland has less influence than other small nation-states such as the Republic of Ireland, Denmark, or Luxembourg. As an interim measure, these politicians have called for the establishment of a Scottish-European Joint Assembly. This would consist of Members of the Scottish Parliament and Scottish Members of the European Parliament. These would jointly direct Scottish policy in Europe. In common with their counterparts in Northern Ireland, Scottish nationalists anticipate that as the relationship with Brussels increases in significance, Westminster's influence will decrease. This 'may not make Scottish independence inevitable, but it gives the nationalists some good arguments' (supplement to *The Economist*, 6 November 1999, 7).

Not all nationalists in Northern Ireland are equally open to the concept of the EU, but while SF may be less favourably disposed towards it than the SDLP, both parties are aware that Europeanisation could engender a variety of opportunities for greater co-operation with Dublin. It is for precisely the same reason that unionists are less inclined to welcome greater collaboration with other European states although the UU are probably more appreciative than the DUP of the advantages of such co-operation. But some Protestants have religious anxieties regarding the promotion of goodwill towards Europe. According to Bruce (1999b), there is a concern that evangelical Protestantism will be overwhelmed by a predominantly secular European culture. Furthermore, considerable sections of the EU are Catholic and could engender expressions of support or empathy for Catholics in Northern Ireland.

Overall, while the promotion of citizenship of the EU could alleviate tensions regarding cultural traditions in Northern Ireland, it is my view that it will be difficult to develop in the short-term. As long as unionists consider the procedure with suspicion and nationalists regard it with false expectations they will fail to grasp the genuine opportunities afforded by the promotion of a European identity. Many people view Europe through the lenses of their preferred parliaments. While Britain hesitates on the question of Europe, it is highly unlikely that unionists will approach it with great fervour. Nationalists also appear to reflect the influence of the Dublin parliament in their interpretation of its significance. But in recent years both Britain and Ireland appear to be adopting a more favourable approach towards the concept of federalisation and as time passes Brussels is likely to gain a new significance while that of Westminster or Dublin may diminish.

A common regional tradition

While globalisation might generate an overall global identity that would replace the national one, it is also likely to spawn new local traditions that operate in tandem with the transnational one (Hall 1992). For this reason it is important to consider the regional identities that could be promoted in conjunction with a supra-national tradition. As sovereignty is no longer necessarily aligned with specific territories or boundaries, people could focus on the revitalisation of a common culture, but whether this actually implies the existence of a 'common' culture is another issue. Spencer and Wollman question whether such a concept has any validity at all in any context. They argue that 'the very idea of a common culture after all has some political undertones or associations. It brings with it traces of egalitarianism – sharing a common culture implies that all have the same or equal access to it, equal ownership of it (shares in it?) have equally contributed in making or creating it' (1999: 104). It is their viewpoint that such homogeneity is forged only in relation to high cultures, which are usually defended against old or rival cultures.

In the case of Northern Ireland, attempts to impose a British high culture on all groups have resulted in conflict and led to the emergence of various counter cultures. Some minority groups, such as the Ulster Vanguard Movement, have been very keen to affirm the concept of a common regional culture with a view to weakening links with both Westminster and Dublin, but overall many unionists and nationalists reject the idea. In the initial chapter of a joint anthology of poetry by the Protestant John Hewitt and the Catholic John Montague, the unionist J.W. Foster argues that

> It is less than helpful, indeed it is positively harmful, even with the best will in the world, merely to assert that beneath the orange and green camouflage Protestants and Catholics are all Irishmen and only political scoundrels prevent their mutual recognition of the fact. This is a pious delusion that short-circuits the arduous and hazardous business of trying to forge a genuine cultural synthesis (which involves recognising real antithesis).
>
> (in Watson 1991: 5)

Nationalists sometimes argue that they do not share a common culture with unionists as the latter have no interest in cultural affairs. According to Nairn (1981: 233), 'the unacknowledged kernel of the real problem is the character of Protestant Ulster. Hidden under its bowler hat, the physiognomy of this particular band of tonguetied sons of bastards' ghosts has remained curiously unknown'. Some unionists would endorse the view that they have little affection for cultural symbols but violent confrontations in Portadown and Belfast have demonstrated that loyalists are distressed by restrictions on emblems of British culture in Northern Ireland. This particularly applies in the case of Orange parades.

My examination of the cultural practices of Protestants and Catholics, unionists and nationalists reveals that many of their traditions have, at one point, been shared across the community and that genuine differences between them are very small. But it is for precisely this reason that they appear important; 'the smaller the real differences between two people the larger they are bound to loom in their imagination' (McGarry and O'Leary 1995: 253). Moreover, the two traditions model has emphasised these differences, generating an impression of two distinct communities with disparate cultures.

It is not only the case that variations between larger ethnic groups are often quite minute, but customs that endorse an impression of difference are frequently practised by subgroups rather than the community at large. For example, all nationalists do not necessarily speak Irish. Only a small proportion of unionists supports Ulster-Scots. Some nationalists do not participate in the GAA. Not all unionists are members of the Orange Order. Many of the cultural practices that define people as belonging to an apparent tradition are 'in practice, only a small proportion of what most Catholics and Protestants actually do' (Buckley and Kenney 1995: 200).

Culture operates in a social context and it is surely far better to speak of cultural traits as pertaining to a particular locality or social group rather than assuming it differentiates Irish from British, Catholics from Protestants, or nationalists from unionists. In the past certain cultural traditions may have had their origin in particular countries, but this situation no longer applies and it is frequently the case that customs pertain to social classes rather than specific denominations or locations. A particular example of this is the practice of mural painting, which is predominantly the prerogative of working class-unionists and nationalists. More economically privileged individuals do not indulge in it. Cultural fusion has already occurred at a variety of levels and many traits of Northern Irish society are not particularly representative of an Irish or British cultural tradition. 'Within each region is a culture in which all of the people participate, whatever their politics, religion, or ethnicity' (Buckley and Kenney 1995: 197).

But what is proposed in this context is the active promotion of a particular single tradition with which all would identify. The successful generation of this concept would rely heavily on aspects of the social infrastructure of Northern Ireland, especially on integrated education and on the cross-curricular themes such as *Education for Mutual Understanding* and *Cultural Heritage*. Cultural fusion differs from that of the 'melting pot' in that no one identity is expected to adapt to the other. Very often the concept of the 'melting pot' is a myth and 'the different cultures which go into the pot don't dissolve into a national soup' (Buruma 1998: 39). In the context of Northern Ireland the promotion of a common identity would emphasise integration, without assimilation producing a non-discriminatory regional identity. Assimilation to either of the dominant cultures is not an issue as everybody is aware that this cannot work. Such a policy has blatantly failed in many regions and catastrophes, such as that in Kosovo, were a consequence of policies of assimilation. In the case of Northern Ireland a new single tradition could only be forged on regional rather than national identities.

An Ulster identity

The concept of a regional identity for Northern Ireland has already been mooted on several different occasions. One of its most ardent promoters was the poet, John Hewitt, who considered an Ulster identity as being perfectly compatible with his sense of Irishness, Britishness, and that of

Europe. Hewitt outlined his layers of identity in the following manner (in Arthur 1991: 274):

> I'm an Ulsterman of planter stock. I was born in the island of Ireland, so secondarily I'm an Irishman. I was born in the British archipelago and English is my native tongue, so I am British. The British archipelago is offshore to the continent of Europe, so I'm European. This is my hierarchy of values and as far as I'm concerned, anyone who omits one step in that sequence of values is falsifying the situation.

Hewitt's narrative of overlapping identities differs little from that of John Hume (1996: 133) who suggested that 'simultaneously or successively, we can be Europeans, British, Irish, Northern Irish, Derrymen or Derrywomen – whatever we choose'.

But while Hume was keen to emphasise that 'there are no incomparabilities between identities, there is no superiority of one identity over another', Hewitt preferred to review his layers of identity in order of priority, with primary significance being attached to that of the Region. Because it would not stand as a symbol of any particular tradition or denomination, Hewitt believed that this construct could 'command the loyalty of every one of its inhabitants' (in Clyde 1991: 255) and it would represent what Estyn Evans (1984) called the 'Common Ground'. This construct would generate a loyalty that was rooted in its own place, and would reflect local traditions, dialects and, cultures. Such an identity would enhance the diversity of Europe by recovering a cultural tradition that evolved solely in an Ulster context.

In the case of Hewitt and Evans, the regional concept already existed in the construct of an Ulsterman or -woman. Rather than seeking affirmation from either Dublin or Westminster, the people of Northern Ireland could renew their sense of place by affirming their status as Ulstermen and -women. Such a model has one distinct advantage. As pointed out by Delanty (1996b: 133), Ulster is not a 'geographical fit' with the six counties of Northern Ireland. This is 'all the more reason why it would be appropriate to a post-national Europe of regions, at the same time enhancing the democratisation of a new Europe'. The regeneration of a sense of Ulster identity could further the federalist dimension that has already occurred in Britain.

However, I believe that there may be problems for some with the concept of an Ulsterman or Ulsterwoman. In the first instance I feel that an emphasis on the distinctiveness of the locality could be perceived as an affirmation that Ulster is different from the rest of Ireland. If this were the case, extremists could construe the concept of an Ulster person as legitimating the partition of Ireland (O'Sullivan See 1986). While unionists might welcome such implications, nationalists might feel uneasy with it.

Moreover, some nationalists have difficulty separating the concept of 'Ulsterman' from the image of 'Protestant Ulsterman'. Ulster is a term with

powerful emotional resonance for many Protestants and it cannot be easily substituted with the concept of Northern Irish. Explaining the emotive
power of the idea of this concept, Cox (1988: 35) says that it is as Ulstermen
that many Protestants carry 'a weight of reverberations down the centuries', linking them with their forefathers. The Ulster Plantation created
them. In the days of the anti-Home Rule bill, Protestants were motivated
by the slogan that 'Ulster will fight and Ulster will be right' and 'it was the
36th Ulster Division that did fight, on the Somme'. Compared to the idea
encouraged by the term 'Ulster', Northern Ireland lacks much resonance.
Cox explains that while ' "Northern Ireland" is for the Tourist Board;
"Ulster" is for the heart'.

Nationalists believe that many Protestants in the past viewed Ulster in
monolithic terms – 'an "Ulster" conceived as the Protestant people's
homeland' (Ruane and Todd 1996: 304). But if the concept of an Ulsterman
or Ulsterwoman is perceived as predominantly a Protestant construct, its
appeal to Catholics is minimal. It does not represent a genuinely shared
local cultural tradition and would have to be re-conceptualised as a territory for all denominations.

A Northern Irish identity

As an alternative, the term 'Northern Irish' might prove more attractive.
In my initial chapter I reviewed the acceptability of the term 'Northern
Irish' across all community groups. Currently it appears that some 15 percent of Protestants identify themselves as Northern Irish. As this term is
derived from the dominion state of the UK, it does not compromise the
British identity of Protestants in Northern Ireland. Many nationalists do
not identify with the six-county state feeling that it was established primarily as a concession to unionists. But the NISAS demonstrated that the
phrase 'Northern Irish' is also acceptable to a substantial minority of them
because the ambiguity of terminology does not legitimate the Border
between Northern Ireland and the Republic. Neither does it compromise
their aspirations to a united Ireland. For these reasons it is possible that the
concept of a Northern Irish cultural tradition is more acceptable to nationalists than that of an Ulster one, although the latter resonates more power-
fully with unionists.

If the concept of a single regional tradition were widely accepted, one
might ask what symbols could usefully serve as reinforcers of a new
Northern Irish tradition? Perhaps the Assembly could serve as such a symbol, but until its legitimacy is widely accepted it will hardly unite the communities symbolically. Thus far, attempts at devising other new symbols
have failed. Gaffney (1998) reported on the efforts of the Institute in
London to devise a modern flag that would prove acceptable to all
groups. That Institute had already sketched the modern flag of

Bosnia-Herzegovina and had worked on that of post-apartheid South Africa. Yet because it combined emblems associated with the two traditions in Northern Ireland, the end result did not particularly appeal to any group. SF rejected it on the basis that the tricolour fulfilled their needs for a flag. Neither the PUP nor the UUP were in favour of the idea. The Alliance Party correctly stated that Northern Ireland was not yet in a position to hold a rational debate on an issue as sensitive as flags.

Rather than insisting on the generation of a common culture that is shared equally by all, the Northern Irish Assembly could consider the promotion of a 'cultural corridor' as proposed by Edna Longley. This perspective emphasises the vertical rather than the horizontal dimension of a united Northern Ireland. It does not assume that all equally share similar cultural traits and recognises the existence of extremists who are ultra-British or ultra-Irish. Allowing for variations in degree, this model emphasises the connections between the Irishness and Britishness in Northern Ireland and suggests that 'inhabitants might accept this province-in-two-contexts as a cultural corridor. Unionists want to block the corridor at one end, republicans at the other. Culture, like common sense, insists it can't be done' (1987: 144). In this context Northern Ireland is conceived of as a frontier between Britain and Ireland. Not only are the connections between the inhabitants within the state of Northern Ireland stressed, emphasis is also placed on relations between the states of Britain and the Republic of Ireland. 'Only by promoting circulation within and through Ulster will the place ever be part of a healthy system' (Longley 1987: 144).

Longley's model provides an image that astutely emphasises the similarities and differences between cultural practices of various groups. It also has value in that it does not set apparently intransigent traditions in opposition to one another. Whether nationalists or unionists would actually accept it in the short term is questionable because it affirms the inextricable links between Northern Ireland and its neighbouring states. Nationalists would be forced to acknowledge the British input into the development of an Irish identity. Unionists would have to accept Irish influences on British identity. Neither may particularly care to accept this affirmation of hybridity in the short term. In the long term I feel that this concept will become more acceptable and can be promoted in the context of alternatives.

Re-conceptualising the model

Perhaps Westminster should reject the concept of a fixed number of cultural traditions and adopt a more inclusive discourse of multiculturalism – a symbol that has become 'the hegemonic credo of the late twentieth century, invoked as a global solution to national practices of education, science, politics and social policy' (Samad 1997: 240). Parry and Parry (1999:

230) state that 'multiculturalism raises questions about the claims of each and every self-defining culture to equal and fair treatment and to due recognition vis-à-vis other cultures'.

In my initial chapter I referred to the variety of cultural traditions in Northern Ireland. These included traditions of the indigenous Travellers and non-indigenous Chinese, Jewish, and Pakistani groups. It is possible to envisage a Northern Ireland that is redefined as comprising a great variety of traditions such as British, Irish, Ulster-Scots, Travellers, Chinese, Pakistani, Jewish, and so on. Politicians could refrain from constantly speaking of one, two or even three traditions and sometimes, at least, promote an alternative vision of a mosaic of identities.

But multiculturalism in Northern Ireland as elsewhere must be accompanied by policies of anti-racism. Without this it could not withstand the force of repression. In this context multiculturalism aims 'not only to allow national, ethnic and immigrant minorities a voice, but to protect them from offensive, symbolic as well as civic and material exclusions and violations' (Werbner 1997: 263).

Apart from the recognition and inclusion of established minorities in Northern Ireland it is also important to acknowledge the increasing range of 'hyphenated' identities. These are usually applied to migrant or settler communities and several examples, such as German-Turks or French-Algerians, are regularly used in a European context. They are also commonly used to describe minority identities, particularly in the context of a second or third generation minority group. Ulster-Scots is the most commonly accepted hyphenated identity in Northern Ireland and is generally assumed to refer to Ulster people of Scottish descent. But the term refers not only to genetic composition; it is a concept rooted in both territory and culture and implies the original existence of two separate and distinct locations (Gupta and Ferguson 1992). From that point of view dual loyalties could prove problematic thereby heightening rather than dissolving problems.

In recent critiques of culture the concepts of creolisation and hybridisation have received a lot of attention (e.g. Hannerz 1987). Caglar (1997: 172) defines the concept of creolisation as a metaphor derived from the discipline of linguistics which 'places emphasis on internal heterogeneity, cultural mixtures and new positions of identification'. During this process, components of various cultural traditions are synthesised in a manner that permits the retention of their original differences (Parkin 1993). In a similar fashion hybridisation is defined as 'the ways in which forms become separated from existing practices and recombine with new forms in new practices' (Pieterse 1995: 49). These concepts have been commended as recognising the new forms of identity that are produced when old borders are weakened.

But while hybridity is often lauded as the solution to the fossilisation of cultural traditions, it can actually serve to endorse the essentialisation of such constructs and 'these concepts are in danger of embracing the very reifications they seek to overcome' (Caglar 1997: 172). Although such a process serves to deconstruct the rigidity of larger cultural groupings, new constructs can become similarly fossilised. In the context of Northern Ireland it could be assumed that all Ulster-Scots endorse the same cultural tradition when it fact there is no such internal homogeneity. Despite an apparent opportunity to celebrate difference, the concepts of British-Pakistani, Northern Irish-Chinese or Irish Traveller might actually predetermine the confines of these differences. In such circumstances 'the "sources of diversity" are pre-given rather than being practice-bound' (Caglar 1997: 173).

Turner (1993) endorses the concept of multiculturalism as a means of harmonising relations among various cultural communities, but 'the tendency towards reification of ethnic identity is an aspect of multiculturalist policies' that has generated considerable controversy (Samad 1997: 244). In recognition of this problem of reification, Turner usefully distinguishes between 'difference' and 'critical' multiculturalism. 'Difference' multiculturalism' focuses on the distinction between cultural groups and emphasises the distance between them. Consequently, it lays great stress on the 'the internal homogeneity of cultures in terms that potentially legitimise repressive demands for communal conformity' (1993: 412). In contrast, the concept of 'critical' or 'polycentric' multiculturalism focuses on internal dynamics rather than external boundaries. Individuals are construed as open and polycentric rather than fixed and unchanging. Critical multiculturalism sets 'no limits to the kind of social groups, networks, or relations that can guarantee a cultural identity of their own' (1993: 419). In this process the creation of new groups is always possible. New cultural communities are created (Caglar 1997: 178).

This process prioritises the individual rather than the tradition to which he or she is deemed to belong. Its success relies on the determination of men and women to express their own needs and concerns even in those circumstances where the wider group views such expressions with hostility. In principle, critical multiculturalism ensures the expression and rejuvenation of a full spectrum of cultural traditions. Its success would provide the catalyst for the emergence of new cross-community networks grounded in mutual affairs. This would ensure that new inclusive communities are forged not only in Northern Ireland but also throughout the British Isles (Ruane and Todd 1996). But unless there is a far greater articulation of pluralism in Great Britain and the Republic of Ireland, such multiculturalism cannot be expected to succeed in Northern Ireland (Cox 1988).

Of course it could be countered that such a spectacle could ultimately lead to chaos, as the variety of alternatives could prove immeasurable. In one sense this argument contests the principle of democracy itself and in any event is hardly likely to occur *ad infinitum*. But it has merit in that the 'problem' of diversity has led to the collapse of some states such as former

Yugoslavia. It has also had a major impact on other existing states such as Canada where multiculturalism was introduced as a resolution to the continuing tension between English and French nationalism. As a consequence of increased recognition for all traditions, and especially for the 'first nations', the state of Nunavut was officially created in 1993. Indigenous Inuit people formally govern this very large country (Sykes 1999: 13). In order to achieve coherence, the accommodation of multiculturalism in Northern Ireland must be structured. Perhaps this could involve special legal or constitutional measures to protect forms of cultural difference – through what Young (1989: 258) call 'differentiated citizenship'. In these circumstances the constitution is designed to protect not only individual rights, but also minority rights. This process is already in place in Canada and in many federal systems in Europe, Asia, and Africa.

What types of group rights should be implemented is the focus of my future, rather than current research. Kymlicka (1995) has outlined some mechanisms for the protection of cultural difference that are already in place in many states. The first of these categories of group-differentiated rights is the right to self-government for minorities. No group in Northern Ireland is seeking the right to self-determination and it is unlikely to become a federal state.

Kymlicka (1995) also raises the question of polyethnic rights. Many groups are now challenging the 'Anglo-conformity' model, which presumed that they would readily assimilate to the cultural norm. In this instance the procedure aims to ensure that all individuals effectively exercise the common rights of citizenship. In the context of Northern Ireland, the Irish community has sought and received public funding for their cultural practices. Irish groups in Northern Ireland have defended these demands not on the basis of separatism but simply a means of ensuring that they are not discriminated against. These funding mechanisms preserve the richness and diversity of cultural resources in Northern Ireland.

But it is imperative that a voice is given to many more of those who feel the need to express cultural difference. These group-specific rights will help minorities to express their cultural particularity without hampering their success in Northern Irish social, political, and economic institutions. Obviously this involves funding activities that express a Gaelic identity. But unless it is also applied to other groups such as the Travellers, the Chinese, and the Pakistani, this mechanism will merely reinforce the two traditions paradigm and will be perceived in a zero-sum game context. Moreover, it also involves greater recognition of the significance of social structures such as integrated education.

Westminster or Stormont should also consider affording special representation to particular groups. Is it possible that a very small number of seats should be reserved for disadvantaged groups? But I feel that this raises many questions, not least of which is whether a Hindu from India would be happy with his representation by a Muslim from Pakistan or whether either would accept that their interests could be protected by a member of another minority group. Sometimes this mechanism of special representation is criticised as being the corollary of self-government but in the case of Northern Ireland the proportion of ethnic minorities is so small that it would hardly attract any serious objections.

Despite the merits of Kymlicka's and other multiculturalist models, there are still problems that need to be addressed. The emphasis throughout is on collectivities that are primarily identified by their culture. Multiculturalism does not simply imply the recognition of collective cultural difference. It also aims to ensure the survival of groups bearing these differences. Unfortunately, 'this implies the institutionalisation of cultures in the public sphere, a freezing of cultural differences and a reifying of cultural "communities"' (Caglar 1997: 179). Moreover, as Finlay (2000: 38) points out, 'the two traditional hegemonic identities in Ireland – Irish Nationalist and Ulster Unionism – might attempt to appropriate the more visible presence of racialised minorities in Ireland to their own hegemonic ends or to silence each other'.

In view of these problems, greater consideration could be given to Nancy Fraser's alternative – the 'status model of recognition'. According to this, 'what requires recognition is not group specific identity but rather the status of individual group members as full partners in social interaction' (Fraser 2000: 113). In this context, the definition of misrecognition changes. It no longer applies to the depreciation or lack of parity of esteem for any particular group identity and refers instead to 'social subordination – in the sense of being prevented from participating as a peer in social life' (Fraser 2000: 113).

The focus is on institutional patterns and the importance of enabling all parties to participate as peers in social life. As the emphasis is no longer on particular cultural identities, no specific group has an advantage. Instead, the focus is on the entrenchment of new value patterns that promote parity of participation – as opposed to parity of esteem in social life. In contrast with the 'identity model' as promoted in the GFA, the 'status model' interprets the concept of justice as having dimensions of both recognition and distribution. It does not confine itself to the effects of institutionalised norms on the status of individuals but also reviews the allocation of resources to them.

Concepts of recognition and justice are set in a larger social framework. Injustice is not merely defined as misrecognition, but concerns itself with economic structures, property regimes, and labour markets. 'Today's struggles for recognition often assume the guise of identity politics. Aimed at countering demeaning cultural representations of subordinated groups, they abstract misrecognition from its institutional matrix and sever its links with political economy and, insofar as they propound "authentic" collective identities, serve less to foster interaction across differences than to enforce separation, conformism, and intolerance' (Fraser 2000: 119).

Conclusion

Fraser's model appears to offer the ideal solution to the conflict in Northern Ireland. Yet in practice I feel it would be impossible to implement in the short term. British identity has dominated the Region for centuries. While unionists have reluctantly witnessed the inclusion of expressions of Irishness in the public sphere, it is highly unlikely in my view that they would accept a model that shifts the focus from British identity to nationalist concerns. In this context, unionists could no longer claim the majority prerogative, as the terms 'majority' and 'minority' would have no relevance. As nationalists have fought very hard to gain any state recognition for their collective cultural identity, I think it unlikely that they would accept any model in the short term that shifts the focus from collective cultural identities. That could be perceived as a diminution in status for expressions of Gaelic or Irish culture.

But Fraser's model is significant in that culture is placed in an economic and social context. A variety of social and religious institutions could contribute to the enhancement of mutual understanding between various groups in Northern Ireland. For example churches could play a more positive role in defusing tension. In this context, Loughlin (1989: 311) has suggested that the Catholic church could radically restructure its hierarchical relationships while Protestant groups could take a more critical look at social institutions such as the Orange Order. Efforts such as these would help to ensure greater emphasis on the factors that unite rather than divide individuals.

In the short term there is no doubt that unionists and nationalists will continue to vie with one another over the status of the two traditions in Northern Ireland, although it is increasingly recognised that such binary oppositions do not necessarily correspond to reality. Cultural differences in Northern Ireland are not primordial. While historical, religious, and social factors have generated an impression of separate cosmologies, they have been constructed with a particular purpose. Historically politicians and others have sought to construe small differences between groups as evidence of distinct and separate bodies of tradition and have reified cultures as separate entities belonging to specific communities. In my analysis of the concepts of separate Celtic, Scottish, and English traditions I have come to the conclusion that no community can lay an exclusive claim to them. Geographical, historical, and demographic factors have determined that groups throughout the British Isles have had a considerable influence on one another.

In this book I am not arguing for the total eradication of the two traditions paradigm or the identity model. Concepts of distinct British and Irish cultural traditions cannot simply be eliminated, but it is necessary to be aware of the pitfalls associated with identity models and to consider the alternatives. An increasing appreciation of the extent of cultural diversity in Northern Ireland and the greater inclusion of other minority groups such as the Travellers, Chinese, and Pakistani would ensure that concepts of essential British and Irish cultural traditions would no longer totally dominate political discussion. They would not be positioned in constant opposition to each other.

The solution appears to be a multi-layered approach to tradition that does not confine itself simply to the erection of dual symbols of Britishness and Irishness or the redefinition of a single local or global tradition. It is also important to re-affirm that peoples in Northern Ireland and throughout the British Isles share many common narratives. The real question is not the purging of opposing traditions. Rather, the dichotomy must be redefined in terms of alliance rather than opposition and in this context all traditions, indigenous and non-indigenous, can be made compatible with other local/regional and supra-national identities.

This means that traditional group boundaries have to be recognised as flexible and open to questioning. Ethnic identities are neither pure nor static. 'Rather they change in new circumstances or by sharing social space with other heritages and influences' (Modood 1999: 34). The new sense of uncertainly will possibly be perceived with anxiety by those who feel more comfortable with traditional classifications, but anxiety is a feature of the postmodern era and it is time to eliminate the dualistic thinking promoted by the two traditions paradigm. The dissolution of traditional boundaries will encourage the pursuit of new community frameworks and lessen the emphasis on traditional differences. It will encourage the people of Northern Ireland to understand the true extent of their shared heritage and traditions. It would also allow them to enjoy their cultural differences in a non-threatening fashion and appreciate the vast cultural resources of their society.

SELECT BIBLIOGRAPHY

Adams, G. (1986) *Free Ireland: Towards A Lasting Peace*, Dingle.
—— (1988) *A Pathway to Peace*, Cork.
—— (1992) *Towards a Lasting Peace in Ireland*, Dublin.
Adams, G.B. (1965) 'Materials for a Language Map of 17th Century Ireland', *Ulster Dialect Archive Bulletin*, 4, pp. 15–28.
—— (1977) 'The Dialects of Ulster'. In D Ó Muirithe ed., *The English Language in Ireland*, Dublin and Cork, pp. 56–70.
Adamson, I. (1991a) [1981] *The Identity of Ulster: the Land, the Language and the People*, Bangor.
—— (1991b) *The Ulster People: Ancient, Medieval and Modern*, Bangor.
—— (1995) [1974] *The Cruthin: the Ancient Kindred*, Bangor.
Ager, D. (1999) *Identity, Insecurity and Image: France and Language*, Clevedon.
Aikin, L. (1822) *Memoirs of the Court of King James the First*, 2 vols, London.
Akenson, D. (1969) *The Irish Education Experiment: the National System of Education in the Nineteenth Century*, London and Toronto.
—— (1988) *Small Differences: Irish Catholics and Irish Protestants, 1815–1922: an International Perspective*, Kingston and Montreal.
—— (1992) *God's Peoples: Covenant and Land in South Africa, Israel, and Ulster*, Ithaca and London.
Akenson, D. and Crawford, W. (1977) *Local Poets and Social History: James Orr, Bard of Ballycarry*, Belfast.
Alcock, A. (1975) *Protection of Minorities: Three Case Studies South Tyrol, Cyprus, Quebec*, Belfast.
—— (1986) 'The Making of a Nation', *Ulster: an Ethnic Nation*, Lisburn, pp. 13–23.
—— (1991) 'Italy – the South Tyrol', *Minorities and Autonomy in Western Europe: a Minority Rights Group Report*, London, pp. 6–12.
—— (1994) *Understanding Ulster*, Armagh.
Alexander, R. (1985) 'Navan Fort: Why Armagh Council Should Reconsider', *Ulster*, July/August, pp. 8–9.
Anderson, B. (1991) [1983] *Imagined Communities: Reflections on the Origin and Spread of Nationalism*, London, New York.
Andric I. (1995) [1945] *The Bridge over the Drina*, London.
Arnold, M. (1867) *On the Study of Celtic Literature*, London.
Arthur, P. (1991) 'John Hewitt's Hierarchy of Values'. In G. Dawe and J.W. Foster, eds, *The Poet's Place: Ulster Literature and Society: Essays in Honour of John Hewitt, 1907–87*, Belfast, pp. 273–84.

Ascherson, N. (1996) *Black Sea: the Birthplace of Civilisation and Barbarism*, London.
Aughey, A. (1991) 'Unionism and Self-Determination'. In P. Roche and B. Barton, eds, *The Northern Ireland Question: Myth and Reality*, Aldershot, pp. 1–16.
———— (1995a) *Irish Kulturkampf*, Belfast.
———— (1995b) 'The Idea of the Union'. In J.W. Foster, ed., *The Idea of the Union: Statements and Critiques in Support of the Unions of Great Britain and Northern Ireland*, Vancouver, pp. 8–19.
Back, L. and Solomos J. (2000) 'Introduction: Theorising Race and Racism'. In L. Back and J. Solomos, eds, *Theories of Race and Racism*, London, pp. 1–28.
Balibar, E. (1991) 'Racism and Nationalism'. In E. Balibar and I. Wallerstein, eds, *Race, Nation, Class — Ambiguous Identities*, London, pp. 86–106.
Banner, B. (1990) 'This We Will Maintain', *The Belfast: 1990: Tercentenary Issue*, Belfast.
Banton, M. (2000) 'The Idiom of Race'. In L. Back and J. Solomos, eds, *Theories of Race and Racism*, London, pp. 51–63.
Bardon, J. (1997) 'Jonathon Bardon'. In G. Lucy and E. McClure, eds, *The Twelfth: What it Means to Me*, Belfast, pp. 10–13.
Barth, F. (1969) *Ethnic Groups and Boundaries: the Social Organisation of Culture Difference*, Oslo.
Bauman, Z. (1973) *Culture as Praxis*, London.
Bauman, Z. (1992) 'Soil, Blood and Identity', *Sociological Review*, 40 (4), pp. 675–701.
Baumgarten, R. (1990) 'Etymological Aetiology in Irish Tradition', *Ériu*, 41, pp. 115–23.
Bausinger, H. (1990) [1971] *Folk Culture in a World of Technology*, translated by E. Dettmer, Bloomington and Indianapolis.
Bean, K. (1994) *The New Departure: Recent Developments in Irish Republican Ideology and Strategy*, Liverpool.
Bell, G. (1976) *The Protestants of Ulster*, London.
Bellow, S. (1998) *To Jerusalem and Back: a Personal Account*, New York.
Ben-Amos, D. (1984) 'The Seven Strands of Tradition', *Journal of American Folklore*, 21, pp. 97–131.
Benveniste, E. (1969) *Le Vocabulaire des Institutions Indo-Européennes*, vol. 1, Paris.
Benvenisti, M. (1990) 'The Peace Process and Intercommunal Strife'. In H. Giliomee and J. Gagiano, eds, *The Elusive Search for Peace*, Oxford, pp. 117–31.
Biberaj, E. (1993) 'Kosova: the Balkan Powder Keg'. In P. Janke, ed., *Ethnic and Religious Conflicts: Europe and Asia*, Aldershot, pp. 1–27.
Billig, M. (1995) *Banal Nationalism*, London.
Binchy, A. (1994) 'Travellers' Language: A Sociolinguistic Perspective'. In M. McCann, S. Ó Síocháin and J. Ruane, eds, *Irish Travellers: Culture and Ethnicity*, Belfast, pp. 134–54.
Blok, A. (1998) 'The Narcissm of Minor Differences', *European Journal of Social Theory*, 1 (1), pp. 33–56.
Bord na Gaeilge (1986) *The Irish Language in a Changing Society: Shaping the Future*, Dublin.
Bossuyt, M. and Leonard, D. (1991) 'Belgium', *Minorities and Autonomy in Western Europe: a Minority Rights Group Report*, London, pp. 19–23.
Bossy, J. (1982) 'Some Elementary forms of Durkheim', *Past and Present*, xcv, pp. 3–18.
Bourdieu, P. (1977) *Outline of a Theory of Practice*, Cambridge.

—— (1990) *The Logic of Practice*, Cambridge.

Bowen, K. (1983) *Protestants in a Catholic State: Ireland's Privileged Minority*, Dublin.

Bowers, S. (1994) 'Ethnic Politics in Eastern Europe'. In P. Janke, ed., *Ethnic and Religious Conflicts: Europe and Asia*, Aldershot, pp. 29–53.

Bowie, F. (1993) 'Conflicting Interpretations of Welsh Identity'. In S. Macdonald, ed., *Inside European Identities: Ethnography in Western Europe*, Oxford, pp. 167–93.

Boyce, D. (1996a) '1916, Interpreting the Rising'. In D.G. Boyce and A. O'Day, eds, *The Making of Modern Irish History*, London, pp. 163–87.

—— (1996b) 'Past and Present: Revisionism and the Northern Ireland Troubles'. In D. Boyce and A. O'Day, eds, *The Making of Modern Irish History*, London, pp. 216–38.

—— (1997) 'Bigots in Bowler Hats? Unionism since the Downing Street Declaration, 1993–95'. In A. O'Day, ed. *Political Violence in Northern Ireland – Conflict and Conflict Resolution*, London, pp. 51–65.

Bradley, I. (1996) *Columba: Pilgrim and Penitent*, Glasgow.

Bradley, J. (1995) *Ethnic and Religious Identity in Modern Scotland: Culture, Politics and Football*, Avebury.

Bragg, M. (1999) 'How We Lost the Battle of Hastings but Then Won the War of Words', *The Mail on Sunday*, October 17, p. 58.

Braidwood, J. (1964) 'Ulster and Elizabethan English', *Ulster Dialects – An Introductory Symposium*, Holywood, Ulster, pp. 5–45.

Brearton, F. (1997) 'Dancing unto Death: Perceptions of the Somme, the Titanic and Ulster Protestantism', *The Irish Review*, 20, pp. 89–103.

Breen, R., Devine P., and Dowds, L., eds (1996) *Social Attitudes in Northern Ireland*, Belfast.

Brewer, J. and Bullen, W., eds (1873) *Calendar of the Carew Manuscripts, Preserved in the Archiepiscopal Library at Lambeth*, London.

British-Irish Parliamentary Body (1994) *Report from Committee D on Culture, Education and Environment*, 32, London.

Brooke, C. (1816) [1789] *Reliques of Irish Poetry: Consisting of Heroic Poems, Odes, Elegies and Songs, translated into English Verse*, Dublin.

Brooke, P. (1986) *Ulster Presbyterianism – The Historical Perspective 1610–1970*, Dublin, New York.

Brooks, R. (1999) 'BBC Ban on Word "British" ', *Sunday Times* (Irish), 4 April, p. 9.

Brow, J. (1990) 'Notes on Community, Hegemony and the Uses of the Past', *Anthropological Quarterly*, 63 (1), pp. 1–5.

Brow, J. and Swedenberg, T. eds (1990) (Special Issue) Tenditious Revisions of the Past in the Construction of Community, *Anthropological Quarterly*, 63 (1).

Brown, R. (1969) *The Ecumenical Revolution: an Interpretation of the Catholic-Protestant Dialogue*, London.

Brubaker, R. (1992) *Citizenship and Nationhood*, Cambridge, Mass.

Bruce, S. (1987) 'The Northern Ireland Conflict is a Religious Conflict'. Paper presented at Annual Meeting of the British Association for the Advancement of Science, Belfast, 24–8 August.

—— (1992) *The Red Hand: Protestant Paramilitaries in Northern Ireland*, Oxford.

—— (1999a) 'Inspection of the Facts Points to a Ready Assimilation', *The Herald*, 10 August, p. 3.

—— (1999b) 'Unionists and the Border'. In M. Anderson and E. Bort, eds, *The Irish Border: History, Politics, Culture*, Liverpool, pp. 127–37.

Bryan, D. (1998) 'Ireland's Very Own "Jurassic Park": the Mass Media, Orange Parades and the Discourse on Tradition'. In A. Buckley, ed., *Symbols in Northern Ireland*, Belfast, pp. 23–42.

Bryan, D., Fraser, T., and Dunn, S. (1995) *Political Rituals: Loyalist Parades in Portadown*, Coleraine.

Bryson, L. and McCartney, C. (1994) *Clashing Symbols: A Report on the Use of Flags, Anthems and Other National Symbols in Northern Ireland*, Belfast.

Buchanan, R. (1982) 'The Planter and the Gael: Cultural Dimensions of the Northern Ireland Problem'. In F. Boal and J. Douglas, eds, *Integration and Division: Geographical Perspectives on the Northern Ireland Problem*, London, pp. 49–73.

Buckley, A. (1986) 'The Chosen Few: Biblical Texts in the Regalia of an Ulster Secret Society', *Folk Life*, 24 (19), pp. 5–24.

——— (1988) 'Collecting Ulster's Culture: are There *Really Two* Traditions?'. In A. Gailey, ed., *The Use of Tradition: Essays Presented to G. B. Thompson*, Holywood, pp. 49–60.

——— (1989) ' "We're Trying to Find Our Identity": Uses of History among Ulster Protestants'. In E. Tonkin, M. McDonald, and M. Chapman, eds, *History and Ethnicity*, London and New York, pp. 183–97.

——— (1991) 'Uses of History among Ulster Protestants'. In G. Dawe and J.W. Foster eds, *The Poet's Place: Ulster Literature and Society*, Belfast, pp. 259–71.

Buckley, A. and Kenney, M. (1995) *Negotiating Identity: Rhetoric, Metaphor and Social Drama in Northern Ireland*, Washington and London.

Bunting, E. (1983) [1796], *Bunting's Ancient Music of Ireland*, Cork.

Buruma, I. (1998) 'National Success', *Prospect*, December, pp. 36–40.

Byrne, C. (1993) 'Protestants Ignore Taunts to Learn Irish', *Sunday Times*, 9 May, p. 7.

Caglar, A. (1997) 'Hyphenated Identities and the Limits of "Culture" '. In T. Modood and P. Werbner, eds, *The Politics of Multiculturalism in the New Europe: Racism, Identity and Community*, London and New York, pp. 169–85.

Canavan, T. (1994) 'The Protestants in Eighteenth-Century Ireland'. In J. Elvert, ed., *Nordirland in Geschichte und Gegenwart/Northern Ireland – Past and Present*, Stuttgart, pp. 43–52.

Cannadine, D. (1983) 'The Context, Performance and Meaning of Ritual: the British Monarchy and the "Invention of Tradition", c. 1820–1977'. In E. Hobsbawm and T. Ranger eds, *The Invention of Tradition*, Cambridge, pp. 101–64.

Canny, N. (1989) 'Early Modern Ireland, c. 1500–1700'. In R.F. Foster, ed., *The Oxford Illustrated History of Ireland*, Oxford, pp.104–60.

Cearr, D. (1997) 'And You Think We've Got Problems with Yankee Interference', *Ulster Nation: a Third Way for Ulster*, 2 (15), p. 7.

Chaney, D. (1994) *The Cultural Turn: Scene-Setting Essays on Contemporary Cultural History*, London.

Chapman, A. (1998) 'The Religious Society of Friends (Quakers)'. In N. Richardson, ed., *A Tapestry of Beliefs: Christian Traditions in Northern Ireland*, Belfast, pp. 184–8.

Chapman, M. (1978) *The Gaelic Vision in Scottish Culture*, London.

——— (1992) *The Celts – The Construction of a Myth*, London.

Charles-Edwards, T. (1996) 'Language and Society Among the Insular Celts AD 400–1000'. In M.J. Green, ed., *The Celtic World*, London, pp. 703–36.

Chaucer, G. (1830) *The Canterbury Tales*, London.

Chenevix-Trench, C. (1986) [1984] *The Great Dan: a Biography of Daniel O'Connell*, London.

Clark, G. (1966) 'The Invasion Hypothesis in British Archaeology', *Antiquity*, 40, pp. 172–89.

Clarke, A. (1967) 'The Colonisation of Ulster and the Rebellion of 1641'. In T.W. Moody and F.V. Martin, eds, *The Course of Irish History*, Cork, pp. 189–203.

––––– (1978) 'Colonial Identity in Early Seventeenth-Century Ireland', *Historical Studies*, 11, pp. 55–71.

Clarke, L. and Woods, R. (1999) 'Irish Eyes are English not Celtic', *Sunday Times*, 14 November, p. 8.

Clarke, R. (1999) 'On Doing Things Differently: a Church of Ireland Glance at the Past'. In D. Carroll, ed., *Religion in Ireland: Past, Present and Future*, Dublin, pp. 29–39.

Claude, I. (1955) *National Minorities: An International Problem*, Cambridge, Mass.

Clayton, P. (1998) 'Religion, Ethnicity and Colonialism as Explanations of the Northern Ireland Conflict'. In D. Miller, ed., *Rethinking Northern Ireland*, Essex, pp. 40–54.

Cleeve, B. (1983) 'The Secret Language', *Studies*, lxxii (287), pp. 251–63.

Clyde, T. (1991) 'A Stirring in the Dry Bones: John Hewitt's Regionalism'. In S. Dawe and J. Wilson, eds, *The Poet's Place: Ulster Literature and Society, Essays in Honour of John Hewitt, 1907-1987*, Belfast, pp. 249–58.

Cochrane, F. (1997) *Unionist Politics and the Politics of Unionism since the Anglo-Irish Agreement*, Cork.

Cohen, A., ed. (1986) *Symbolising Boundaries: Identity and Diversity in British Cultures*, Manchester.

Cohen, R. (1994) *Frontiers of Identity: the British and the Others*, London.

Colley, L. (1992) 'Britishness and Otherness', *Journal of British Studies*, 31, pp. 309–29.

––––– (1996) *Britons: Forging the Nation 1707–1837*, London.

––––– (1999) 'This Country is not so Special', *New Statesman*, 3 May, pp. 27–9.

Collins, M. (2000) 'Travellers: Culture and Identity'. In R. Lentin, ed., *Emerging Irish Identities*, Dublin, pp. 66–8.

Collis, J. (1992) 'Celts and Politics'. In P. Graves-Brown, S. Jones, and C. Gamble, eds, *Culture, Identity and Archaeology: the Construction of European Communities*, London and New York, pp. 167–78.

Colvin, I. (1936) *The Life of Lord Carson*, 3 vols, London.

Connall, (1988) 'Myth and Reality', *Ulster*, July/August, pp. 9–10.

Connerton, P. (1989) *How Societies Remember*, Cambridge.

Connor, W. (1978) 'A Nation is a Nation, is a State, is an Ethnic Group is a . . .', *Ethnic and Racial Studies*, 1 (4), pp. 377–400.

Conversi, D. (1997) *The Basques, the Catalans and Spain: Alternative Routes to Nationalist Mobilisation*, London.

Coolahan, J. (1981) *Irish Education: its History and Structure*, Dublin.

Cooper, J. (1998) 'The Moravian Church in Ireland'. In N. Richardson, ed., *A Tapestry of Beliefs: Christian Traditions in Northern Ireland*, Belfast, pp. 197–202.

Corish, P. (1985) *The Irish Catholic Experience: a Historical Survey*, Dublin.

Cornell, S. (1996) 'The Variable Ties that Bind: Content and Circumstance in Ethnic Processes', *Ethnic and Racial Studies*, 19 (2), pp. 265–89.

Corry, E. (1985) 'Irish Ireland through the Gaelic Way', *Fortnight*, 223, pp. 5, 8.

Cosgrove, A. (1967) 'The Gaelic Resurgence and the Geraldine Supremacy'. In T.W. Moody and F.V. Martin, eds, *The Course of Irish History*, Cork, pp. 158–73.

Coulter, C. (1994) 'The Character of Unionism', *Irish Political Studies*, 9, pp. 1–24.

Cox, W. (1988) 'On Being an Ulster Protestant'. In N. Evans ed., *National Identity in the British Isles*, Gwynedd.

Coyle, D. (1983) *Minorities in Revolt: Political Violence in Ireland, Italy and Cyprus*, Rutherford, Madison, Teaneck.

Coyle, P. (1999) *The Story of Belfast Celtic*, Edinburgh.

Craig, P., ed. (1992) *The Rattle of the North: an Anthology of Ulster Prose*, Belfast.

Crawford, W. (1982) 'The Ulster Irish in the Eighteenth Century', *Ulster Folklife*, 28, pp. 24–32.

Crilly, O. (1998) 'The Catholic Church in Ireland'. In N. Richardson, ed., *A Tapestry of Beliefs: Christian Traditions in Northern Ireland*, Belfast, pp. 23–44.

Cronin, M. (1999) *Sport and Nationalism in Ireland: Gaelic Games, Soccer and Irish Identity since 1884*, Dublin.

Crowley, T. (1996) *Language in History: Theories and Texts*, London and New York.

——— (2000) *The Politics of Language in Ireland 1366–1922*, London and New York.

Cullen, P. (2000) *Refugees and Asylum-Seekers in Ireland*, Cambridge.

Cullen, P., McCann, T., Mann-Kler, D., Goldstone, K., and Sultan-Prnjavorac, F. (2000) 'Irish Identity Formation and Anti-Racism'. In R. Lentin, ed., *Emerging Irish Identities*, Dublin, pp. 71–9.

Currie, D. (1998) 'The Christian Brethren'. In N. Richardson, ed., *A Tapestry of Beliefs: Christian Traditions in Northern Ireland*, Belfast, pp. 114–22.

Curtis, Lewis (1971) *Apes and Angels: the Irishman in Victorian Caricature*, Newton Abbot.

Curtis, L. (1991) [1984] *Nothing but the Same Old Story: the Roots of Anti-Irish Racism*, Belfast.

Darby J. (1983) 'The Historical Background'. In J. Darby, ed., *Northern Ireland: the Background to the Conflict*, Belfast, pp. 13–31.

——— (1997) *Scorpions in a Bottle: Conflicting Cultures in Northern Ireland*, London.

Darby, J., Murray, D., Batts, D., Dunn, S., Farren, S., and Harris, J. (1977) *Education and Community in Northern Ireland: Schools Apart?*, Coleraine.

Davis, P. and Hersh, R. (1990) [1980] *The Mathematical Experience*, London, New York, Victoria.

Day, A. and McWilliams, P., eds (1991) *Ordnance Survey Memoirs of Ireland: Parishes of Co. Londonderry 111 1831–5, Roe Valley Lower*, Belfast.

——— (1992) *Ordnance Survey Memoirs of Ireland: Parishes of Co. Londonderry 1V 1833–5, Roe Valley Upper: Dungiven*, Belfast.

Deacon, B. and Payton, P. (1993) 'Re-Inventing Cornwall: Culture Change on the European Periphery', *Cornish Studies*, 2 (1), pp. 62–79.

Deane, S. (1985), *Celtic Revivals: Essays in Modern Irish Literature 1880–1980*, London, Boston.

——— (1986) 'Civilians and Barbarians', *Ireland's Field Day*, Indiana, pp. 33–44.

De Búrca, S. (1966) 'On the Origin and Language of the Goidels', *Studia Celtica*, 1, pp. 128–37.

De Fréine, S. (1978) *The Great Silence*, Dublin.

Delanty, G. (1995) *Inventing Europe: Idea, Identity, Reality*, Hampshire and London.

——— (1996a)'Habermas and Post-National Identity: Theoretical Perspectives on the Conflict in Northern Ireland', *Irish Political Studies*, 11, pp. 20–32.

———— (1996b) 'Northern Ireland in a Europe of Regions', *Political Quarterly*, 67, pp. 127–34.

Demirdirek, H. (1998) 'Re-Claiming Nationhood through Re-Nativization of Language: the Gagauz in Moldova', Paper delivered at the Conference of the European Association of Social Anthropologists, Frankfurt, 4–7 September.

De Paor, L. (1970) *Divided Ulster*, Middlesex.

———— (1990) *Unfinished Business: Ireland Today and Tomorrow*, London.

Department of Foreign Affairs (1985) *Agreement between the Government of Ireland and the Government of the United Kingdom*, Dublin.

———— (1995) *Seisiúin Phoiblí: Public Sessions Forum for Peace and Reconciliation: Fórum um Shíocháin agus Athmhuintearas*, Dublin.

Department of Health and Social Services, Registrar General Northern Ireland (1993) *The Northern Ireland Census 1991: Religion Report*, Belfast.

Desmond-Greaves, C. (1991) *1916 as History: the Myth of the Blood Sacrifice*, Dublin.

Deutsch, K. and Faltz, W., eds (1963) *Nation-Building*, New York.

Devine T. and McMillan, J., eds (1999) *Celebrating Columba: Irish-Scottish Connections 597–1997*, Edinburgh.

Devlin, P. (1983) 'A Bogsider's Education'. In P. Craig, ed., (1992) *The Rattle of the North: an Anthology of Ulster Prose*, Belfast, pp. 379–93.

Diffley, S. (1973) *The Men in Green: the Story of Irish Rugby*, London.

Dikötter, F. (1990) 'Group Definition and the Idea of Race in Modern China', *Ethnic and Racial Studies*, 13 (3), pp. 420–31.

Dineley, T. (1870) *Observation in a Voyage through the Kingdom of Ireland: Being a Collection of Several Monuments' Inscriptions, Draughts of Towns, Castles, etc.*, Dublin.

Doherty, R. (1998) *The Williamite War in Ireland 1688–1691*, Dublin.

Donnan, H. and O'Brien, M. (1998) ' "Because You Stick Out, You Stand Out": Perceptions of Prejudice Among Northern Ireland's Pakistanis'. In P. Hainsworth ed. *Divided Society: Ethnic Minorities and Racism in Northern Ireland*, London, pp. 197–221.

Douglas, N. (1998) 'The Politics of Accommodation, Social Change and Conflict Resolution in Northern Ireland', *Political Geography*, 17 (2), pp. 209–29.

Dowling, P. (1971) *A History of Irish Education*, Cork.

Dubourdieu, J. (1802) *Statistical Survey of the County of Down with Observations on the Means of Improvement; drawn up for the consideration and by order of the Dublin Society*, Dublin.

Dudley Edwards, R. (1990) [1977] *Patrick Pearse: the Triumph of Failure*, Dublin.

Dunleavy, J. and Dunleavy, G. (1991) *Douglas Hyde: a Maker of Modern Ireland*, Berkeley, Los Angeles, Oxford.

Dunlop, J. (1999) 'Who are these Irish Presbyterians?' In D. Carroll, ed., *Religion in Ireland: Past, Present and Future*, Dublin, pp. 40–50.

Dunn, S. ed. (1995) *Facets of the Conflict in Northern Ireland*, Basingstoke.

Dunne, T. (1980) 'The Gaelic Response to Conquest and Colonisation: the Evidence of the Poetry' *Studia Hibernica*, 20, pp. 7–30.

———— (1982) *Theobald Wolfe Tone: Colonial Outsider*, Cork.

Durkacz, V. (1983) *The Decline of the Celtic Languages: a Study of the Linguistic and Cultural Conflict in Scotland, Wales and Ireland from the Reformation to the Twentieth Century*, Edinburgh.

Easthope, A. (1998) 'Common Sense', *Prospect*, December, p. 15.

——— (1999) *Englishness and National Culture*, London and New York.

Edwards, J. (1985) *Language, Society and Identity*, Oxford.

Eide, A. (1993) *New Approaches to Minority Protection*, London.

——— (1996) *A Review and Analysis of Constructive Approaches to Group Accommodation and Minority Protection in Divided or Multicultural Societies*, Dublin.

El-Assal, R. (1999) *Caught in Between: the Extraordinary Story of an Arab Palestinian Christian Israeli*, London.

Elliott, M. (1982) *Partners in Revolution: the United Irishmen and France*, New Haven and London.

——— (1997) 'Religion and Identity in Northern Ireland'. In W.A. Horner ed. *Global Convulsions: Race, Ethnicity and Nationalism at the End of the Twentieth Century*, pp. 149–67.

——— (1989) *Wolfe Tone: Prophet of Irish Independence*, New Haven, London.

——— (2000) *The Catholics of Ulster, a History*, London.

Ellis Evans, D. (1991) 'Celticity, Identity and the Study of Language – Fact, Speculation and Legend', *Archaeologia Cambrensis*, cxl, pp. 1–13.

——— (1996) 'The Early Celts – the Evidence of Language'. In M. Green, ed., *The Celtic World*, London, pp. 8–20.

Elvert, J., ed. (1994) *Nordirland in Geschichte und Gegenwart/ Northern Ireland – Past and Present*, Stuttgart.

Eriksen, T. (1993) *Ethnicity and Nationalism: Anthropological Perspectives*, London.

Estyn Evans, E. (1951) 'The Past in the Present'. In P. Craig, ed., (1992) *The Rattle of the North: an Anthology of Ulster Prose*, Belfast, pp. 215–7.

——— (1984) *Ulster: The Common Ground*, Mullingar.

European Commission (1999) *The Amsterdam Treaty: a Comprehensive Guide*, Brussels.

Evans, L. (2000) *Kingdom of the Ark*, New York.

Falaky Nagy, J. (1981/82) 'Liminality and Knowledge in Irish Tradition', *Studia Celtica*, xvi/xvii, pp. 135–43.

Farren, S. (1991) 'Culture, Curriculum and Educational Policy in Northern Ireland', *Language, Culture and Curriculum*, 4 (1), pp. 43–57.

——— (1994) 'English – Caught in the Crossfire'. In M. Hayhoe and S. Parker, eds, *Who Owns English*, Buckingham and Philadelphia, pp. 24–32.

Fennell, D. (1986) 'Creating A New British Identity', *Studies*, 300, pp. 392–400.

Fenton, J. (1995), *The Hamely Tongue – A Personal Record of Ulster-Scots in County Antrim*, Belfast.

Fenton, S. (1999) *Ethnicity: Racism, Class and Culture*, Basingstoke.

Finlay, A. (2000) 'Identity, Criticism and Decadent Strata'. In R. Lentin, ed., *Emerging Irish Identities*, Dublin, pp. 35–39.

Finlayson, A. (1996) 'Nationalism as Ideological Interpellation: the Case of Ulster Loyalism', *Ethnic and Racial Studies*, 19 (1), pp. 88–112.

Finney, B. (1995) 'An Englishman on the Union'. In J.W. Foster, ed., *The Idea of the Union: Statements and Critiques in Support of the Union of Great Britain and Northern Ireland*, Vancouver, pp. 53–9.

Fishman, J. (1989) *Language and Ethnicity in Minority Sociolinguistic Perspective*, Clevedon, Philadelphia.

Fitzpatrick, R. (1989) *God's Frontiersmen: the Scots-Irish Epic*, London.

Flanagan D. and Flanagan L. (1994) *Irish Place Names*, Dublin.

Follis, B. (1996) 'Friend or Foe? Ulster Unionists and Afrikaner Nationalists', *Southern African-Irish Studies*, 3, pp. 171–89.

Foster, J.W. (1988) 'Culture and Colonisation: View from the North', *The Irish Review*, 5, pp. 17–26.

—— (1995a) 'The Task for Unionists'. In J.W. Foster ed. *The Idea of the Union: Statements and Critiques in Support of the Union of Great Britain and Northern Ireland*, Vancouver, pp. 69–74.

—— (1995b) 'Why I am a Unionist'. In J W. Foster, ed., *The Idea of the Union: Statements and Critiques in Support of the Unions of Great Britain and Northern Ireland*, Vancouver, pp. 59–64.

Foster, R. (1988) *Modern Ireland 1600–1972*, Middlesex.

—— (1993) *Paddy & Mr Punch: Connections in Irish and English History*, London.

Fraser, M. (1974) *Children in Conflict*, Harmondsworth.

Fraser, N. (2000) 'Rethinking Recognition', *New Left Review*, 2, pp. 107–20.

Friel, B. (1981) *Translations*, London.

Fritz, P. (1998) 'The Lutheran Church in Ireland'. In N. Richardson, ed., *A Tapestry of Beliefs: Christian Traditions in Northern Ireland*, Belfast, pp. 203–5.

Fujitani, T. (1993) 'Inventing, Forgetting, Remembering: Towards a Historical Ethnography of the Nation-State'. In H. Befu, ed., *Cultural Nationalism in East Asia: Representation and Identity*, Berkeley, pp. 77–106.

Gaffney, D. (1998) 'New North Flag will Cause quite a Flutter', *Sunday Tribune*, 4 October, p. 3.

Gailey, A. (1975) 'The Scots Element in North Irish Popular Culture', *Ethnologia Europaea*, viii, pp. 2–22.

Gallagher, M. (1995) 'How Many Nations are there in Ireland?', *Ethnic and Racial Studies*, 18 (4), pp. 715–39.

Gandhi, L. (1998) *Postcolonial Theory: a Critical Introduction*, Edinburgh.

Gannon, M. (1994) *Understanding Global Cultures: Metaphorical Journeys through 17 Countries*, London, New Delhi.

Garvin, T. (1987a) *Nationalist Revolutionaries in Ireland 1858–1928*, Oxford.

—— (1987b) 'The Politics of Language and Literature in Pre-Independence Ireland', *Irish Political Studies*, 2, pp. 49–63.

Gaskill, H. (1991) *Ossian Revisited*, Edinburgh.

Geertz, C. (1973) *The Interpretation of Culture*, New York.

Gellner, E. (1983) *Nations and Nationalism*, Oxford.

GFA: see Government of the United Kingdom of Great Britain and Northern Ireland and Government of Ireland (1998).

Gibbons, L. (1996) *Transformations in Irish Culture*, Cork.

Gielke, A. (1990) 'International Norms and Divided Societies'. In H. Giliomee and J. Gagiano, eds, *The Elusive Search for Peace*, Oxford, pp. 95–116.

Giliomee, H. (1990) 'The Elusive Search for Peace'. In H. Giliomee and J. Gagiano, eds, *The Elusive Search for Peace*, Oxford, pp. 299–318.

Gilroy, P. (1987) *There Ain't No Black in the Union Jack*, London.

Girvin, B. (1994) 'The Act of Union, Nationalism and Religion: 1780–1850'. In J. Elvert, ed., *Nordirland in Geschichte und Gegenwart/ Northern Ireland – Past and Present*, Stuttgart, pp. 53–81.

Glendinning, R. (1997) 'Robin Glendinning'. In G. Lucy and E. McClure, eds, *The Twelfth: What it Means to Me*, Belfast, pp. 57–8.

Glenny, M. (1990) *The Rebirth of History, Eastern Europe in the Age of Democracy*, Harmondsworth.

—— (1992) *The Fall of Yugoslavia: the Third Balkan War*, London.

Gorter, D. (1989) 'Dutch State Policy towards the Frisian Language', *Ethnic Studies Report*, 8 (1), pp. 36–47.

Government of the United Kingdom of Great Britain and Northern Ireland and Government of Ireland (1998) *Agreement Reached in the Multi-Party Negotiations*, Belfast.

Graham, B. (1998) 'Contested Images of Place among Protestants in Northern Ireland', *Political Geography*, 17 (2), pp. 129–44.

Gramsci, A. (1971) *Selections from the Prison Notebooks and the Study of Philosophy*, London.

Graves-Brown, P., Jones, S., and Gamble, G., eds, (1996) *Cultural Identity and Archaeology: the Construction of European Communities*, London and New York.

Gray, B. (1999) 'Steering a Course Somewhere between Hegemonic Discourses of Irishness'. In R. Lentin, ed., *The Expanding Nation: Towards a Multi-Ethnic Ireland*, Dublin, pp. 66–73.

Greene, D. (1964) 'The Celtic Languages'. In J. Raftery, ed., *The Celts*, Cork, Dublin, pp. 9–21.

Gregg, J. (1943) *The Ne Temere Decree*, Dublin.

Gregg, R. (1972) 'The Scotch-Irish Dialect Boundaries in Ulster'. In M.F. Wakelin, ed., *Patterns in the Folk Speech of the British Isles*, London, pp. 132–4.

Grillo, R. (1989) *Dominant Languages: Language and Hierarchy in Britain and France*, Cambridge.

Guelke, A. (1988) *Northern Ireland: the International Perspective*, Dublin.

Gupta, A. and Ferguson, J. (1992) 'Beyond "Culture": Space, Identity and the Politics of Difference', *Cultural Anthropologist*, 7 (1), pp. 6–23.

Habermas, J. (1986) 'The Limits of Neo-Historicism'. In P. Dews, ed., *Autonomy and Solidarity: Interviews with Jürgen Habermas*, London, pp. 237–43.

—— (1994) 'Struggles for Recognition in the Democratic Constitutional State'. In A. Gutmann, ed., *Multiculturalism: Examining the Politics of Recognition*, Princeton, pp. 107–48.

—— (1996) 'The European Nation-State: its Achievements and its Limits'. In G.H. Balakrishnan and B. Anderson, eds, *Mapping the Nation*, London, pp. 281–94.

Haddick-Flynn, K. (1999) *Orangeism: the Making of a Tradition*, Dublin.

Hale, A. (1997) 'Rethinking Celtic Cornwall: an Ethnographic Approach', *Cornish Studies*, 2 (5), pp. 85–99.

Hall, M. (1986) *Ulster: the Hidden History*, Belfast.

—— (1993) *Ulster's Scottish Connection*, Antrim.

—— (1994) *The Cruthin Controversy*, Antrim.

—— (1995) *The Battle of Moira: an Adaptation of Sir Samuel Ferguson's Congal*, Antrim.

Hall, S. (1977) *Encoding/Decoding*, Birmingham.

Hall, S. (1992) 'The Question of Cultural Identity'. In S. Hall, D. Held, and A. McGrew, eds, *Modernity and Its Futures*, Cambridge, pp. 273–316.

—— (1996) 'Introduction: Who Needs "Identity"?' In S. Hall and P. du Gay, eds, *Questions of Cultural Identity*, London, New Delhi, pp. 1–17.

Handleman, D. (1977) 'The Organization of Ethnicity', *Ethnic Groups*, 1, pp. 187–200.

Handler, R. and Linnekin, J. (1984) 'Tradition: Genuine or Spurious', *Journal of American Folklore*, 97 (385), pp. 273–90.

Hanna, C. (1902) *The Scotch-Irish or the Scot in North Britain, North Ireland and North America*, New York.

Hanna, W. (2000) *Intertwined Roots: an Ulster-Scot Perspective*, Dublin.

Hannerz, U. (1987) 'The World in Creolisation', *Africa*, 57, pp. 546–59.

Harkness, D. (1990) 'Identities'. In M. Crozier, ed., *Cultural Traditions in Northern Ireland: Varieties of Britishness*, Belfast, pp. 46–9.

Harris, R. (1986) [1972] *Prejudice and Tolerance in Ulster: a Study of Neighbours and 'Strangers' in a Border Community*, Manchester.

Harris, W. (1744) *The Ancient and Present State of the County of Down: Containing a Chronological Description, with the Natural and Civil History of the Same*, Dublin.

Harrison, J. (1888) *The Scot in Ulster*, Edinburgh.

Harrison, S. (1992) 'Ritual as Intellectual Property', *Man*, 27 (2), pp. 225–44.

——— (1995) 'Four Types of Symbolic Conflict', *Journal of the Royal Anthropological Institute*, 1 (2), pp. 255–72.

——— (1999) 'Identity as a Scarce Resource', *Social Anthropology*, 7 (3), pp. 239–51.

Hartnett, M. (1998) *Ó Rathille*, Meath.

Haseler, S. (1996) *The English Tribe: Identity, Nation and Europe*, London.

Hastings, A. (1997) *The Construction of Nationhood: Ethnicity, Religion and Nationalism*, Cambridge.

Haugen, E. (1966) 'Dialect, Language, Nation', *American Anthropologist*, 68 (4), pp. 922–35.

Heaney, S. (1999) *Beowulf*, London.

Heffer, S. (1999) *Nor Shall my Sword: the Reinvention of England*, London.

Helleiner, J. (1995) 'Gypsies, Celts and Tinkers: Colonial Antecedents of Anti-Traveller Racism in Ireland', *Ethnic and Racial Studies*, 18 (3), pp. 532–54.

Hennessey, T. (1997) *A History of Modern Ireland 1920–1996*, Hampshire and London.

Herbert, M. (1988) *Iona, Kells and Derry: the History and Hagiography of the Monastic Family of Columba*, Oxford.

Herbison, I. (1980) *Webs of Fancy: Poems of David Herbison, The Bard of Dunclug*, Oxford and Ballymena.

——— (1992) 'Language, Literature and Cultural Identity: an Ulster-Scots Perspective'. In J. Lundy and A. Mac Póilin, eds, *Styles of Belonging: The Cultural Identities of Ulster*, Belfast, pp. 54–62.

Heslinga, M. (1962) *The Irish Border as a Cultural Divide – a Contribution to the Study of Regionalism in the British Isles*, Assen.

Hewitt, J. (1972) 'No Rootless Colonist'. In P. Craig, ed., (1992), *The Rattle of the North: an Anthology of Ulster Prose*, Belfast, pp. 121–31.

Hewitt, J., ed. (1974) *Rhyming Weavers and Other Country Poets of Antrim and Down*, Belfast.

Hill, J. (1993) 'The Origins of the Scottish Plantations in Ulster to 1625: A Reinterpretation', *Journal of British Studies*, 32, pp. 24–43.

Hindley, R. (1990) *The Death of the Irish Language*, London.

Hobsbawm, E. (1983) 'Introduction: Inventing Traditions'. In E. Hobsbawm and T. Ranger, eds, *The Invention of Tradition*, Cambridge, pp. 1–14.

——— (1992) 'Ethnicity and Nationalism in Europe Today', *Anthropology Today*, 8 (1), pp. 3–8.

——— (1996) 'Language Culture and National Identity', *Social Research*, 63 (4), pp. 1065–80.

———, (1997) *On History*, London.

Hobsbawm, E. and Ranger, T., eds, (1983) *The Invention of Tradition*, Cambridge.

Holmes, R. (1985) *Our Irish Presbyterian Heritage*, Belfast.

Holub, M. (1999) 'Introduction'. In Olbracht I., *The Sorrow Eyes of Hannah Karajicj*, Budapest, London, New York, pp. vii–xxii.

Hume, D. (1986) 'Remembering Ferguson & Our Culture', *New Ulster*, 12, pp. 11–2.

Hume, J. (1986) 'A New Ireland – the Acceptance of Diversity', *Studies*, 300, pp. 378–83.

——— (1988) 'Europe of the Regions'. In R. Kearney, ed., *Across the Frontiers: Ireland in the 1990s*, Dublin, pp. 45–57.

——— (1996) *Personal Views: Politics, Peace and Reconciliation in Ireland*, Dublin.

Hunter, B. (1987) 'Ulster Characteristics', *Ulster*, May, p. 12.

Husserl, E. (1970) *The Crisis of European Science*, translated by D. Carr, Evanston.

Hutchinson, B. (1997) 'Billy Hutchinson'. In B. Lander, ed., *Irish Voices, Irish Lives*, Kerry, pp. 55–69.

Hutchinson, J. (1987) *The Dynamics of Cultural Nationalism – the Gaelic Revival and the Creation of the Irish Nation State*, London.

——— (1996) 'Irish Nationalism'. In D.G. Boyce and A. O'Day, eds, *The Making of Modern Irish History*, London, pp. 100–19.

Hutchinson, J. and Smith, A., eds, (1994) *Nationalism*, Oxford, New York.

——— (1996) *Ethnicity*, Oxford, New York.

Hyde, D. (1986) 'The Necessity for De-Anglicising Ireland'. In B. Ó Conaire, ed., *Language, Lore and Lyrics: Essays and Lectures*, Dublin, pp. 153–70.

Hymes, D. (1975) 'Folklore's Nature and the Sun's Myth', *Journal of American Folklore*, 88, pp. 345–69.

Ichijo, A. (1999) 'Scotland and Europe: Three Visions of Contemporary Scottish Nationalism'. In K. Brehony and N. Rassool, eds, *Nationalisms Old and New*, Basingstoke and New York, pp. 208–20.

Ignatieff, M. (1994) *Blood and Belonging: Journeys into the New Nationalism*, London.

——— (1998) 'Identity Parades', *Prospect*, April, pp. 18–23.

——— (1999) [1998] *The Warrior's Honour: Ethnic War and the Modern Conscience*, London, Sydney, Auckland.

Independent Commission on Policing in Northern Ireland, (1999) *A New Beginning: Policing in Northern Ireland – the Report of the Independent Commission on Policing in Northern Ireland* [Patten Report], Belfast.

Irwin, G. (1996) *Ethnic Minorities in Northern Ireland*, Coleraine.

——— (1998) 'The Indian Community in Northern Ireland'. In P. Hainsworth, ed., *Divided Society: Ethnic Minorities and Racism in Northern Ireland*, London, pp. 184–96.

Irwin, G. and Dunn, S., eds, (1997) *Ethnic Minorities in Northern Ireland*, Coleraine.

Ivey, A. and Payton, P. (1994) 'Towards a Cornish Identity Theory', *Cornish Studies*, 2 (2), pp. 151–73.

Jackson, A. (1996) 'Irish Unionism'. In D.G. Boyce and A. O'Day, eds, *The Making of Modern Irish History*, London, pp. 120–40.

Jackson, H. (1972) *The Two Irelands: The Double Minority – A Study of Intergroup Tensions*, London.

Jackson Lears, T. J. (1985) 'The Concept of Cultural Hegemony: Problems and Possibilities', *American Historical Review*, 90 (3), pp. 567–93.

Jakubowska, L. (1990) 'Political Drama in Poland', *Anthropology Today*, 6 (4), pp. 10–3.

James, S. (1999) *The Atlantic Celts: Ancient People or Modern Invention*, London.

Jarman, N. (1992) 'Troubled Images', *Critique of Anthropology*, 12 (2), pp. 133–65.

———— (1997) *Material Conflicts: Parades and Visual Displays in Northern Ireland*, Oxford.

———— (1998) 'Painting Landscapes: the Place of Murals in the Symbolic Construction of Urban Space'. In A. Buckley, ed., *Symbols in Northern Ireland*, Belfast, pp. 81–98.

———— (1999) *Displaying Faith: Orange, Green and Trade Unions in Northern Ireland*, Belfast.

Jarman, N. and Bryan, D. (1998) *From Riots to Rights Nationalist Parades in the North of Ireland*, Coleraine.

Jarman, N., Bryan, D., Caleyron, N., and de Rosa, C. (1998) *Politics in Public: Freedom of Assembly and the Right to Protest – A Comparative Analysis*, Belfast.

Jenkins, R. (1997) *Rethinking Ethnicity: Arguments and Explorations*, London.

Johnson, R.W. (1990) 'The Politics of International Intervention'. In H. Giliomee and J. Gagiano, eds, *The Elusive Search for Peace*, Oxford, pp. 276–98.

Jones, G. and Sharrock, D. (2000) 'RUC Stripped of Royal Title', *The Daily Telegraph*, 20 January, p. 1.

Jones, S. (1997) *The Archaeology of Ethnicity: Constructing Identities in the Past and Present*, London.

Joyce, C. and O'Brien, B. (1998) *Confronting Racism in Ireland: Travellers and Socio-Economic Development*, Belfast.

Joyce, J. (1977) [1916] *A Portrait of the Artist as a Young Man*, London.

Kachuk, P. (1994) 'A Resistance to British Cultural Hegemony: Irish-Language Activism in West-Belfast', *Anthropologica*, xxxvi, pp. 135–54.

Kadare, I. (1997) *The File on H*, translated by D. Bellos, London.

Kahn, J. (1995) *Culture, Multiculture, Postculture*, London.

Kay, B. (1997) 'Shamrock and Thistle Entwined'. In J. Erskine and G. Lucy, eds, *Cultural Traditions in Northern Ireland: Varieties of Scottishness*, Belfast, pp. 7–24.

Kearney, R. (1984) *Myth and Motherland*, Derry.

———— (1988) 'Introduction: Thinking Otherwise'. In R. Kearney, ed., *Across the Frontiers: Ireland in the 1990s*, Dublin.

———— (1997) *Postnationalist Ireland: Politics, Culture, Philosophy*, London, New York.

Keating, M. (1988) *State and Regional Nationalism – Territorial Politics and the European State*, New York, London.

Kennedy, B. (1995) *The Scots-Irish in the Hills of Tennessee*, Belfast.

———— (1996) *The Scots-Irish in the Shenandoah Valley*, Belfast.

———— (1997) *The Scots-Irish in the Carolinas*, Belfast.

Kennedy, F. (1998) 'Italians Ask: 'What Did the Romans Ever Do for Us?', *Sunday Independent* (English), 15 November, p. 19.

Kenney, M. (1998) 'The Phoenix and the Lark: Revolutionary Mythology and Iconographic Creativity in Belfast's Republican Districts'. In A. Buckley, ed., *Symbols in Northern Ireland*, Belfast, pp. 153–70.

Keogh, D. (1998) *Jews in Twentieth-Century Ireland: Refugees, Anti-Semitism and the Holocaust*, Cork.

Keogh, D. (1999) 'The Jewish Contribution to Twentieth-Century Ireland'. In D. Carroll, ed., *Religion in Ireland: Past, Present and Future*, Dublin, pp. 60–85.

Kiberd, D. (1986) 'Anglo-Irish Attitudes', *Ireland's Field Day: Field Day Theatre Company*, Indiana: University of Notre Dame, pp. 83–106.

———— (1996) *Inventing Ireland: the Literature of the Modern Nation*, London.

King, A. (1999) 'Future of the Union: Most Scots Have No Wish to Separate from their "Fellow Citizens" the English', *The Daily Telegraph*, 15 April, pp. 14–5.

Kinsella, T., trans. (1969) *The Táin*, Dublin.

Kirk, J. (1997) 'Ethnolinguistic Differences in Northern Ireland'. In A. Thomas, ed., *Issues and Methods in Dialectology*, Bangor (Wales), pp. 55–68.

Klíma, I. (1994) *The Spirit of Prague and other Essays*, London.

Kloss, H. (1967) ' "Abstand Languages" and "Ausbau Languages" ', *Anthropological Linguistics*, 9 (7), pp. 29–41.

Knox, C. (1989) *Local Government Leisure Services: Planning and Politics in Northern Ireland*, unpublished D.Phil thesis, University of Ulster.

Kockel, U. (1994) 'Mythos und Identität. Der Konflikt im Spiegel der Volkskultur'. In J. Elvert, ed., *Nordirland in Geschichte und Gegenwart/ Northern Ireland – Past and Present*, Stuttgart, pp. 495–517.

———— (1995) 'The Celtic Quest: Beuys as Hero and Hedge School Master'. In D. Thistlewood, ed., *Joseph Beuys: Diverging Critiques*, Liverpool, pp. 129–48.

———— (1999a) *Borderline Cases: the Ethnic Frontiers of European Integration*, Liverpool.

———— (1999b) 'Braveheart and the Irish Border: Ulster-Scottish Connections'. In M. Anderson and E. Bort, eds, *The Irish Border: History, Politics, Culture*, Liverpool, pp. 159–73.

———— (1999c) 'Nationality, Citizenship and Identity: Reflecting on Europe at Drumcree Parish Church', *Ethnologia Europaea*, 29 (2), pp. 97–108.

Kofos, E. (1989) 'National Heritage and National Identity in Nineteenth- and Twentieth-Century Macedonia', *European History Quarterly*, 19, pp. 229–67.

Kohn, H. (1945) *The Idea of Nationalism*, New York.

Kristeva, J. (1991) *Strangers to Ourselves*, trans. L. Roudiez, London.

Kymlicka, W. (1995) *Multicultural Citizenship: a Liberal Theory of Rights*, Oxford.

Lacey, B. (1997) *Colum Cille and the Columban Tradition*, Dublin.

Lambkin, B. (1994) 'The Ulster Cycle, the Navan Centre and the Improvement of Community Relations in Northern Ireland', *Ulidia: Proceedings of the First International Conference on the Ulster Cycle of Tales*, pp. 281–90.

———— (1996) *Opposite Religions Still? Interpreting Northern Ireland After the Conflict*, Avebury.

Leach, E. (1982) *Social Anthropology*, Glasgow.

Lebow, N. (1976) *White Britain and Black Ireland: the Influence of Stereotypes on Colonial Policy*, Philadelphia.

Lee, J. (1973) *The Modernisation of Irish Society 1848–1918*, Dublin.

Lee, R. (1981) *Interreligious Courtship and Marriage in Northern Ireland*, unpublished PhD thesis, University of Edinburgh.

Lee, S. (1993) *The Way Forward*. Speech at Celebration of Tenth Anniversary of the Chinese Chamber of Commerce (Northern Ireland), Belfast.

Leerssen, J. (1996) 'Celticism'. In T. Brown, ed., *Celticism*, Amsterdam, pp. 1–20.

Lenihan, P. (1997) ' "Celtic" Warfare in the 1640s'. In J.R. Young, ed., *Celtic Dimensions of the British Civil Wars*, Edinburgh, pp. 116–40.

Lentin, R., ed. (1999) *The Expanding Nation: Towards a Multi-Ethnic Ireland*, Dublin.

———— ed. (2000) *Emerging Irish Identities*, Dublin.

———— (2000) 'Introduction – Racialising the Other, Racialising the "Us": Emerging Irish Identities as Processes of Racialisation'. In R. Lentin, ed., *Emerging Irish Identities*, Dublin, pp. 4–16.

Levine, S. (1990) 'Cultural Politics in New Zealand. Responses to Michele Dominy', *Anthropology Today*, 6 (3), pp. 4–6.

Lévy-Bruhl, L. (1975) *The Notebooks on Primitive Mentality*, Oxford.

Leyburn, J. (1962) *The Scotch-Irish, a Social History*, Chapel Hill.

Lhuyd, E. (1707) *Archaeologia Britannica*, Oxford.

Liechty, J. (1993) *Roots of Sectarianism in Ireland*, Belfast.

——— (1999) 'Sectarianism and the Churches: the Legacy and the Challenge'. In D. Carroll, ed., *Religion in Ireland: Past, Present and Future*, Dublin, pp. 86–96.

Lisburn Museum (1985) *The Huguenots & Ulster 1685–1985*, Lisburn.

Litton Falkiner, C. (1904) *Illustrations of Irish History and Topography, Mainly of the Seventeenth Century*, London, New York, Bombay.

Llobera, J. (1998a) 'The Role of Historical Memory in Catalan National Identity', *Social Anthropology*, 6 (3), pp. 331–42.

——— (1998b) 'The Force of Nationalism in National Identity. The Experience of Western Europe', Paper delivered at the Conference of the European Association of Social Anthropologists, September.

Loane, P. (1985) 'True History of Ireland and Ulster', *Ulster*, November, p. 3.

Loftus, B. (1994) *Mirrors: Orange and Green*, Down.

London Hibernian Society (1825) *The Nineteenth Annual Report of the London Hibernian Society for Establishing Schools and Circulating the Holy Scriptures in Ireland – with Interesting Extracts of Correspondence*, London.

Longley, E. (1987) 'Opening Up: a New Pluralism'. In R. Johnstone and R. Wilson, eds, (1991) *Fortnight Magazine and the Troubles in Northern Ireland 1970–91*, Belfast, pp. 141–4.

——— (1990) 'Literature'. In M. Crozier, ed., *Cultural Traditions in Northern Ireland: Varieties of Britishness*, Belfast, pp. 23–7.

Longley, M. (1996) 'Michael Longley'. In A. Thomson, ed., *Faith in Ulster*, Belfast, pp. 74–5.

Loughlin, J. (1995) *Ulster Unionism and British National Identity Since 1885*, London and New York.

Loughlin, S. (1989) 'The Role of the Churches in the Conflict in Northern Ireland: a Reply to John Hickey', *Studies*, 78 (311), pp. 306–11.

——— (1998) 'Culture, Nation and Region in Western Europe: a Comparative Approach,' Paper delivered at Cardiff University, September.

Lowry, D. (1991) ' "The Ulster of South Africa": Ireland, the Irish and the Rhodesian Connection', *Southern African-Irish Studies*, 1, pp. 122–45.

Lydon, J. (1967) 'The Medieval English Colony'. In T.W. Moody and F.V. Martin, eds, *The Course of Irish History*, Cork, pp. 144–57.

Lynch, D. (1998) 'Cultured Words from Unionist Shock', *Sunday Independent* (Irish), 20 December, p. 17.

Lyon, W. (1997) Defining Ethnicity: Another Way of Being British'. In T. Modood and P. Werbner, eds, *The Politics of Multiculturalism in the New Europe: Racism, Identity and Community*, London and New York, pp. 186–206.

Lyons, F. (1971) *Ireland since the Famine*, London.

——— (1979) *Culture and Anarchy in Ireland 1890–1939*, Oxford.

Macafee, W. and Morgan, V. (1981) 'Population in Ulster, 1600–1760'. In P. Roebuck, ed., *Plantation to Partition – Essays in Ulster History in Honour of J.L. McCracken*, Belfast, pp. 46–63.

MacAlister, R. and MacNeill, J., eds (1916) *Leabhar Gabhála: the Book of Conquests of Ireland*, Dublin.

Mac Aodha, B. (1985/6) 'Aspects of the Linguistic Geography of Ireland in the Early Nineteenth Century', *Studia Celtica*, xx/xxi, pp. 205–20.

Mac Cormaic, E. (1986) 'The Key'. In *The Role of the Language in Ireland's Cultural Revival*, Belfast, pp 11–20.

MacDonagh, O. (1983) *States of Mind, a Study of Anglo-Irish Conflict 1780–1980*, London.

MacDonald, D. (1998) *The Sons of Levi*, Monaghan.

MacDonald, H. (2000) 'The Wrath Pack', *Magill*, March, pp. 29–30.

Mac Eoin, G. (1986) 'The Celticity of Celtic Ireland'. In K.H. Schmidt, ed., *Geschichte und Kultur der Kelten*, Heidelberg, pp. 161–74.

Mac Giolla Chríost, D. and Aitchison, J. (1998) 'Ethnic Identities and Language in Northern Ireland', *Area*, 30 (4), pp. 301–9.

Mac Laughlin, J. (1995) *Travellers and Ireland: Whose Country, Whose History?*, Cork.

——— (1996) 'The Evolution of Anti-Traveller Racism in Ireland', *Race and Class* 37 (3), pp. 47–63.

Macleod, I. and MacNeacail, A. (1995) *Scotland – a Linguistic Double Helix*, Dublin.

MacMathúna, S. (1992) 'Observations on Class and Culture in Ireland', In S. Mac Grianna and P. Ua Conchubhair, eds, *Essays on Class and Culture in Ireland*, Derry, pp. 37–48.

Mac Neill, E. (1921) *Celtic Ireland*, Dublin, London.

Mac Neill, E. (1933) 'The Pretanic Background in Britain and Ireland', *The Journal of the Royal Society of Antiquaries of Ireland for the Year LXIII*, 1, pp 2–28.

Mac Póilin, A. (1990a) 'Embers of Cultural Liberalism Faded', *Fortnight*, 288, p. 31.

——— (1990b) 'From the Token Teague to the Patronised Prod', *Fortnight*, 282, p. 29.

——— (1990c) 'Rescuing the Protestant Gaeilgeoirí', *Fortnight*, 286, pp. 27–8.

——— (1990d) 'The Most "Expressive and Polished" Language', *Fortnight*, 287, p. 29.

——— (1994a) ' "Spiritual Beyond the Ways of Men" – Images of the Gael', *The Irish Review*, 16, pp. 1–22.

——— (1994b) 'The Work of the ULTACH Trust in Promoting the Irish Language', *Ulster Local Studies*, 16 (2), pp. 29–37.

——— (1994c) *Second Report/An Dara Tuairisc 1991–93*, Belfast.

Mac Póilin, A. ed. (1997) *The Irish Language in Northern Ireland*, Belfast.

Madden, K. (1998) *Ten Troubled Years: Settlement, Conflict and Rebellion in Forkhill, County Armagh, 1778–1798*, unpublished MA thesis, Queen's University, Kingston, Canada.

Maguire, G. (1991) *Our Own Language: an Irish Initiative*, Clevedon, Philadelphia, Adelaide.

Malcolm, I. (1997) 'Living with Irish'. In A. Mac Póilin, ed., *The Irish Language in Northern Ireland*, Belfast, pp. 7–30.

Malcomson, W. (1999) *Behind Closed Doors: the Hidden Structure with the Orange Order [the Royal Arch Purple Order] Examined from an Evangelical Perspective*, Banbridge.

Mallory, J. and McNeill, T. (1991) *The Archaeology of Ulster: from Colonisation to Plantation*, Belfast.

Mari MacArthur, E. (1995) *Columba's Island: Iona from Past to Present*, Edinburgh.

Markale, J. (1978) *Celtic Civilization*, London.

Martin, F. (1967) 'The Anglo-Norman Invasion'. In T.W. Moody and F.V. Martin, eds, *The Course of Irish History*, Cork, pp. 123–43.

Maxwell, C. (1954) *The Stranger in Ireland – from the Reign of Elizabeth to the Great Famine*, London.

Mayo, P. (1974) *The Roots of Identity*, London.

McA Scott, E. and Robinson, P. (1992) 'Introduction'. In *The Country Rhymes of Samuel Thomson, The Bard of Carngranny 1766–1816*, Bangor, pp. viii–xvii.

McAuley, J. (1995) *Changing faces of Loyalism?: Political Reactions to the 'Peace Process'*, Aldershot.

McAuley, J. (1990) 'The Hound of Ulster and the Re-Writing of Irish History', *Études Irlandaises*, 15 (2), pp. 149–64.

———— (1991) 'Cuchullain and an RPG-7: the Ideology and Politics of the Ulster Defence Association'. In E. Hughes, ed., *Culture and Politics in Northern Ireland 1960–1990*, Milton Keynes, pp. 45–68.

McBride, I. (1996) 'Ulster and the British Problem'. In R. English and G. Walker, eds, *Unionism in Modern Ireland: New Perspectives on Politics and Culture*, Hampshire and London, pp. 1–18.

———— (1997) *The Siege of Derry in Ulster Protestant Mythology*, Dublin.

McCartney, D. (1967) 'From Parnell to Pearse'. In T.W. Moody and F.V. Martin, eds, *The Course of Irish History*, Cork, pp. 294–312.

McCausland, N. (1991) '1641–1991: the Ulster Massacre 350th Anniversary', *The Twelfth: Silver Jubilee Issue*, Belfast, pp. 36–41.

———— (1997) *Patrick Apostle of Ulster: a Protestant View of Patrick*, Belfast.

McCavitt, J. (1994) 'The Wars of the Seventeenth Century and the Colonisation of Ulster'. In J. Elvert, ed., *Nordirland in Geschichte und Gegenwart/ Northern Ireland—Past and Present*, Stuttgart, pp. 27–42.

McClelland, J. (1994) *Searching for Hillbillys: an Ulsterman in the Appalachians*, Belfast.

McClure, J. (1997) *Why Scots Matters*, Edinburgh.

McClure, J. (1981) 'Scottis, Inglis, Suddroun: Language Labels and Language Attitudes'. In J. R. Lyall and F. Riddy, eds, *Proceedings of the Third International Conference on Scottish Language and Literature (Medieval and Renaissance)*, Stirling, Glasgow, pp. 52–69.

McCoy, G. (1997a) 'Protestant Learners of Irish in Northern Ireland'. In A. Mac Póilin, ed. *The Irish language in Northern Ireland*, Belfast, pp. 131–69.

———— (1997b) 'Rhetoric and Realpolitik: the Irish Language Movement and the British Government'. In H. Donnan and G. McFarlane, eds, *Culture and Policy in Northern Ireland: Anthropology in the Public Arena*, Belfast, pp. 117–39.

McCracken, J. (1967) 'Northern Ireland'. In T.W. Moody and F.V. Martin, eds, *The Course of Irish History*, Cork, pp. 313–23.

McCrone, D. (1998) *The Sociology of Nationalism: Tomorrow's Ancestors*, London.

McCrum, R., Cran, W., and MacNeil, R. (1987) 'The Scots-Irish Migrations', *English Today*, 9, pp. 23–5.

McCusker, H. (1987) 'Gaelic Dead as the Dodo', *Orange Standard*, December 1986/ January 1987, p. 3.

McDonald, H. (1997) 'Back to the Craic my Father Wore', *Observer*, 9 November.

McDonald, M. (1989)*'We are not French!' Language, Culture and Identity in Brittany*, London and New York.

McDowell, D. (n.d.) *Ulster's Ancient Past: The Glittering Lies*, Hampshire.

McDowell, R. (1967) 'The Protestant Nation'. In T.W. Moody and F.V. Martin, eds, *The Course of Irish History*, Cork, pp. 232–47.

McGarry, J. and O'Leary, B. (1995) *Explaining Northern Ireland: Broken Images*, Oxford.

McGimpsey, C. (1994) 'The Irish Language and the Unionist Tradition'. In P. Mistéil, ed., *The Irish Language and the Unionist Tradition*, Belfast, pp. 7–16.

McKay, S. (2000) *Northern Protestants: an Unsettled People*, Belfast.

McKee, V. (1995) 'Contemporary Gaelic Language Politics in Western Scotland and Northern Ireland since 1950: Comparative Assessments', *Contemporary Politics*, 1, pp. 92–113.

McLoughlin, D. (1994) 'Ethnicity and Irish Travellers: Reflections on Ní Shúinéar'. In M. McCann, S. Ó Síocháin, and J. Ruane, eds, *Irish Travellers: Culture and Ethnicity*, Belfast, pp. 54–77.

McMaster, J. (1995) *Understanding Irish Churches: Historical and Political Perspectives*, Belfast.

—— (1997) 'Johnston McMaster'. In G. Lucy and E. McClure, eds, *The Twelfth: What it Means to Me*, Armagh.

McMillan, D. (1998) 'The Baptist Union of Ireland'. In N. Richardson, ed., *A Tapestry of Beliefs: Christian Traditions in Northern Ireland*, Belfast, pp. 104–13.

McNamee, P. (1986) *Divided Societies*, Belfast.

McVeigh, R. (1998) ' "There's no Racism because There's no Black People Here": Racism and Anti-Racism in Northern Ireland'. In P. Hainsworth, ed., *Divided Society: Ethnic Minorities and Racism in Northern Ireland*, London, pp. 11–32.

—— (1999) 'Is Sectarianism Racism? The Implications of Sectarian Division for Multi-Ethnicity in Ireland'. In R. Lentin, ed., *The Expanding Nation: Towards a Multi-Ethnic Ireland*, Dublin, pp. 16–20.

—— (2000) 'The Green Tiger and the Orange Sloth: the North of Ireland and New Formations of Irishness'. In R. Lentin, ed., *Emerging Irish Identities*, Dublin, pp. 24–34.

Meier, H. (1977) 'Scots is not Alone: the Swiss and Low German Analogues'. In A.J. Aitken, M.P. McDiarmid and D.S. Thomson, eds, *Bards and Makars*, Glasgow, pp. 201–13.

Megaw, R. and Megaw, V. (1999) 'Celtic Connections Past and Present: Celtic Ethnicity Ancient and Modern'. In R. Black, W. Gillies, and R. Ó Maolalaigh, eds, *Celtic Connections: Proceedings of the Tenth International Congress of Celtic Studies*, 1, East Lothian, pp. 19–81.

Memmi, A. (1965) *The Colonizer and the Colonized*, New York.

Meyer, K. (1909) 'The Secret Languages of Ireland', *Journal of Gypsy Lore Society*, 2, pp. 241–6.

Miles, R. (1989) *Racism*, London.

Miller, David (1978) *Queen's Rebels: Ulster Loyalism in Historical Perspective*, Dublin.

Miller, D. (1995) 'Reflections on British National Identity', *New Community*, 21 (2), pp. 153–66.

—— (1998) 'Colonialism and Academic Representations of the Troubles'. In D. Miller, ed., *Rethinking Northern Ireland*, Essex, pp. 3–39.

Milroy, J. (1981) *Accents of English*, Belfast.

Mistéil, P., ed. (1994) *The Irish Language and the Unionist Tradition*, Belfast.

Modood, T. (1997) 'Introduction: the Politics of Multiculturalism in the New

Europe'. In T. Modood and P. Werbner, eds, *The Politics of Multiculturalism in the New Europe: Racism, Identity and Community*, London, New York, pp. 1–25.
—— (1999) 'New Forms of Britishness: Post-Immigration Ethnicity and Hybridity in Britain'. In R. Lentin, ed., *The Expanding Nation: Towards a Multi-Ethnic Ireland*, Dublin, pp. 34–40.
Modood, T., Berthoud, R., Lakey, J., Nazroo, J., Smith, P., Virdee, S., and Reishon, S. (1997) *Ethnic Minorities in Britain: Diversity and Disadvantage*, London.
Moloney, E. and Collins, S. (1999) 'British Give Back Land to GAA in Crosmaglen', *Sunday Times* (Irish), 4 April, p. 4.
Montague, J., ed. (1974) *The Faber Book of Irish Verse*, London.
Montgomery, G. and Whitten, J. (1995) *The Orange on Parade*, Belfast.
Montgomery, M. (1991) 'The Anglicization of Scots in Seventeenth-Century Ulster', *Studies in Scottish Literature – The Language and Literature of Early Scotland*, xxvi, pp. 50–64.
—— (1993) 'The Lexicography of Hiberno-English'. In J. Doan, J. Weaver, J., and M. Montgomery, eds, *Scotch-Irish and Hiberno-English Language and Culture*, Nova University, pp. 20–35.
Montville, J. (1993) 'The Healing Function in Political Conflict Resolution'. In J.D. Sandole and H. van der Merwe, eds, *Conflict Resolution Theory and Practice: Integration and Application*, Manchester, pp. 112–27.
Moody, T. (1939) 'The Treatment of the Native Population under the Scheme for the Plantation of Ulster', *Irish Historical Studies*, 1, 1938–9, pp. 59–63.
—— (1974) *The Ulster Question 1603–1973*, Cork.
Moore, R. (1973) 'Race Relations in the Six Counties: Colonialism, Industrialization, and Stratification in Ireland', *Race*, xiii, pp. 21–42.
Morgan, H. (1993) 'Deceptions of Demons', *Fortnight*, 320, pp. 34–6.
Morgan, P. (1983) 'From a Death to a View: the Hunt for the Welsh Past in the Romantic Period'. In E. Hobsbawm and T. Ranger, eds, *The Invention of Tradition*, Cambridge, pp. 43–100.
Morgan, V., Smith, M., Robinson, G., and Fraser, G. (1996) *Mixed Marriages in Northern Ireland*, Coleraine.
Moxon-Browne, E. (1983) *Nation, Class and Greed in Northern Ireland*, Aldershot.
Mulhearn, F. (1998) *The Present Lasts a Long Time: Essays in Cultural Politics*, Cork.
Mullan, D. (1998) [1997] *Eyewitness Bloody Sunday*, Dublin.
Nairn, T. (1981) [1977] *The Break-Up of Britain*, London.
Nandy, A. (1983) *The Intimate Enemy: Loss and Recovery of Self under Colonialism*, Delhi.
Napier, C. (1989) 'Address'. In M. Crozier, ed., *Cultural Traditions in Northern Ireland: Varieties of Irishness*, Belfast, pp. 41–4.
Nekvaplu, J. and Neustupný, J. (1998) 'Linguistic Communities in the Czech Republic'. In C.B. Paulston and D. Peckham, eds, *Linguistic Minorities in Central and Eastern Europe*, pp. 116–34.
Neuberger, B. (1990) 'Nationalisms Compared'. In H. Giliomee and J. Gagiano, eds, *The Elusive Search for Peace*, Oxford, pp. 54–77.
Nic Craith, M. (1988) *An tOileánach Léannta*, Dublin.
—— (1994) [1993] *An Ghaeilge i gCorcaigh sa Naóú hAois Déag*, Bremen.
—— (1995) 'The Symbolism of Irish in Northern Ireland'. In U. Kockel, ed., *Landscape, Heritage and Identity: Case Studies in Irish Ethnography*, Liverpool, pp. 11–46.

———— (1996/7) 'Irish in Primary and Post-Primary Education: North and South of the Border', *Irish Studies Review*, 17, pp. 35–9.

———— (1999a) 'Irish Speakers in Northern Ireland, and the Good Friday Agreement', *Journal of Multilingual and Multicultural Development*, 20 (6), pp. 1–14.

———— (1999b) 'Linguistic Policy in Ireland and the Creation of a Border.' In M. Anderson and E. Bort, eds, *The Irish Border: History, Politics, Culture*, Liverpool, pp. 175–200.

———— (1999c) 'Primary Education on the Great Blasket Island 1864–1940', *Journal of the Kerry Historical and Archaeological Society*, 28, 1995, pp. 77–137.

———— (2001) 'Politicised Linguistic Consciousness: the Case of Ulster-Scots', *Nations and Nationalism*, 7 (1), pp. 21–37.

Nic Craith, M. and Shuttleworth, I. (1996) 'Irish in Northern Ireland: the 1991 Census'. In M. Nic Craith, ed., *Watching One's Tongue: Aspects of Celtic and Romance Languages*, Liverpool, pp. 163–76.

Nicholls, K. (1972) *Gaelic and Gaelicised Ireland in the Middle Ages*, Dublin, London.

Nic Éinrí, U. (1971) *Stair na Teanga Gaeilge*, Dublin.

Ní Cheallacháin, M., ed. (1962) *Filíocht Phádraigín Haicéad*, Dublin.

Ní Shúinéar, S. (1994) 'Irish Travellers, Ethnicity and the Origins Question'. In M. McCann, S. Ó Síocháin, and J. Ruane, eds, *Irish Travellers: Culture and Ethnicity*, Belfast, pp. 54–77.

Noonan, P. (1998) 'Pathologisation and Resistance: Travellers, Nomadism and the State'. In P. Hainsworth, ed., *Divided Society: Ethnic Minorities and Racism in Northern Ireland*, London, pp. 152–83.

Nordland, R. (1999) 'Vengeance of a Victim Race', *Newsweek*, cxiii (15), pp. 35–6.

Northern Ireland Council for the Curriculum, Examination and Assessment (1997) *Mutual Understanding and Cultural Heritage: Cross-Curricular Guidance Materials*, Belfast.

Northover, M. and Donnelly, S. (1996) 'A Future for English/Irish Bilingualism in Northern Ireland?', *Journal of Multilingual and Multicultural Development*, 17 (1), pp. 33–48.

Ó Baoill, D. (1994) 'Travellers' Cant – Language or Register?' In M. McCann, S. Ó Síocháin and J. Ruane, eds, *Irish Travellers: Culture and Ethnicity*, Belfast, pp. 155–69.

O'Brien, C. (1988) *God Land: Reflections on Religion and Nationalism*, Massachusetts.

O'Brien, J. (1998) 'GAA Decides in Secret on Rule 21', *Sunday Tribune*, 31 May, p. 5.

Ó Casaide, S. (1930) *The Irish Language in Belfast and County Down a.d. 1601–1850*, Dublin.

O'Casey, S. (1966) *Three Plays by Sean O'Casey*, London.

O'Connell, J. (1994) 'Ethnicity and Irish Travellers'. In M. McCann, S. Ó Síocháin, and J. Ruane, eds, *Irish Travellers: Culture and Ethnicity*, Belfast, pp. 110–20.

O'Connor, F. (1993) *In Search of a State: Catholics in Northern Ireland*, Belfast.

O'Connor, F. (1999a) 'A Trimble of Anticipation', *Magill*, February, pp. 14–6.

———— (1999b) 'An Imperfect Peace Process', *Magill*, October, pp. 26–7.

O'Conor, C. (1753) *Dissertations on the Ancient History of Ireland*, Dublin.

Ó Cuív, B. (1951) *Irish Dialects and Irish-Speaking Districts – Three Lectures*, Dublin.

O'Day, A. (1996) 'Home Rule and the Historians'. In D.G. Boyce and A. O'Day, eds, *The Making of Modern Irish History*, London, pp. 141–62.

O'Day, A., ed. (1997) *Political Violence in Northern Ireland: Conflict and Conflict Resolution*, Westport, Connecticut, London.

Ó Dónaill, É. (1995) *Now You're Talking*, Dublin.

Ó Donnaile, A. (1997) 'Can Linguistic Minorities Cope with a Favourable Majority?' In A. Mac Póilin, ed., *The Irish Language in Northern Ireland*, Belfast, pp. 191–209.

O'Dowd, L. (1998) ' "New Unionism", British Nationalism and the Prospects for a Negotiated Settlement in Northern Ireland'. In D. Miller, ed., *Rethinking Northern Ireland*, London and New York, pp. 70–93.

———— (1999) 'British Nationalism and the Northern Ireland "Peace Process" '. In K.J. Brehony and N. Rassool, eds, *Nationalisms Old and New*, Basingstoke and New York.

Ó Glaisne, R. (1981) 'Irish and the Protestant Tradition'. In M. Hederman, R. Kearney, eds, *The Crane Bag Book of Irish Studies*, Dublin, pp. 864–75.

O'Grady, S.H., ed. (1857) *Tóruigheacht Dhiarmada agus Ghráinne: the Pursuit after Diarmuid O'Duibhne and Gráinne, the Daughter of Cormac MacAirt*, Dublin.

———— ed. (1892) *Silva Gadelica: a Collection of Tales in Irish*, London.

Ó hAdhmaill, F. (1985) *Report of a Survey Carried Out on the Irish Language in West Belfast in the Winter of 1984/5*, Coleraine.

———— (1990) *The Function and Dynamics of the Ghetto: a Study of Nationalist West Belfast*, unpublished PhD thesis, University of Ulster.

Ó hAdhmaill, F. (1989) 'Irish And The New Educational Reforms', *British Journal Of Educational Studies*, xxxvii (1), pp. 72–7.

O'Hickey, M. (n.d.) *The True National Idea*, Dublin.

Ó Huallacháin, C. (1994) *The Irish and Irish – a Sociolinguistic Analysis of the Relationship between a People and their Language*, Dublin.

Ó hUiginn, R. (1989) 'Tongue Twisting: the Language Question', *Fortnight*, 269, pp. 24–5.

———— (1992) 'The Background and Development of *Táin Bó Cuailgne*'. In J.P. Mallory, ed., *Aspects of the Táin*, Belfast, pp. 29–67.

O'Leary, P. (1970) *My Story*, Cork.

Ó Maolchraoibhe, P. (1986) 'The Role of the Language in Ireland's Cultural Revival', *The Role of the Language in Ireland's Cultural Revival*, Belfast, pp. 1–10.

Ó Muilleoir, M. (1986) 'The Necessity for Cultural Liberation', *The Role of the Language in Ireland's Cultural Revival*, Belfast, pp. 20–3.

———— (1990) *Comhad Comhairleora*, Dublin.

Ó Muirithe, D. (1996) *A Dictionary of Anglo-Irish Words and Phrases from the Gaelic in the English of Ireland*, Dublin.

Ó Murchú, D. (1997) *Reclaiming Spirituality*, Dublin.

Ó Néill, E. (1990) 'Personally Speaking', *Fortnight*, 281, p. 32.

———— (1997) 'Dropped Signs Fuel Equality Debate', *Irish News*, 24 August.

O' Rahilly, T. (1946) *Early Irish History and Mythology*, Dublin.

O' Reilly, C. (1999) *The Irish Language in Northern Ireland: the Politics of Culture and Identity*, Hampshire and New York.

O' Reilly, C. (1993), 'Political Speech', *Fortnight*, 319, pp. 38–9.

———— (1997) 'Nationalists and the Irish Language in Northern Ireland: Competing Perspectives'. In A. Mac Póilin, ed., *The Irish Language in Northern Ireland*, Belfast, pp. 95–130.

———— (1998), 'The Irish Language as Symbol: Visual Representations of Irish in Northern Ireland'. In A. Buckley, ed., *Symbols in Northern Ireland*, Belfast, pp. 43–62.

Ó Riagáin, P. (1997) *Language Policy and Social Reproduction: Ireland 1893–1993*, Oxford.

O Riordan, M. (1990) *The Gaelic Mind and the Collapse of the Gaelic World*, Cork.

Ó Ríordáin, J. (1980) *Irish Catholics: Tradition and Transition*, Dublin.

—— (1998) *Irish Catholic Spirituality*, Dublin.

Orr, J. (1935) *Poems on Various Subjects*, Belfast.

Ó Snodaigh, P. (1973) *Hidden Ulster (The Other Hidden Ireland)*, Dublin.

—— (1995) *Hidden Ulster: Protestants and the Irish Language*, Belfast.

Ó Snodaigh, P. (1981) 'Hidden Ulster Revisited'. In M. Hederman and R. Kearney, eds, *The Crane Bag Book of Irish Studies*, Dublin, pp. 876–7.

O'Sullivan See, K. (1986) *First World Nationalisms: Class and Ethnic Politics in Northern Ireland and Quebec*, Chicago and London.

O'Toole, F. (2000) 'Green, White and Black, Race and Irish Identity'. In R. Lentin, ed., *Emerging Irish Identities*, Dublin, pp. 17–23.

Ó Tuathaigh, G. (1972) *Ireland before the Famine 1798–1848*, Dublin.

Ó Tuathaigh, G. (1986) 'An Chléir Chaitliceach, an Léann Dúchais agus an Cultúr in Éirinn, C.1750–C.1850'. In P. Ó Fiannachta, ed., *Léann na Cléire – Léachtaí Cholm Cille*, xvi, pp. 110–39.

—— (1988) 'The Irish Nation-State in the Constitution'. In B. O'Farrell, ed., *De Valera's Constitution and Ours*, Dublin, pp. 46–60.

Palmer, H. (1976) 'Mosaic versus Melting Pot?: Immigration and Ethnicity in Canada and the United States', *International Journal*, 31, pp. 488–528.

Parkin, D. (1993) 'Nemi in the Modern World', *Man* 28 (1), pp. 79–99.

Parry, N. and Parry, J. (1999) 'Nationalism, Culture and the End of Civilization?'. In K. Brehony and N. Rassool, eds, *Nationalisms Old and New*, Basingstoke and New York, pp. 221–40.

Patten Report: see Independent Commission on Policing in Northern Ireland, (1999).

Paulin, T. (1984), 'Paisley's Progress'. In P. Craig, ed. (1992) *The Rattle of the North: an Anthology of Ulster Prose*, Belfast, pp. 410–24.

—— (1986) 'A New Look at the Language Question', *Ireland's Field Day: Field Day Theatre Company*, Indiana, pp. 3–22.

Paxman, J. (1998) *The English: A Portrait of a People*, London.

Pedersen, K. (1991) 'Denmark and Germany – the German Minority in Denmark and the Danish Minority in Germany', *Minorities and Autonomy in Western Europe: a Minority Rights Group Report*, London, pp. 16–9.

Pells R. (1998) 'Us and Them', *Visions of Europe: Time*, Special Issue, Winter, p. 126.

Pender, S. ed. (1939) *A Census of Ireland, circa 1659, with supplementary material from the Poll Money Ordinances (1660–1661)*, Dublin.

Penrose, J. (1995) 'Globalization, Fragmentation and a Dysfunctional Concept of Nation: the Death Knell of "Nation States" and the Salvation of Cultural Diversity?' In B. Synak, ed., *The Ethnic Identities of European Minorities: Theory and Case Studies*, Gdansk, pp. 11–25.

Pentland Mahaffy, R., ed. (1900) *Calendar of the State Papers relating to Ireland, of the Reign of Charles I – 1625–1632*, London.

—— (1901) *Calendar of the State Papers Relating to Ireland, of the Reign of Charles I – 1633–1647*, London.

—— (1905) *Calendar of the State Papers Relating to Ireland Preserved in the Public Record Office —1660–1662*, London.

—— (1908) *Calendar of the State Papers Relating to Ireland Preserved in the Public Record Office – 1666–1669*, London.

Perceval-Maxwell, M. (1973) *The Scottish Migration to Ulster in the Reign of James I*, London.

Phillipson, R., and Skutnabb-Kangas, T. (1995) 'Language Rights in Postcolonial Africa'. In T. Skutnabb-Kangas, R. Phillipson, and M. Rannut, eds, *Linguistic Human Rights: Overcoming Linguistic Discrimination*, Berlin and New York, pp. 335–45.

Pieterse, J. (1995) 'Globalisation as Hybridisation'. In M. Featherstone and S. Lash, eds, *Global Modernities*, London, pp. 45–68.

Pike, L. (1866), *The English and Their Origin: a Prologue to Authentic English History*, London.

Pinkerton, A. (1984) 'Message Understood', *Ulster*, pp. 3–4.

Policy Planning and Research Unit, Statistics and Social Division (1988) *The Irish Language In Northern Ireland 1987 – Preliminary Report of a Survey of Knowledge, Interest and Ability*, 17, Belfast.

Pollock, A., Opsahl, T., O'Malley, P., Gallagher, E., Elliott, M., Faulkner, L., Lister, R., and Gallagher, E. (1993) *A Citizens' Inquiry: the Opsahl Report on Northern Ireland*, Dublin.

Popper, K. (1972) *Objective Knowledge: an Evolutionary Approach*, Oxford.

Porter, B. (1997) 'Concepts of Nationalism in History'. In W.A. Van Horne, ed., *Global Convulsions – Race, Ethnicity, and Nationalism at the End of the Twentieth Century*, New York, pp. 93–113.

Porter, N. (1996) *Rethinking Unionism: an Alternative Vision for Northern Ireland*, Belfast.

Pringle, D. (1997) 'Diversity, Asymmetry and the Quest for Consensus', *Political Geography*, 17 (2), pp. 231–8.

Purdon, E. (1999) *The Story of the Irish Language*, Cork.

Raftery, B. (1994) *Pagan Celtic Ireland: the Enigma of the Iron Age*, London and New York.

Raftery, J. (1964) 'The Archaeology of the Celts in Ireland'. In J. Raftery, ed., *The Celts*, Cork, Dublin, pp. 47–58.

Ray, C. (1998) 'Scottish Heritage Southern Style', *Southern Cultures*, 4 (2), pp. 28–45.

Renan, E. (1882) *Qu'est-ce que'une Nation?*, Paris.

Renfrew, C. (1987) *Archaeology and Language*, Harmondsworth.

—— (1996) 'Prehistory and the Identity of Europe or Don't Let's Be "Beastly to the Hungarians" '. In P. Graves-Brown, S. Jones, and C. Gamble, eds, *Culture, Identity and Archaeology: the Construction of European Communities*, London and New York, pp. 125–37.

Rex, J. (1987) 'The Concept of a Multicultural Society', *New Community* 14 (1/2), pp. 218–29.

—— (1994) 'Ethnic Mobilization in a Multicultural Society'. In R. Pohoryles, L. Giorgi, H. Kreutz, J. Rex, and P. Schlesinger, eds, *European Transformations: Five Decisive Years at the Turn of the Century: an 'Innovation' Reader 1988–1992*, Avebury, pp. 215–26.

Rhys, J. (1990) [1889] *The Rhind Lectures in Archaeology in Connection with the Society of Antiquaries of Scotland, Delivered in December, 1889, on the Early Ethnology of the British Isles*, Llanerch.

Richardson, J. (1712) *A Proposal for the Conversion of the Popish Natives of Ireland to the*

Established Religion: with the Reasons upon Which it is Grounded: and an Answer to the Objections made to it, London.

Robinson, G. (1992) *Cross-Community Marriage in Northern Ireland*, Belfast.

Robinson, M. (1987a) 'Programme Responses', *Fortnight*, 253, p. 28.

——— (1987b) 'The Politics of Language', *Fortnight*, 252, p. 24.

Robinson, P. (1984) *The Plantation of Ulster: British Settlement in an Irish Landscape, 1600–1670*, Dublin.

——— (1986) 'Hanging Ropes and Buried Secrets', *Ulster Folklife*, 32, pp. 3–15.

——— (1988) 'The Geography of Tradition: Cultural Diversity in the Ards Peninsula'. In A. Gailey, ed., *The Use of Tradition: Essays Presented to G. B. Thompson*, Holywood, pp. 13–32.

——— (1989) 'The Scots Language in Seventeenth-Century Ulster', *Ulster Folklife*, 35, pp. 87–99.

——— (1997) *Esther, Quaen o tha Ulidian Pechts*, Belfast.

——— (1998) *Wake the Tribe O' Dan*, Belfast.

Roche, P. (1994) 'Contemporary Irish Nationalism'. In J. Elvert, ed., *Nordirland in Geschichte und Gegenwart/ Northern Ireland – Past and Present*, Stuttgart, pp. 309–33.

Roe, M., Pegg, W., Hodges, K., and Trimm, R. (1999) 'Forgiving the Other Side: Social Identity and Ethnic Memories in Northern Ireland'. In J.P. Harrington and E. Mitchell, eds, *Politics and Performance in Contemporary Northern Ireland*, Amherst, pp.122–56.

Rolston, B. (1992) *Drawing Support: Murals in the North of Ireland*, Belfast.

——— (1995) *Drawing Support 2: Murals of War and Peace*, Belfast.

——— (1998) 'What's Wrong with Multiculturalism? Liberalism and the Irish Conflict'. In D. Miller, ed., *Rethinking Northern Ireland*, London, pp. 253–74.

——— (1999) 'Music and Politics in Ireland: the Case of Loyalism'. In J.P. Harrington and E. Mitchell, eds, *Politics and Performance in Contemporary Northern Ireland*, Amherst, pp. 29–56.

Rose, R. (1971) *Governing Without Consensus*, London.

Ruane, J. and Todd, J. (1996) *The Dynamics of Conflict in Northern Ireland: Power, Conflict and Emancipation*, Cambridge.

Rushe, D. (1921) *History of Monaghan for Two Hundred Years 1660–1860*, Dundalk.

Russell, C. and Prendergast, J. eds, (1874) *Calendar of the State Papers, Relating to Ireland, of the Reign of James I – 1608–1610*, London.

——— (1877) *Calendar of the State Papers, Relating to Ireland, of the Reign of James I – 1611–1614*, London.

——— (1880) *Calendar of the State Papers, Relating to Ireland, of the Reign of James I – 1615–1625*, London.

Ryan, M. (1996) *Another Ireland: an Introduction to Ireland's Ethnic-Religious Minority Communities*, Belfast.

Said, E. (1999) *Out of Place*, London.

Samad, Y. (1997) 'The Plural Guises of Multiculturalism: Conceptualising a Fragmented Paradigm'. In T. Modood and P. Werbner, eds, *The Politics of Multiculturalism in the New Europe: Racism, Identity and Community*, London and New York, pp. 240–60.

Sampson, G. (1802) *Statistical Survey of the County of Londonderry, with Observations on the Means of Improvement; Drawn up for the Consideration and under the Direction of the Dublin Society*, Dublin.

Sands, B. (1982) *Skylark Sing Your Lonely Song – An Anthology of the Writings of Bobby Sands*, Dublin, Cork.

Schmidt, K. (1993) 'Insular Celtic: P and Q Celtic'. In M.J. Ball with J. Fife, eds, *The Celtic Languages*, London and New York, pp. 64–98.

Schwimmer, E. (1972) 'Symbolic Competition', *Anthropologia*, 14, pp. 117–55.

Scullion, F. (1981) 'History and Origins of the Lambeg Drum', *Ulster Folklife*, 27, pp. 19–38.

Segre, D. (1980) *Crisis of Identity: Israel and Zionism*, Oxford.

Sheehan, E. ed. (2000) *Travellers: Citizens of Ireland*, Dublin.

Shanks, A. (1990) 'Northern Irish Gentry Culture: an Anomaly'. In M. Hill and S. Barber, eds, *Aspects of Irish Studies*, Belfast, pp. 85–91.

Shaw, G. (1924) *John Bull's Other Island; and Major Barbara; also how He Lied to her Husband*, London.

Simms, J. (1967) 'The Restoration and the Jacobite Wars'. In T.W. Moody and F.V. Martin, eds, *The Course of Irish History*, Cork, pp. 204–16.

Sims-Williams, P. (1998) 'Celtomania and Celtosceptism', *Cambrian Medieval Studies*, 36, pp. 1–35.

Sinha, S. (1999) 'The Right to Irishness: Implications of Ethnicity, Nation and State towards a Truly Multi-Ethnic Ireland'. In R. Lentin, ed., *The Expanding Nation: Towards a Multi-Ethnic Ireland*, Dublin, pp. 21–5.

Skutnabb-Kangas, T. and Bucak, S. (1995) 'Killing a Mother Tongue – How the Kurds are Deprived of Linguistic Human Rights'. In T. Skutnabb-Kangas, R. Phillipson, and M. Rannut, eds, *Linguistic Human Rights: Overcoming Linguistic Discrimination*, Berlin and New York, pp. 347–70.

Skutnabb-Kangas, T. and Phillipson, R. (1995) 'Linguistic Human Rights, Past and Present'. In T. Skutnabb-Kangas, R. Phillipson, and M. Rannut, eds, *Linguistic Human Rights: Overcoming Linguistic Discrimination*, Berlin and New York, pp. 71–110.

Sluka, J. (1996) 'The Writing's on the Wall', *Critique of Anthropology*, 16 (4), pp. 381–94.

Smiles, S. (1870) *The Huguenots: Their Settlements, Churches, and Industries in England and Ireland*, London.

Smith, A. (1981) *The Ethnic Revival*, Cambridge.

——— (1986) *The Ethnic Origins of Nations*, Oxford.

——— (1988) 'The Myth of the "Modern Nation" and the Myths of Nations', *Ethnic and Racial Studies*, 11 (1), pp. 1–26.

——— (1992) 'Chosen Peoples: Why Ethnic Groups Survive', *Ethnic and Racial Studies*, 15 (3), pp. 436–56.

——— (1993a) 'The Nation: Invented, Imagined, Reconstructed'. In M. Ringrose and A. Lerner, eds, *Reimagining the Nation*, Buckingham, Philadelphia, pp. 9–28.

——— (1993b) 'The Ethnic Sources of Nationalism'. In M. Brown, ed, *Ethnic Conflict and International Security*, Princeton, pp. 27–41.

——— (1994) 'The Problem of National Identity: Ancient, Medieval and Modern?', *Ethnic and Racial Studies*, 17 (3), pp. 375–99.

——— (1999) *Myths and Memories of the Nation*, Oxford, New York.

Smith, D. (1999) *Zygmunt Bauman: Prophet of Postmodernity*, Cambridge.

Smith, P. (1998) 'The Elim Pentecostal Church and other Pentecostal Churches'. In N. Richardson, ed., *A Tapestry of Beliefs: Christian Traditions in Northern Ireland*, Belfast, pp. 142–50.

Smith, W. (1994) 'The Irish Language and the Unionist Tradition'. In P. Mistéil, ed., *The Irish Language and the Unionist Tradition*, Belfast, pp. 17–23.

Smyth, A. (1996) 'The Hamely Tongue: a Personal Record of Ulster-Scots in County Antrim', *Ullans: the Magazine for Ulster-Scots*, 4, pp. 61–3.

Smyth, D. (1994) 'Glimpses of Erin', *Fortnight*, 334, p. 5.

Smyth, J. (1992) *The Men of No Property: Irish Radicals and Popular Politics in the Late Eighteenth Century*, Hampshire.

Smyth, J. (1997) 'Dropping Slow: the Emergence of the Irish Peace Process'. In A. O'Day, ed., *Political Violence in Northern Ireland – Conflict and Conflict Resolution*, London, pp. 67–79.

Smyth, L. (1998) 'The Salvation Army'. In N. Richardson, ed., *A Tapestry of Beliefs: Christian Traditions in Northern Ireland*, Belfast pp. 164–8.

Smyth, W. (1988) 'Society and Settlement in Seventeenth Century Ireland: the Evidence of The "1659 Census" '. In W.J. Smyth and K. Whelan, eds, *Common Ground— Essays on the Historical Geography of Ireland*, Cork, pp. 55–83.

Smyth, W. (1996) 'Foes without – Fears Within', *The Twelfth: Special Edition to Celebrate her Majesty's 70th Birthday*, Belfast.

Spencer, P. and Wollman, H. (1999) 'Blood and Sacrifice: Politics Versus Culture in the Construction of Nationalism'. In K. Brehony and N. Rassool, eds, *Nationalisms Old and New*, Basingstoke and New York, pp. 87–124.

Stewart, D. (1952) *The Scots in Ulster – Their Denization and Naturalisation 1605 to 1634*, Belfast.

Stevens, D. (1997) 'Nationalism as Religion', *Studies*, 86 (343), pp. 248–59.

Strachan, J. and O'Keefe, J.G. (1912) *The Táin Bó Cuailgne from the Yellow Book of Lecan*, Dublin.

Sugden, J. and Bairner, A. (1995) *Sport, Sectarianism and Society in a Divided Ireland*, Leicester, London and New York.

Sweeney, K. (1990) 'Seminar Discussion 5: Sport'. In M. Crozier, ed., *Cultural Traditions in Northern Ireland: Varieties of Britishness*, Belfast, pp. 107–16.

Swift, R. (1990) *The Irish in Britain 1815–1914: Perspectives and Sources*, London.

Sykes, L. (1999) 'Drink, Drugs and a Caribou Stew', *Geographical*, 71 (3), pp. 12–9.

Tarrant, D. (1998) 'The Church of the Nazarene'. In N. Richardson, ed., *A Tapestry of Beliefs: Christian Traditions in Northern Ireland*, Belfast, pp. 169–73.

Taylor, C. (1992) *Multiculturalism and the Politics of Recognition*, Princeton.

Thompson, E. (1991) [1963] *The Making of the English Working Class*, Middlesex.

Thompson, J. (1990) *Ideology and Modern Culture*, Cambridge.

Thomson, A. ed. (1996) *Faith in Ulster*, Belfast.

Thomson, D. (1974) *An Introduction to Gaelic Poetry*, London.

Thomson, R. (1977) 'The Emergence of Scottish Gaelic'. In A. Aitken, M. McDiarmid, and D. Thomson eds, *Bards and Makars*, Glasgow, pp. 127–35.

Thomson, S. (1992). In E. McA Scott and P. Robinson, eds, *The Country Rhymes of Samuel Thomson: the Bard of Carngranny 1766–1816*, Bangor.

Todd, J. (1987) 'Two Traditions in Unionist Political Culture', *Irish Political Studies* 2, pp. 1–26.

——— (1988) 'The Limits of Britishness', *The Irish Review*, 5, pp. 11–6.

——— (1990) 'Northern Irish Nationalist Political Culture', *Irish Political Studies*, 5, pp. 31–44.

——— (1994) 'Irish Pluralism in a European Perspective', *Études Irland*, xix, pp. 155–65.

Todd, L. (1984) 'By their Tongue Divided: Towards an Analysis of Speech Communities in Northern Ireland', *English World-Wide*, 5, pp. 159–80.
—— (1999) *Green English: Ireland's Influence on the English Language*, Dublin.
Tóibín, C. (1987) *Walking Along the Border*, London.
Tonkin, E. (1992) *Narrating our Pasts: the Social Construction of Oral History*, Cambridge.
Tovey, H., Hannan, D., and Abramson, H. (1989) *Why Irish? Irish Identity and Irish Language*, Dublin.
Tranter, N. (1987) *The Story of Scotland*, Glasgow.
Trevor-Roper, H. (1983) 'The Invention of Tradition: the Highland Tradition of Scotland'. In E. Hobsbawm and T. Ranger, eds, *The Invention of Tradition*, Cambridge, pp. 15–42.
Trew, K. (1996) 'National Identity'. In R. Breen, P. Devine, and L. Dowds, eds, *Social Attitudes in Northern Ireland – The Fifth Report*, Belfast, pp. 140–2.
Trimble, D. (1989) 'Address'. In M. Crozier, ed., *Cultural Traditions in Northern Ireland: Varieties of Irishness*, Belfast, pp. 45–50.
Tschernokoshewa, E. (1997) 'Blending Worlds: on Ethnic Identities in Late Modernity', *Ethnologia Europaea*, 27, pp. 139–52.
Turner, T. (1993) 'Anthropology and Multiculturalism: What is Anthropology that Multiculturalists Should Be Mindful of it?', *Cultural Anthropology* 8 (4), pp. 411–29.
Tylor, E. (1871) *Primitive Culture: Researches into the Development of Mythology, Philosophy, Religion, Art and Custom*, London.
Ulster Democratic Party (1997) *Northern Ireland and the Talks Process*, Belfast.
Ulster Heritage Agency (1991) 'A Sense of Belonging Can Take Us Beyond the Religious Divide', *New Ulster Defender*, 1 (6), pp. 13–6.
Ulster Independence Committee (n.d.) ' "United" Kingdom or Family of Nations?', *Ulster Patriot*, 1, p.16.
—— (1989) 'Ulster – Part of the Irish Nation?', *Ulster*, 2, p. 16.
Ulster Independence Movement (n.d.) *Ulster's Right to Self-Determination: One Island— Two Nations*, Belfast.
Ulster Information Service (1984) 'Ulster – the Land of no Surrender', *Ulster*, July/August, p. 8.
Ulster-Scots Language Society and the Ulster-Scots Academy (1996) *The Ulster-Scots Language: a Submission to the Forum*, October.
Ulster Loyalist Association (1970) *The Massacre of the Protestants in 1641 and the Siege of Londonderry*, Belfast.
Ulster Vanguard Publication (1972) *Ulster – a Nation*, Belfast.
Ulster Young Unionist Council (1986) *Cuchulain: the Lost Legend, Ulster: the Lost Culture*, Belfast.
Valarasan-Toomey, M. (1998) *Irish Celtic Tiger: from the Outside Looking In*, London.
Van Den Berghe, P. (1973) 'Pluralism'. In J. Honigmann, ed., *Handbook of Social and Cultural Anthropology*, Chicago, pp. 959–77.
Van Esbeck, E. (1974) *One Hundred Years of Irish Rugby*, Dublin.
Vannais, J. (1999) *Post-Ceasefire Political Murals in Northern Ireland: a Process of Legitimisation*, unpublished MA thesis, Queen's University, Belfast.
Vansittart, P. (1998) *In Memory of England: a Novelist's View of History*, London.
Volf, M. (1996) *Exclusion and Embrace*, Abingdon.
Wagner, H. (1918) *Linguistic Atlas and Survey of Irish Dialects*, vol. 1, Dublin.

Wagner, H. (1987) 'The Celtic Invasions of Ireland and Great Britain – Facts and Theories', *Zeitschrift für Celtische Philologie*, 42, pp. 1–40.

Wai Kuen Mo (1998) 'The Belfast Chinese Christian Church'. In N. Richardson, ed., *A Tapestry of Beliefs: Christian Traditions in Northern Ireland*, pp. 211–3.

Wakefield, E. (1812) *An Account of Ireland, Statistical and Political*, London.

Walker, B. (1997) [1996] *Dancing to History's Tune: History, Myth and Politics in Ireland*, Belfast.

Walker, G. (1995) *Intimate Strangers: Political and Cultural Interaction Between Scotland and Ulster in Modern Times*, Edinburgh.

—— (1997) 'Scotland and Ulster: Political Interactions since the Late Nineteenth Century and Possibilities of Contemporary Dialogue'. In J. Erskine and G. Lucy, eds, *Varieties of Scottishness*, Belfast, pp. 91–109.

—— (1999) 'The Northern Ireland Problem and Scottish-Irish Relations'. In T.M. Devine and J.F. McMillan, eds, *Celebrating Columba: Irish-Scottish Connections 597-1997*, Edinburgh, pp. 155–62.

Walker, S. (1992) 'Old History: Protestant Ulster in Lee's Ireland', *Irish Review*, 12, pp. 65–71.

Wall, M. (1967) 'The Age of the Penal Laws'. In T.W. Moody and F.V. Martin, eds, *The Course of Irish History*, Cork, pp. 217–31.

Wallerstein, I. (1991) 'The Construction of Peoplehood: Racism, Nationalism, Ethnicity'. In E. Balibar and I. Wallerstein, eds, *Race, Nation, Class: Ambiguous Identities*, London, pp. 71–85.

Wallman, S., ed. (1979) *Ethnicity at Work*, London.

Walsh, D. (2000) *Bloody Sunday and the Rule of Law in Northern Ireland*, Dublin.

Warm, D. (1998) 'The Jews of Northern Ireland'. In P. Hainsworth, ed., *Divided Society: Ethnic Minorities and Racism in Northern Ireland*, London, pp. 222–39.

Warner, R. (1994) 'The Navan Archaeological Complex: a Summary', *Ulidia: Proceedings of the First International Conference on the Ulster Cycle of Tales*, pp. 165–70.

Watson, A. and McKnight, E. (1998) 'Race and Ethnicity in Northern Ireland: the Chinese Community'. In P. Hainsworth, ed., *Divided Society: Ethnic Minorities and Racism in Northern Ireland*, London, pp. 127–52.

Watson, G, (1986) 'Cultural Imperialism: an Irish View', in P. Craig, ed. (1992), *The Rattle of the North: an Anthology of Ulster Prose*, Belfast, pp. 274–86.

—— (1996) 'Celticism and the Annulment of History'. In T. Brown, ed., *Celticism*, Amsterdam, pp. 207–20.

—— (1991) 'Landscape in Ulster Poetry'. In G. Dawe and J.W. Foster, eds, *The Poet's Place: Ulster Literature and Society*, Belfast, pp. 1–16.

Watson, S. (1988) 'Coimhlint an Dá Chultúr – Gaeil agus Gaill i bhFilíocht Chúige Uladh san Ochtú hAois Déag', *Eighteenth Century Ireland – Iris an Dá Chultúr*, iii, pp. 85–104.

Weber, M. (1978) [1968]. In G. Roth and C. Wittich, eds, *Economy and Society: an Outline of Interpretative Sociology*, New York.

Weir, P. (1997) 'Peter Weir'. In G. Lucy and E. McClure, eds, *The Twelfth: What it Means to Me*, Belfast, pp.143–5.

Welsh, J. (1994) 'The Role Of The Inner Enemy in European Self-Definition: Identity, Culture and International Relations Theory', *History of European Ideas*, 19 (1–3), pp. 53–61.

Werbner, P. (1997) 'Afterword: Writing Multiculturalism and Politics in the New

Europe'. In T. Modood and P. Werbner, eds, *The Politics of Multiculturalism in the New Europe: Racism, Identity and Community*, London and New York, pp. 261–7.

Westerkamp, M. (1988) *Triumph of the Laity: Scots-Irish Piety and the Great Awakening 1625–1760*, Oxford.

Whelan, P. (1986) 'Irish on the Blanket: from the Language of Resistance to the Language of Life', *Éirí na Gealaí: Reflections on the Culture of Resistance*, Belfast, pp. 1–5.

Whitside, L. (1997) *In Search of Columba*, Dublin.

Whyte, J. (1967) 'The Age of Daniel O'Connell'. In T.W. Moody and F.V. Martin eds, *The Course of Irish History*, Cork, pp. 248–74.

——— (1971) *Church and State in Modern Ireland 1923–1970*, Dublin.

Wichert, S. (1991) *Northern Ireland Since 1945*, London and New York.

Wilde, O. (1899) *The Importance of Being Earnest*, Oxford.

Williams, C. (1984) 'More than Tongue can Tell: Linguistic Factors in Ethnic Separatism'. In J. Edwards ed., *Linguistic Minorities, Policies and Pluralism*, London, pp. 179–219.

——— (1994) *Called unto Liberty: On Language and Nationalism*, Clevedon.

——— (1996) 'Ethnic Identity and Language Issues in Development'. In D. Dwyer, and D. Drakakis-Smith, eds, *Ethnicity and Development: Geographical Perspectives*, Chichester, pp. 45-85.

——— (1998) 'Room to Talk in a House of Faith: on Language and Religion'. In B. Graham, ed., *Modern Europe: Place, Culture and Identity*, London, pp. 186–209.

Williams, G. (1989) *Sport in Britain: a Social History*, Cambridge.

Williams, R. (1961) *The Long Revolution*, London.

Williams, Ronald (1997) [1984] *The Lords of the Isles: the Clan Donald and the Early Kingdom of the Scots*, Argyll.

Withers, C. (1984) *Gaelic in Scotland 1618-1981: the Geographical History of a Language*, Edinburgh.

Wood, M. (1999) *In Search of England: Journeys into the English Past*, Viking Press.

Woodburn, J. (1914) *The Ulster Scot*, London.

Woods, O. (1995), *Seeing is Believing: Murals in Derry*, Derry.

Worsley, P. (1984) *The Three Worlds: Culture and World Development*, London.

Wright, F. (1973) Protestant Ideology and Politics in Ulster', *Archives Européennes de Sociologie*, 14 (2), pp. 213–80.

——— (1987) *Northern Ireland: a Comparative Analysis*, Dublin.

Yoruk, Z. (1997) 'Turkish Identity Form Genesis to the Day of Judgement'. In K. Dean, ed., *Politics and the Ends of Identity*, Avebury.

Young, I. (1989) 'Polity and Group Difference: a Critique of the Idea of Universal Citizenship', *Ethics*, 99 (2), pp. 250–75.

Young, R. (1997) 'Hybridism and the Ethnicity of the English'. In K.A. Pearson, B. Parry and J. Squire, eds, *Cultural Readings of Imperialism: Edward Said and the Gravity of History*, London, pp. 127–50.

Zapatero, G. (1996) 'Celts and Iberians: Ideological Manipulations in Spanish Archaeology'. In P. Graves-Brown, S. Jones, and G. Gamble, eds, *Cultural Identity and Archaeology: the Construction of European Communities*, London and New York, pp. 179–95.

Žižek, S. (1991) *For They Know Not What They Do*, London.

NEWSPAPERS

An Phoblacht
Daily Record
Examiner
Irish News
New Ulster Defender
New Statesman and Society
Orange Standard
Red Hand
Sunday Independent (English)
Sunday Independent (Irish)
Sunday Tribune
The Herald
The Economist
The Mail on Sunday
The Daily Telegraph
The Irish Times
The Sunday Times
Ulster
Ulster Nation: a Third Way for Ulster
Ulster Patriot

RADIO PROGRAMMES

Powell, E. (1989) *The History-Makers* (BBC Radio Ulster, 5 February).

INDEX